BASEBALL RESEARCH JOURNAL

Volume 53, Number 2
Spring 2024

Published by the Society for American Baseball Research

BASEBALL RESEARCH JOURNAL, Volume 53, Number 2

Editor: Cecilia M. Tan
Interior design and production: Lisa Hochstein
Copyediting assistance: King Kaufman
Proofreader: Keith R.A. DeCandido
Fact checker: Clifford Blau

Front cover art by Gary Cieradkowski / Studio Gary C

Published by:
Society for American Baseball Research, Inc.
Cronkite School at ASU
555 N. Central Ave. #406C
Phoenix, AZ 85004

Phone: (602) 496–1460
Web: www.sabr.org
Email: BRJsubscribe@sabr.org

Paper: ISBN 978-1-960819-11-6
E-book: ISBN 978-1-960819-10-9

Contents

From the Editor

First, a little housekeeping. The SABR main office has created a new email address: BRJsubscribe@sabr.org. If you have any questions, concerns, or problems with your *BRJ* subscription, including lost or missing issues, credit card updates, or if you didn't sign up to get the print edition at first, but you've decided now you'd enjoy taking it in on paper, email BRJsubscribe@sabr.org and the staff can help you.[1]

In this issue, we're pleased to present all the baseball research we can squeeze in! SABR membership has grown since 2020, and so have submissions. Members have asked me why recently there were fewer statistical articles and more historical ones, as if I influenced that balance intentionally. But I do very little to influence what SABR members submit.

If there are more stats articles in this issue, it means more stats articles were received this year. Ultimately, the interests of SABR members are wide and varied, and in any given issue you might find anything from a biomechanical breakdown of batter swings to the coinage of a new term.[2] This issue includes some longtime SABR veterans like Herm Krabbenhoft, who has authored dozens of articles, and who is promoting a new term this time—the pitcher's cycle—and Mark Armour, who not only has award-winning books on his resume, he also happens to be serving as the president of SABR's board, which means I don't know where he found the time to thoroughly research the campaign to get Satchel Paige in the Hall of Fame.

Working his way toward veteran status is John Racanelli, who has published articles on disparate topics including Hack Wilson, the San Diego Chicken, and baseball card litigation. He does double duty here with two articles on unrelated topics, but which both sit at the intersection of SABR interests in history and statistics, one on the "gap years" of 1929–31 in MVP award voting, and one on players who almost hit for the cycle but were missing just the single.

And we have some rookies this issue, as well. A typical *BRJ* usually contains a few first-timers, some of whom join SABR specifically to be able to publish their work, others who may have been in SABR for a while before they decided to try their hands at a research article. Barrett Snyder brings us a detailed and comprehensive look at pioneer Rachel Balkovec, while Rick Reiff looks back at Deadball Era slugger Clifford "Cactus" "Gavy" Cravath.

I know I just implied above that maybe we have too many submissions coming in for the amount of space we have in the journal. Please do not let that discourage you from submitting, though. Problems of abundance are good ones to have.

But also remember the *BRJ* is not the only way to get involved with research, writing, and publishing through SABR. By the time this issue appears, we'll have begun soliciting articles for 2025's issue of *The National Pastime*, which will have a Texas theme, since the SABR national convention will be held June 25–29 in Dallas-Fort Worth. The BioProject and the Games Project are adding new articles to their online collections every week. And of course we have anywhere from 8 to 10 new books and themed web projects coming out every year. And that isn't even counting committee newsletters, *Turnstyle*, or the baseball cards blog!

To put it mildly, there's a lot going on. Many members are content to just read and enjoy the publications, and that's wonderful. But if you want to get more involved, send me a query if you have an article idea, or sign up with the BioProject to research and write a bio of player, or with the Games Project to write up a game, maybe even one you attended. My first year in SABR I volunteered to write an article for something called The Fenway Project. The Fenway Project turned into a book, the book turned into an inspiration for more books, and here we are 22 years later. Get involved and you never know where it might lead.

— Cecilia M. Tan
Cambridge, Massachusetts

Notes

1. Since 2011, SABR has been publishing the *Baseball Research Journal* in three formats: paperback, ebook, and as articles on the SABR website. Last year, because the cost of printing and shipping has risen so drastically since 2020, SABR instituted a separate subscription fee of $7 per issue for those members who wish to continue receiving the printed edition. There's been some lingering confusion over the new system, and also the notifications that the system sends out, and the new email address should help anyone with questions to get help quickly.
2. Takeyuki Inohiza, "Hitting Mechanics: The Twisting Model and Ted Williams's 'The Science of Hitting,'" *Baseball Research Journal*, Spring 2014; Wade Kapszukiewicz, "Golden Pitches: The Ultimate Last-at-Bat, Game Seven Scenario," *Baseball Research Journal*, Spring 2016.

Satchel's Wild Ride

How Satchel Paige Finally Made the Hall of Fame

Mark Armour

On July 25, 1966, Casey Stengel and Ted Williams were inducted into the National Baseball Hall of Fame in Cooperstown. Although most observers likely assumed that Casey would steal the show, as he usually did, it was Williams who provided the audience with the indelible memory. He spoke fewer than 500 words, taking just three minutes, thanking people from his childhood all through his wonderful career. And in the middle of his speech, he said this:

> The other day Willie Mays hit his 522nd home run. He has gone past me, and he's pushing, and I say to him, 'go get 'em Willie.' Baseball gives every American boy a chance to excel, not just to be as good as someone else, but to be better than someone else. This is the nature of man and the name of the game, and I've always been a very lucky guy to have worn a baseball uniform, to have struck out or hit a tape-measure home run. And I hope that someday the names of Satchel Paige and Josh Gibson in some way can be added as a symbol, to the great Negro players that are not here, only because they were not given a chance.[1]

These are some of the most famous words Williams ever spoke, and among the most impactful and memorable ever spoken at any of the dozens of Hall of Fame inductions. And, make no mistake, this was an extraordinary gesture.

"These were brave, eloquent words, spoken by a man who was in a position to know," wrote Charles Livingston days later in the *Louisville Defender*. "A lesser man than Williams, preoccupied with his own hour of glory, would have completely forgotten or ignored other contemporary greats, particularly those of the Negro race. Ted, however, is no small man when it comes to accessing the worth of others."[2]

Although I have found no evidence that Williams ever met Gibson, Ted and Satchel were quite friendly. Williams often told the story of seeing Paige pitch in San Diego when Ted was a boy, likely in the early 1930s. (When Paige finally was allowed to pitch in the American League, when he was in his 40s and Williams was the best hitter in the world, Ted managed just two singles in nine at bats against him.[3]) In 1956, when Paige was pitching for Triple-A Miami in the International League, writer Jimmy Burns ran into Williams at the All-Star Game in Washington. As Burns was walking away, Ted stopped him. "Be sure and give Satchel Paige my best regards when you get back to Miami."[4]

Williams' words in Cooperstown should not have been a total surprise because he had made related comments to *The Sporting News* in January when he was first elected. "I feel there should be no hard and fast rules that can't be bent once in a while," he said. "There's one man who should be in and that's Satchel Paige."[5]

Still, Ted's generous remarks have made me wonder about whether any others might have held similar views in 1966, how his remarks were received at the time, and why, if Williams's words were so compelling and effective, did it take five more years for Paige to have his own moment on that grand baseball stage?

I focus on Paige, rather than some of his illustrious Black contemporaries, because most of the discussion at the time focused on him. He was by far the best-known Black player in white America during his Negro League career. But he was also the most prominent such player who went on to play in integrated leagues. In the 1950s, great players like Gibson, Oscar Charleston, Rube Foster, and Buck Leonard were either retired or deceased, while Paige was making All-Star teams for the Browns and winning 31 games in three years for Miami. More than one commentator would come away from a Paige outing and wonder, "Imagine how good he must have been."[6] Satchel Paige was the introductory course in white baseball fans' appreciation of the Negro Leagues, while remaining a walking advertisement to their greatness.

Prior to Williams' speech, at least one other prominent player had touted Paige for the Hall of Fame: Bob Feller, who did so in the runup to his own election to the Hall in 1962. In a first-person account for the *Saturday Evening Post* that January, Feller said: "I believe very strongly that there should be a niche for Satchel Paige. To be sure, his major league record doesn't qualify him, but that was only because the old color line kept him out of the majors for so many years."

"I barnstormed with Satch annually," Feller continued, "starting back in '37, when both of us could really hum that ball. Satch had a team of relatively untrained Negro players. My men bore down to see what they could do against the fabled Satch Paige. They couldn't do much. By the time he came to the major leagues, Paige was getting by mostly on savvy. Still, nobody stopped Joe DiMaggio as cold as he did."[7] (To Feller's point, DiMaggio hit .342 with 11 home runs off Feller, while he was 0-for-8 against Paige with three strikeouts.)

But Ted Williams's public support of Paige predated Feller's. He had lobbied for Paige way back in 1953. Williams was a captain in the US Marine Corps. While stationed at a base in El Toro, California, awaiting transport to Korea, he gave a far-ranging interview to the *Army Times*. Williams praised Paige as a brilliant pitcher, and expressed the hope that there could be a niche in the Hall of Fame for him.[8]

It is important to remember that at that time the Hall of Fame had been around barely 15 years, and Williams was not really concerned with (or maybe even aware of) the Hall's rules and procedures. Paige was still an active pitcher, but so what? The way Williams saw it, Paige had been a great player for many years and what else really mattered?

Baseball writers were the principal voices in both shaping and reflecting public opinion on baseball segregation. To that end, there were voices in the Black press who had lamented from the Hall's earliest days that their heroes were being left out. In January 1939, in a column outlining his hopes for the upcoming year, Art Carter in the *Baltimore African-American* included this wish: "Newspapermen forget prejudice and vote Rube Foster a niche in baseball's Hall of Fame."[9]

The *Norfolk Journal and Guide* wrote as early as 1942 that "Satchel Paige will hardly be among those granted a place in baseball's coveted hall of fame, but both his ability and sportsmanship will find a place."[10] In 1947, upon the death of Josh Gibson, the *Kansas City Call* wrote: "He earned the right to a place in baseball's Hall of Fame. His color alone can keep him out."[11] All three of these men—Foster, Paige, Gibson— were frequently cited as players who "would have" had Hall of Fame careers had they been allowed.

Although Satchel had a few cameos in professional baseball in later years, his three years with Miami was his last sustained stint.

A shift in the dialogue took place about 1950, when serious writers began suggesting that these men *did* have Hall of Fame careers. The first such argument that I have seen was put forth by Joe Williams of the *New York World Telegram and Sun* in February 1950, when Paige had just been released by the Indians, seemingly ending his major-league career.

Come to think of it, why should old Satch be kept from the Hall simply because it takes so long to right an ancient social wrong? From now on he becomes…an automatic write-in on my ballot. In this way baseball, through the press box, can help make amends for the artistic recognition and fiscal rewards denied him down through the years when he was as good as any pitcher in the country. Possibly better.[12]

True to his word, Williams remained a tireless Paige advocate for the next 20 years.

Many in the Black press took up the cause, often making the case for Negro League stars generally, not just Paige. Joe Bostic wrote on this issue as early as 1951 in the New York *Amsterdam News*. "It's high time that Sir James Crow be voted out of membership on the voting board for the Hall of Fame," he wrote. "Either that or continue the glorification of the mediocre."[13] Like Joe Williams, Bostic beat this drum for years.[14]

Other vocal allies included Marty Richardson in the *Cleveland Call*,[15] Russ Cowans in the *Chicago Defender*,[16] and John Johnson in the *Kansas City Call* ("If there is no place there for him, then none are worthy"[17]).

White writers, who were more likely to be voters, also began writing articles advocating for Paige. Gordon Cobbledick of the *Cleveland Plain-Dealer* was making the case by 1952.[18] The editor of the *Detroit Times* sounded the call soon after.[19] Gayle Talbot of the Associated Press, read all over the country, weighed in for Paige in August that year.[20] Harold Kaese in the *Boston Globe*, Dave Condon in the *Chicago Sun-Times*—syndicated writers with reaches that extended far beyond their local metro areas— wrote about Paige and the Hall often.

In November 1952, the National Sports Editors reported the results of a poll of their members on the question: "Should Satchel Paige Make the Baseball Hall of Fame?"[21] The results (I have not found precise vote totals):

- 69% Should

- 13% Should Not

- 9% Undecided

- 9% No Opinion

Then and now a player needed 75% on the writer's ballot to be inducted, so these results strongly suggest that Paige would have had a good shot at election as early as 1952, had he been eligible.

Was the Paige "campaign" touted or covered less in the white Southern papers? Undoubtedly, since the most prominent advocates were from the north—the Southern papers printed the columns that they chose to syndicate. But, while one can't read every newspaper, I did find examples of pro-Paige arguments in Southern newspapers. For example, in August 1952 the *Hattiesburg American* ran an AP story from Talbot that began, "A movement is afoot to vote Satchel Paige, the practically ageless Negro pitcher, into baseball's Hall of Fame, and after considerable thought we have decided it is the thing to do." The story closed: "…Who can doubt what the man would have done 20–25 years ago if he had had the opportunity."[22]

The poll cited above was touted in several Southern newspapers, including the *Foley Onlooker*, the *Pascagoula Chronicle*, and the *Green County Democrat* (Eutaw, AL). The *Huntsville Times* published Joe Williams regularly, including several columns on Paige. In early 1954, the *Monroe Journal*, from Monroeville, Alabama, published an editorial touting Paige for the Hall of Fame: "He has been a towering figure in the mythology of the game for a couple of decades, and he should not be left out of the Hall of Fame simply because the color of skin kept him out of the Majors."[23]

Ed Fitzgerald was the longtime editor of *SPORT*, a highly respected national magazine unafraid to weigh in on racial matters. In the November 1952 issue, Fitzgerald wrote a three-page editorial asking his readers to contact their local baseball writer and urge a vote for Paige immediately. "There is no rule," wrote Fitzgerald, "which would bar Satchel from membership because of his race or because of the relatively few seasons he has played in organized ball."[24]

This last part might be a surprise. As of 1952, the only instructions on the writers' ballot were that the player had to have played in the past 25 years, and that he had to be retired for at least one season.[25] Paige would be eligible one year after he finally hung up his uniform. Many observers wanted the Hall of Fame to ignore even that requirement—the Hall was still very young, and certainly capable of modifying or waving the rules as it saw fit. "This is an exceptional case and should be treated as one," wrote L.B. Davis in the *Wichita Post-Observer*. But Paige's primary advocates, like Joe Williams, would often write that Paige's largest obstacle might be that he was never going to stop pitching.[27]

In July 1953 the Hall of Fame board of directors enacted several procedural changes, including the creation of another version of what has come to be called the Veteran's Committee. The latest VC was a group in charge of electing players, managers, and umpires who had finished their careers more than 25 years ago. More important to our story, the board also changed the eligibility for the writers' ballot to require that a player be retired for five years, rather than just one.[28]

After the 1953 season Bill Veeck sold the Browns to a group who moved the team to Baltimore. One of the new owners' first acts was to release Satchel Paige from his contract. Paige spent the next several years pitching and hoping for another shot at the big leagues. The closest he came was the three years he pitched, very well, for the Triple-A Miami Marlins, where observers continually made the case that he could help a big-league team. But as things stood in 1954, Satchel would become eligible for the Hall of Fame in 1959.

This remained the situation until July 1956, when the Hall board made additional rules changes, importantly one that required that any candidate have played parts of at least ten major league seasons.[29] Unless he somehow signed up with a major league team and tacked on five more seasons of pitching, Paige's candidacy was over barring special consideration. The ten-year rule applied to both the writers' ballot and the Veterans group that was considering older players.

This changed the story considerably. Before the two rules changes (often called the "five-year rule" and the "ten-year rule"), the writers were in charge. All the columns urging that Paige be elected had been aimed at the BBWAA: "once he is eligible, please vote for Satchel." The decision was no longer in the writer's hands, it was in the hands of the Hall's Board of Directors. Instead of "please vote for Satchel," the message had become "please change the rules."

So, who was the Board of Directors?

The Hall of Fame was and is run by people associated with or appointed by the Clark Foundation. Although the board of directors today is mainly made up of people from the baseball world, that was not always so. In 1958, for example, there were ten members of the board. Three were from major league baseball: the commissioner (Ford Frick), and the two league presidents (Warren Giles and Will Harridge). The other seven were Foundation people, many of them Cooperstown residents. The president was still Stephen C. Clark, who had founded the Hall of Fame in 1936. The vice president was Paul Kerr, who helped run the Hall for nearly 40 years, including 18 as president. Other directors included Stephen Clark Jr., James Bordley, Rowan Spraker, Howard C. Talbot, and Clyde S. Becker.[30] Their names are less important than the point that the board was composed of mainly businessmen. To get Satchel Paige and other Negro Leaguers into the Hall of Fame, these are the men who needed to be convinced.

Ironically, Paige picked up perhaps his biggest endorsement just a few weeks after the 10-year-rule change. *The Sporting News*, the so-called "Bible of Baseball," which had expressed skepticism about the talents of Black players as integration was unfolding, published a full-throated editorial in support of Paige's election. "On the wall of the pantheon honoring the greatest players," they wrote, "there should be room for the likeness and records of Leroy (Satchel) Paige." The editorial was unsigned, but it would have come with the approval (perhaps even the authorship) of J.G. Taylor Spink, the publisher who enjoyed a close relationship with the Hall of Fame as chairman of the Veteran's Committee.[31]

Joe Williams also had no intention of letting up. After Paige got back in the news for throwing a 1-hit shutout for Miami in August 1956, the writer got back to work. "Isn't there anyone at all among the game's leaders who will agree that in view of the prejudice which condemned him to a generation of skid-row baseball, that this incomparable artist is entitled to special consideration? To install Paige in the Hall by executive order—and without further delay—would constitute no more than a simple, belated recognition of a high talent. Atonement, there can never be."[32]

Over the next several years, more writers joined the cause, urging someone, *anyone*, to right this wrong. "How would you like it if you were the world's greatest tenor," asked Jim Murray in 1964, "but had to stand outside the opera house with an organ grinder selling pencils, while a guy who couldn't come within two octaves of you stood on stage receiving curtain calls and showers of money? ...When you have imagined that, you are well into an understanding of 'This is your life, Satchel Paige.'"[33]

Feller's *Saturday Evening Post* column appeared in 1962, sparking new advocates: Jimmy Powers and Dick Young in the *Daily News*, Wells Twombly in the *San Francisco Examiner*, Stan Isaacs in *Newsday*. "Paige for the Hall" was not a fringe position; these were among the most popular and widely syndicated sports writers in the country. It appeared that a decided majority of baseball writers wanted Satchel to get a plaque.

The great Wendell Smith caught up with Paige in 1965 at a Harlem Globetrotters game; Satchel was touring with the team—speaking to the crowds at halftime and acting as a foil for some of their gags. In Smith's glowing profile of the 58-year-old legend you can feel the author's appreciation and joy, yes, but also frustration—after all these years, all Satch's pitching, all Smith's columns, his hero was still not adequately appreciated: "It is regrettable that such a human is not in the Hall of Fame."[34]

That summer Paige was celebrated at Cleveland Stadium before an Indians-Yankees game to mark his induction into the Cleveland Indians Hall of Fame. There were 56,634 people in attendance, the largest Indians crowd in three years. Taking this as proof that he remained the people's choice, the event stirred up more Satchel columns. Coincidence or not, Kansas City Athletics owner Charles Finley soon signed Paige to a major league contract. Paige pitched three innings in a game for Kansas City in September, facing ten batters. The 59-year-old gave up no runs and one hit, a double to Carl Yastrzemski.

The important question, by the time Ted Williams made his speech in July 1966, was this: Who was keeping Paige out? The short answer: the Hall of Fame board of directors. Specifically, there were two big obstacles. The first was Ford Frick, who was the commissioner of baseball through 1965, and a longtime member of the board even after he left his baseball post. Two years before Williams's speech, Frick had said: "We can't alter the rules for old Satchel... If you make one exception, you have to make many."[35]

The second, and more important, were the businessmen who ran the Hall of Fame. While the Hall's board delegated the voting to the writers or a hand-picked committee, the board made and still makes the rules: Who votes? How often do they vote? Who is eligible this year, as opposed to next year? In 1953 and 1956, the board made changes to the eligibility rules that made it impossible for players who played most of their careers outside of the then-extant major leagues to make the Hall. The only mechanism available would have been some sort of special election, and the board had resisted such a step even in the face of years of pleading.

"Sure, Satchel has done a lot for the game," Hall director Ken Smith said in 1964, "but he just doesn't qualify for it on his major league record. We all love the guy, but it just wouldn't be right to bend the rules."[36] The cruel irony that Paige had been denied the opportunity for twenty years and now was being punished for this denial was apparently lost on Smith and his fellow directors.

Within the world of baseball Paige had no greater friend than Bill Veeck. Veeck, as owner of the Cleveland Indians, signed Paige in 1948 when most thought he was too old, and was rewarded with a world championship the Indians almost certainly would not have

otherwise won. Veeck signed Paige in 1951 when he owned the Browns, and signed him a third time in 1956 when he ran the Miami Marlins. On all three occasions Paige pitched very well for multiple seasons.

And Veeck advocated for Paige's inclusion in the Hall of Fame often in interviews, speeches, and newspaper columns. "Why shouldn't Paige be in the Hall of Fame?" Veeck asked in 1965. "Isn't the Hall of Fame for all of baseball? Sometimes we forget that a lot of baseball is played in places other than the major leagues."[37]

In August 1965, following a hip injury he had suffered in a fall, Casey Stengel retired as manager of the New York Mets.[38] Although no great shakes with the Mets, his 10 pennants and 7 World Series titles with the Yankees made him an overwhelmingly deserving candidate for baseball's Hall of Fame. Unfortunately, the 75-year-old Casey was ineligible for immediate election since the rules required that he wait five years. So that was that.

Except that was not that. On December 2, the BBWAA sent a note to Hall president Paul Kerr, as follows: "The Baseball Writers Association has voted unanimously to recommend to the Hall of Fame Committee that it act immediately—and favorably—on the candidacy of Casey Stengel as a member of the Hall of Fame." Many executives throughout the game publicly endorsed the sentiments.[39]

On December 9, longtime big league executive Branch Rickey passed away. There was no provision at the time for bestowing Hall of Fame honors on executives—this was something the Hall had dealt with as needed, but the last general manager inducted had been Ed Barrow back in 1953, before the current Veterans Committee process had been put in place. "It is not within my power to grant a dispensation," said Kerr. "We can't do a thing without changing the rules. If we don't follow protocol, we invite chaos."[40]

"If Stengel and Rickey are to be selected," continued Kerr, "it will have to be by the Veterans' Committee, which will have to change the present rules. The board of directors of the Hall of Fame has the right to revoke, alter, or amend any changes, but this has always been a formality."[41] This last part was at best misleading, at least as it relates to Negro Leagues players. Indeed, the Board had changed the rules to make their election impossible.

So, on January 30, 1966, the Veterans Committee indeed changed their rules to (a) waive the five-year rule for anyone who retired after the age of 65, which took care of Stengel, and

SABR / THE RUCKER ARCHIVE

Paige had no better friend or bigger supporter in the game than Bill Veeck.

(b) added executives to the list of eligible candidates, which took care of Rickey. Easy-peasy. Stengel was elected on March 8, and Rickey a year later. The haste with which these eligibility problems were resolved for these two obviously deserving candidates, when contrasted with the stonewalls constructed for Paige, is remarkable.

At least a few writers made the connection, including A.S. "Doc" Young: "But now that the committee has proven that it is swayed by human, as well as artistic, considerations—a hip fracture forced the great Casey to quit managing—let us hope, let us pray, that it can do something about Satchel Paige."

"For sheer artistry and sheer fun, not to mention his overlooked mental genius, no man was ever superior to Leroy (Satchel) Paige," Young added. "The game has never known a more valuable goodwill ambassador."[42]

That July, Stengel and Ted Williams had their big day in Cooperstown, and Williams made the speech that began our story. Doc Young lamented that he had not been present, as Williams was a man he had admired for many years. "I wish I had been there to glory in that moment," he wrote. "To walk up to my boyhood batting hero and say, 'you're the greatest. You've got soul.'"[43] Many other stalwarts in the Black press agreed, gushing over Williams for his courage and humanity. The *Los Angeles Sentinel*, for example, wrote: "If Satchel Paige never makes it into the Hall of Fame, a spot he richly deserves, it must make him glow inside to know that Ted Williams knows he belongs there."[44] The *Michigan Chronicle* wrote that "Of Williams's many fine moments in baseball, this acceptance speech was perhaps his finest."[45] This might have read like hyperbole in 1966, but not so much today.

It is not obvious whether more writers got on board after Williams's speech since so many were already there. If there was a shift in the debate it was in its tone, suggesting Williams might have emboldened some of them. While many of the pro-Paige voices, certainly including Ted's, had previously been understated, many columnists became decidedly more aggressive. Whereas Joe Williams felt the need to recite some of Paige's qualifications a decade earlier, the need for that seemed to have passed. No one was debating whether Paige was an all-time great pitcher any longer. "He is a walking reproof to the game whenever he turns up," wrote Jim Murray. "It is hard to see how anyone in the Hall of Fame can avoid wincing when they see him coming. I hope they at least have the decency to hide their plaques."[46]

By 1966, Paige's pitching career had mostly come to an end (though he might not have admitted it).

With more time on his hands, and the outcry over his continued shunning by the Hall of Fame, Paige was often called upon the weigh in on the issue of the day.

- **1965**: "Truly, I think I belong in the Hall of Fame. I don't want to do no braggin' on myself you understand, but all the big wheels call me the greatest that ever lived."

- **1968**: "They don't say I'm not worthy. That's the real test—if I'm worthy or not. Put it to a vote of the people and they'll put me in there—you know that."

- **1969**: "The whole world wants me in it. But I didn't play in the major leagues long enough—that's how it's wrote up, even though for years and years I was the world's greatest pitcher. But I'm not saying they'd change the rules for me. Maybe someday before I die I could sorta sneak in. You know, for good conduct or something like that."[49]

Dizzy Dean, like Bob Feller, had barnstormed with Paige for many years and knew him well. Dean had been praising Paige's talents for many years and weighed in to *Jet* magazine in 1968: "I pitched about 12 years against Satchel from coast to coast. He is one of my finest friends—a guy I appreciate being with and playing against and associating with. I certainly think that if anybody belongs in the Hall Fame it is Satchel Paige. He was one of the outstanding pitchers of all times and a guy who has given his life to baseball."[50]

After years of stalemate, in July 1969 the baseball writers finally made a move to break the logjam, creating a committee of experts to recommend the induction of Negro League stars. The plan was announced by BBWAA president Dick Young during induction weekend for Stan Musial, Roy Campanella, Stan Coveleski, and Waite Hoyt. The plan had been proposed by Larry Claflin of Boston and passed overwhelmingly.[51] This committee had no authority, but the writers were hoping to force the issue.

"Certainly no one questions the credentials of [the newest inductees]," said Young, "but there are questions to be asked. Why Waite Hoyt and Stan Coveleski, and not Satchel Paige? Why Roy Campanella and not Josh Gibson?" Campanella immediately volunteered to be part of the committee. Young pledged that the writers would work closely with commissioner Kuhn and Hall president Paul Kerr.[52]

Another key event in this story was the 1970 publication of Robert Peterson's *Only the Ball was White*. Much more than a scholarly study of the Negro Leagues, the book made the case that the leagues were as good, as valuable, and as historically rich as any baseball that had ever been. The book opens with an excerpt from Ted Williams's Cooperstown speech and closes with capsule biographies of several dozen Negro League stars. "So long as the museum excludes some of these greats," wrote Peterson, "the notion that it represents the best in baseball is nonsense."[53]

The Hall of Fame finally lifted a finger for the Negro Leaguers on February 1, 1971, when Kuhn and Kerr announced the formation of a special committee of ten Negro Leagues experts who would select one Negro League player per year. The honoree would get a plaque that would be hung in a special exhibit. The new committee most prominently included Campanella, Monte Irvin, Judy Johnson, Alex Pompez, Sam Lacy, and Wendell Smith.[54]

Alarmingly, no one was claiming that these honorees would be Hall of Fame members. "It was not their fault they didn't play in the majors," admitted Bowie Kuhn, before countermanding his own point. "We can't make them real members because they don't qualify under the rules." Countered one writer: "So they will be set aside in a separate wing. Just as they were when they played. What an outright farce."[55]

Surprising no one, Paige was the first selection just over a week later, on February 9. Hastily assembling for the press at Toots Shor's restaurant in New York, Kuhn and Paige, who was accompanied by his wife LaHoma, each spoke briefly, and the press asked questions—most of them concerning the separate display. Where would it be? How would the plaques compare to the "real" plaques? Kuhn had no answers, and Paige seemed embarrassed. "Technically," admitted Kuhn, "he's not in the Hall of Fame. But I agree with those who say that the Hall of Fame is a state of mind and the important thing is how sports fans view Satchel Paige. I know how I view him."[56]

Kuhn's words satisfied no one, of course. Smith and Lacy, who had covered and celebrated the Negro Leagues their entire lives, put on a brave face and defended the plan. Smith suggested that this segregation could be temporary.[57] For the time being, the acknowledgment of the greatness of players who had, after all, not played in the major leagues, was a fine compromise.

The reaction was unpleasant. Jim Murray, for one, was furious:

To have kept Satchel Paige from playing in the white leagues for 24 years, and then bar him from the Pearly Gates on the grounds that he didn't play the required 10 years is a shocking bit of insolent cynicism, a disservice to America. What is this—1840? Either let him in the front of the Hall—or move the damn thing to Mississippi.[58]

"It's not worth a hill of beans," said a frustrated Jackie Robinson. "If it were me under those conditions, I'd prefer not to be in it. Rules have been changed before. You can change rules like you changed laws if the law's unjust. Satch's contributions deserve the Hall of Fame. Why does it have to be a special Black thing?"[59]

So, whose idea was this, and why didn't they see all this anger coming?

In 1971 there were 14 men on the board of directors: eight baseball people (Ford Frick, the board chairman; commissioner Kuhn; league presidents Joe Cronin and Chub Feeney, ex-league presidents Warren Giles and Will Harridge; and executives Tom Yawkey and Bob Carpenter) and six Hall directors, local men who ran the Hall foundation.[60] Ten votes were needed to change the rules. According to Dick Young, who spent two years fighting for this cause, the directors most adamant against admitting Negro Leaguers were Frick, Hall President Paul Kerr, and all the other Cooperstown people. Other than Frick, all the baseball people wanted full admittance for the Negro Leaguers.

"There were some pretty good shouting matches," revealed Young, "involving directors of the Hall of Fame, Commissioner Kuhn and a representative of the BBWAA, the organization which had originated the drive."[61] Kuhn later told a similar story in *Hardball*, his memoir, agreeing that Frick and Kerr were the roadblocks, and adding the detail that the writer was Young himself. "Young was passionate and unrelenting in support of admitting Black players. Though I categorically agreed with his argument, I was offended by his rudeness to Frick."[62]

Young also revealed that Hall officials had suggested that it would not merely have a separate wing, but it would have two ceremonies—with the Negro League induction happening on a different date. For their part, the writers threatened to break with Cooperstown and set up their own Hall.[63]

Kuhn claimed in *Hardball* that he had pushed for the wing compromise fully knowing that the public outcry would cause Kerr to cave in. This explanation might be self-serving, though it also might be true. Most of the criticism through the decades has been aimed at Kuhn, rather than the Hall, which is almost certainly backwards.

In early July, just a month before the induction, the Hall caved. Kuhn announced that Paige would be inducted as a full member, one of eight honorees. (The others were Dave Bancroft, Jake Beckley, Chick Hafey, Harry Hooper, Joe Kelley, Rube Marquard, and George Weiss.) "I didn't have no kick or no say when they put me in that separate wing," said Paige. "But getting into the real Hall of Fame is the greatest thing that ever happened to me in baseball."[64]

On August 8, the day before his induction, Paige sat on the terrace at Cooperstown's famed Otesaga Hotel and reflected on his long road. "Isn't this something?" the great man asked. "Here I am, a guy who just loved baseball, still loves it. I played because it was all I ever wanted to do. I had no idea where it would take me—and it brought me here to the Hall of Fame."[65]

"People ask me how I feel about all this. It's the big day of my life, but it's hard to talk about. I could play ball in a town but I couldn't eat there. …But that didn't bother me that much. I never had nothing but that. And I don't want to stir up nothing now. I pure love baseball, and I don't want to do nothing to hurt it."[66]

The next day, Paige finally had his great moment on the steps of the Hall of Fame library. "I am the proudest man on earth today," said Paige. "and my wife and sister and sister-in-law and my son all feel the same. It's a wonderful day and one man who appreciates it is Leroy 'Satchel' Paige… Since I've been here I've heard myself called some very nice names. And I can remember when some of the men in there called me some bad names when I used to pitch against them."[67]

There were reportedly 3,000 people at the ceremony, mainly sprawled out in Cooper Park outside the library. There were three other inductees present (Hafey, Hooper, and Marquard), though Paige was surely the most famous and the most remembered. Bill Veeck made the trip, of course. "Satch is the reason I am here," said Veeck. "You have to remember he supported us in several places. The least I can do is show here today."[68]

Paige praised his old friend from the podium. "They wanted to run both Bill and me out of town in 1948," he said. "There was a writer who even said I was too old to vote but I guess, Bill, I got us both off the hook today."[69]

Among the less famous observers were 16 men who had traveled to Cooperstown for an additional purpose. These men would meet again the next day, Tuesday, August 10, in the Hall of Fame library to create the

Society for American Baseball Research. The Negro Leagues Committee, one of SABR's original research committees, was formed a few weeks later. ∎

Notes

1. Drew Silva, "Throwback: Ted Williams' Hall of Fame speech," https://www.nbcsports.com/mlb/news/throwback-ted-williams-hall-of-fame-speech.
2. Charles Livingston, "Williams Praises Negro Stars," *Louisville Defender*, August 11, 1966, a8.
3. Roger Birtwell, "Ted Batted Only .091 vs. Boyhood Idol," *Boston Globe*, July 26, 1966, 25.
4. Jimmy Burns, "Spotlighting Sports," *Miami Herald*, August 9, 1956, 49.
5. Paul McFarlane, "Ted Unlocks Flood of Memories," *The Sporting News*, February 5, 1966, 3–4.
6. For example, see Joe Williams, *Pittsburgh Press*, July 2, 1952, 22.
7. Bob Feller as told to Edward Linn, "The Trouble with the Hall of Fame," *Saturday Evening Post*, January 27, 1962, 49. Feller has been criticized for suggesting in 1946 that he had seen few Negro League players who would succeed in the major leagues. His pessimism even extended to Jackie Robinson, who Feller believed was too muscle-bound to be able to hit fast pitching. Feller was inducted into the Hall of Fame with Robinson, and in the *Saturday Evening Post* Feller freely admitted— "It pains me to confess this"—his misjudgment.
8. Tom Scanlan, "Second Guess," *Army Times*, January 27, 1953, 28.
9. Art Carter, "From the Bench," *Baltimore African-American*, January 7, 1939, 7.
10. Peter Suskind, "'Satch' Lets Himself Out," *Norfolk Journal and Guide*, August 15, 1942, 14.
11. ANP, *Kansas City Call*, February 7, 1947.
12. Joe Williams, "Evans Says Groth Better Than DiMag," *Worcester Evening Gazette*, February 13, 1950, 21.
13. Joe Bostic, "There Are Some Missing Names in the BB Hall of Fame," *New York Amsterdam News*, February 10, 1951, 25.
14. For example, see "Hall of Fame Next Stop for Ageless Satchel Paige," *New York Age*, July 5, 1952, 27.
15. Marty Richardson, *Cleveland Call and Post*, "Let's Have Some Sports," July 19, 1952, 7A.
16. Russ Cowans, "Paige Should Be In the Hall of Fame," *Chicago Defender*, August 30, 1952, 16.
17. John I. Johnson, "Mighty Old Mound Master," *Kansas City Call*, September 26, 1952, 10.
18. "Selkirk," *Milwaukee Journal*, July 16, 1952, 37.
19. Bob Murphy, "Jerry McCarthy Has Great 2-Year-Old," *Detroit Times Extra*, August 7, 1952.
20. Gayle Talbot, "Ageless Satchel Paige Gets Nomination for the Hall of Fame," *Abilene Reporter-News*, August 18, 1952, 8.
21. Cy Rice, "National Sports Editors Poll," *Arkansas State Press*, November 14, 1952, 4.
22. Gayle Talbot, "Sports Roundup," *Hattiesburg American*, August 18, 1952, 9.
23. Buddy Chambers, "Speaking of Sports," *Monroe Journal*, June 30, 1955.
24. Ed Fitzgerald, "Let's Get Old Satch into the Hall of Fame!" *SPORT*, November 1962, 9.
25. Dan Daniel, "Terry, Dean Rapping on Door of Hall of Fame," *The Sporting News*, February 6, 1952.
26. L. B. Davis, "Sports," *Wichita Post-Observer*, August 14, 1953, 7.
27. Joe Williams, "Sports Comment," *Huntsville Times*, January 18, 1953, 27.
28. Dan Daniel, "Pilots, Umps Get Shrine Recognition," *The Sporting News*, August 5, 1953, 1.
29. Ray Gillespie, "Changes Adopted in Balloting Rules for the Hall of Fame," *The Sporting News*, July 25, 1956, 2.
30. "Clark Heads Hall of Fame," *Oneonta Star*, August 13, 1958, 13.
31. Editorial, *The Sporting News*, September 26, 1956, 12.
32. Joe Williams, "After Years and Years of Skid-row Baseball, Hall of Fame for Satchel," *Buffalo Evening News*, August 21, 1956, 10.

33. Jim Murray, "Baseball's Greatest?" *San Jose News*, June 22, 1964, 16.
34. Wendell Smith, "Satchel Paige Still a Man of the Road," *Pittsburgh Courier*, January 9, 1965, 23.
35. Bob Sudyk, "Too Bad They Can't Bend Rules for Satchel," *The Sporting News*, December 19, 1964.
36. Sudyk.
37. Joe McGuff, "Paige Will Pitch In Finley's Next Novelty Number," *The Sporting News*, September 25, 1965, 23.
38. Bill Bishop, "Casey Stengel," SABR's Biography Project, https://sabr.org/bioproj/person/casey-stengel/.
39. Clifford Kachline, "Give Ol' Perfessor Hall of Fame Spot Now, Writers Urge," *The Sporting News*, December 18, 1965, 12.
40. Oscar Kahan, "Will Rickey Be Barred from Shrine?" *The Sporting News*, December 25, 1965, 1.
41. Kahan.
42. A. S. Doc Young, "A Vote for Satch," *New York Amsterdam News*, March 26, 1966, 33.
43. A. S. Doc Young, "I Had a Good Idea," *Chicago Daily Defender*, August 10, 1966, 24.
44. BPJ, "Ted Makes Hall of Fame as a Real Human Being," *Los Angeles Sentinel*, August 11, 1966, B1.
45. Walter Hoye, "Ted Williams Says Paige and Gibson Were the Greatest," *Michigan Chronicle*, August 20, 1966, A23.
46. Jim Murray, "Old Satchel Puts Baseball to Shame," *Detroit Free Press*, February 5, 1966, 22.
47. Joe McGuff, "Paige Will Pitch in Finley's Next Novelty Number," *The Sporting News*, September 25, 1965, 23.
48. John Crittenden, "Marking a Ballot for Favorite Son," *Miami News*, September 4, 1968, 29.
49. "The Great Satchel Paige: 'New Generation Taking Over'," *Poughkeepsie Journal*, March 30, 1969.
50. Robert E. Johnson, "Dizzy Dean Makes Pitch to Get 'Satch' Paige in Hall of Fame," *Jet*, March 14, 1968, 52.
51. Dick Young, "Brooklyn Atmosphere at Hall of Fame Induction," August 9, 1969, 5.
52. Young, "Brooklyn Atmosphere."
53. Robert Peterson, *Only the Ball Was White* (Englewood Cliffs, NJ: Prentice-Hall, 1970), 254.
54. "Place for Ex-Negro Stars in Shrine," *The Sporting News*, February 13, 1971.
55. Wells Twombly, *The Sporting News*, February 20, 1971, 41.
56. Phil Pepe, "Old Satch Makes Hall of Fame, Natch," *Daily News*, February 10, 1971, 55.
57. C. C. Johnson Spink, "we believe…," *The Sporting News*, February 27, 1971, 17.
58. Jim Murray, "J. Crow Enters Baseball Heaven," *Boston Globe*, February 15, 1971, 19.
59. Milton Gross, "Black Isn't So Beautiful In Baseball Hall of Fame," *High Point Enterprise*, February 9, 1971.
60. "Broeg succeeds Stockton on Cooperstown Group," *The Sporting News*, August 28, 1971, 33.
61. Dick Young, "Young Ideas," *Daily News*, August 6, 1971, 107.
62. Bowie Kuhn, *Hardball—The Education of a Baseball Commissioner* (New York: Times Books, 1987), 110.
63. Young, "Young Ideas."
64. UPI, "Satchel Paige Is Accorded Full Hall of Fame Honor," *Casper Star-Tribune*, July 8, 1971, 16.
65. Dick Wade, "Satchel Looks Back," *Kansas City Star*, August 9, 1971, 12.
66. Wade.
67. Bill Francis, "Paige's Induction in 1971 Changed History," Baseball Hall of Fame website, https://baseballhall.org/discover/baseball-history/paiges-induction-changed-history.
68. Dick Wade, "Paige Enters Hall," *Kansas City Star*, August 10, 1971, 18.
69. UPI, "Satchel Paige Pays Tribute to Bill Veeck," *Lansing State Journal*, August 10, 1971, 17.

Rachel Balkovec

A Comprehensive Profile

Barrett Snyder

Rachel Balkovec's résumé includes several firsts: the first woman to serve as a strength and conditioning coordinator in affiliated baseball; the first woman to do so for a major-league team in Latin American baseball; the first woman hitting coach and All-Star Futures Game coach; and the first woman to manage an affiliated team. Today, she is the director of player development for the Miami Marlins.

Still in her 30s, Balkovec has accomplished all this on a foundation of family influences, mentors along the way, and the pivotal experiences that ignited Ωher passion for baseball. She's overcome barriers in a male-dominated sport, earning praise for her resilience and expertise.

CORNHUSKER STATE BEGINNINGS

Born on July 5, 1987, in Omaha, Nebraska, the second of three sisters, Rachel Balkovec was raised by her parents, Jim and Bonnie, in a 1,500-square-foot house with dark shutters and a basketball hoop. Jim, a former customer service manager at American Airlines, would wake up at 3 o'clock every morning to be at the airport by 5 for the start of his shift. He only missed three days of work in his 35-year career. After Jim would return home, Bonnie, a former bookkeeper, would head out the door on her way to night classes. Bonnie would become the first person in her immediate family to earn a college diploma.[1]

Described by Rachel as "practical Midwesterner people," Jim and Bonnie managed to fund a private education for all three of their girls, but designer clothes were out of the question. Rachel and her sisters would wear thrift-store outfits and regular tennis shoes.[2] Jim and Bonnie ingrained in their daughters the principle that achieving their goals required a dedicated effort and constant hard work. Balkovec has echoed that sentiment over the years, saying that all her achievements can be traced back to the unwavering support and life lessons she received from her parents. She once told a room full of reporters, "My father and mother, they deserve an award. They literally raised three girls to be absolute hellions."[3]

During a telephone interview I conducted with Balkovec in the spring of 2022 for the cover story of *Inside Pitch Magazine*, she emphasized the lasting influence her parents have had on her:

My parents grew up relatively poor and were both the first to go to college in their families. They set my sisters and I up for success by making us each get jobs when we were 14 (Rachel's first job was at 14 working at a movie theater serving popcorn). We had to make our own money, pay for our own material possessions, and earn everything we received. They also made it known that at the end of the day, whatever we wanted in life was entirely up to us and the work ethic we put forth. This is a lesson, a mindset, that I carry with me every day, whether it is my job, my personal life, or even my own ambitions. Anything is possible with work.[4]

Stephanie Balkovec, Rachel's older sister, told Fox Sports, "They wanted to make it so that their kids could be completely independent in the world—to be able to do literally anything and not need them [to do it]." Stephanie and Rachel had to purchase their cars from their parents with their own money and pay for the insurance.[5]

Balkovec also credits her resilient demeanor and "thick skin" to the influence of Jim and Bonnie. "I choose to make decisions that thicken my skin," she told me in 2020, "but the only reason I have that decision-making process is because of what my parents taught me really, really young, and they set me up to make those decisions to go into tough situations and thrive in those situations."

All three Balkovec sisters attended Skutt Catholic High School in Omaha, where Rachel played basketball, soccer, and softball.[6] Katie Pope, who met Balkovec in grade school, recounted in 2022 how being friends with Rachel always felt like having your own personal coach: "She saw more potential in me than I saw in myself. She motivated me, and if I've ever been doubtful of anything—career, boys—she was always a very strong sounding board. She'd whip me into shape and pick me back up."[7]

Erin Hartigan, studio anchor for Bally Sports Southwest, met Balkovec in eighth grade. According to Hartigan, their relationship centered around holding one another accountable and pushing one another to be better. "You want to be on her team because she's going to win," said Hartigan, who was a softball teammate at Skutt Catholic. "She wants to win, but she also knows, 'I'm going to kick your you-know-what.'"[8]

Hartigan remembers that even as a young child, it was clear that Balkovec was unique: "Even when she was in the eighth grade, she had this intensity. She was built differently. I knew then she was destined for big things. I don't know if I anticipated her becoming the first female manager in baseball, but I'd tell you today I am not surprised."[9]

As a high school athlete, Balkovec exhibited qualities of assertiveness and concentration, maintaining elevated standards for her softball teammates while setting even loftier goals for herself. According to coach Keith Engelkamp, "She was always driven and never, ever complained. She would go 100 percent until the coach said it was time to leave."[10] Recognizing her take-charge mindset, Engelkamp thought Balkovec would do well as a catcher, allowing her more control and more chances to engage with the ball.[11]

But Balkovec also had a bit of a temper and was known to throw her equipment. One game, Joe Negrete, an assistant coach for Skutt Catholic, berated her for throwing her helmet after she made an out. He yelled, "You don't ever throw a helmet in my dugout ever again!" and removed Balkovec from the game. She never threw another helmet after that. Years later, Hartigan would describe Engelkamp, Negrete, and Larry King, another assistant coach at Skutt Catholic, as "pivotal" to the long-term development of both herself and Balkovec. The coaching staff would help the girls fine-tune their playing skills while teaching them to build trust, manage their passion and work ethic, and "slow down."[12]

Roughly 15 years after graduating from Skutt Catholic, Balkovec was honored with the school's 2019–20 Alumna of the Year award.[13]

COLLEGE YEARS

Balkovec began her college career at Creighton University, about 20 minutes from her home in Omaha. But her time there was brief. She developed a case of the yips—an abrupt and unexplainable loss of throwing accuracy. A transfer to the University of New

Mexico wasn't a cure, though, and after appearing in 13 games as a catcher in 2007 and two more in 2008, Balkovec arrived at the realization that she could be more valuable to the team off the field. She redirected her work ethic toward inspiring and motivating her teammates in the weight room.[14]

"I was an average softball player who really found solace and an ideal means to contribute in the weight room," she told me for *Inside Pitch Magazine*. "That was my place to shine, work hard, and earn the respect of my teammates and coaches, which ultimately turned into a passion and later a career." Balkovec attributes her eventual ascent in coaching to the strength coaches she worked for in college. These coaches demonstrated "what it meant to be a true coach, as opposed to just blowing a whistle and counting reps," she said.[15]

Her tenure at the University of New Mexico introduced her to an industry that had previously been outside her scope: affiliated professional baseball.

> Baseball was never on my radar until I went to the University of New Mexico and several of my friends on the baseball team got drafted. As I kept in touch with them, I began to understand the onion which is professional baseball. So, it wasn't the sport itself that fueled my desire to work in professional baseball, it was actually the journey of the minor league baseball player: coming to terms with an organization, extended bus rides, limited access to weight rooms, pregame hot dogs, and many other everyday struggles that accompany minor leaguers. Pro baseball is such a unique business to me; it's a never-ending jigsaw puzzle to solve.[16]

After graduating with a degree in exercise science in 2009, Balkovec relocated to Arizona to participate in an internship with API (Athletes' Performance, now known as EXOS), then enrolled as a graduate student at Louisiana State University in 2010. She studied sport administration and was a graduate assistant strength and conditioning coach.[17] In a 2022 interview with the LSU Media Center, Balkovec reminisced about her time in Baton Rouge.

"LSU was an absolutely critical point in my career when I learned about elite level standards in championship programs," she said. "The coaches, players, and professors all played a huge role in developing a foundation on which to build a career in professional sports."[18] After graduation, she embarked on a journey to achieve what seemed nearly impossible at the time:

securing a coaching position in affiliated professional baseball as a woman.[19]

WELCOME TO PROFESSIONAL BASEBALL—IS IT "RACHEL" OR "RAE?"

That journey began with an internship with the Johnson City (Tennessee) Cardinals, a St. Louis affiliate in the rookie-level Appalachian League, in 2012.

The differences between college and minor-league baseball were stark. "I went from 110% intensity to, like, not so intense, and very quiet [stadiums] and no fans," she told NPR's *Only a Game*. "And I would say 95% of the players I was working with did not speak English and don't have any idea what SEC football or baseball or softball means. And they don't care."

After the season, Balkovec was named the 2012 Appalachian League Strength Coach of the Year.[20] However, despite her summer success, she did not receive a job offer from the Cardinals or any other affiliated professional organization. While facing a seeming dead end, Balkovec accepted a front-office internship with Los Tigres Del Licey, a team in the Dominican Professional Baseball League.[21]

Following that experience, Balkovec engaged in additional volunteer intern roles as a strength and conditioning coach throughout 2013 and January 2014. She interned in the Arizona Fall League for the Chicago White Sox and on campus at Arizona State University. During that period, she was also a waitress, worked at Lululemon, and began taking classes on campus with the intent of pursuing a PhD in nutrition. When the Arizona Fall League ended, Balkovec returned to the White Sox in another volunteer capacity. At that point, she discontinued her coursework and temporarily stepped away from her academic career.

Balkovec pursued positions in pro baseball in the spring of 2014, only to face a stream of rejections. At the suggestion of her sister Stephanie, she changed the name on her résumé from Rachel to Rae, an experiment to gauge whether a gender-neutral name would impact her response rate. It did. Suddenly, "Rae" began receiving numerous callbacks from organizations about potential job opportunities. The way Balkovec figured it, "Yes, they will find out I am a woman, but if they talk to me, they'll hear that I know what I'm talking about."[22]

Unfortunately, she fell short of persuading teams to look past her sex. One caller said, "Can I speak to Rae?" to which Balkovec replied, "This is she." After that, as Balkovec described to MLB.com years later, "There was an awkward pause on the other end of the line and he stuttered and said, 'I'm sorry, I was calling about a job, and I just wanted to make sure I said your name correctly.' He was just so surprised I was a girl."[23] He never called back.

"I never felt anger," Balkovec told CBS News in 2020. "Necessary frustration and not understanding and 'Give me a chance,' like those were words that came. But not, like, anger. That was a lesson of, like, 'Okay, look, if they're not going to hire me because I'm a woman, I don't wanna work for them anyway.'"[24]

With no prospects in affiliated baseball, Balkovec accepted a job at Cressey Sports Performance, a training facility in Hudson, Massachusetts.[25] But before she could move there, the Cardinals offered her the role of minor-league strength and conditioning coordinator in February 2014. She was the first woman to work full-time as a strength coach in affiliated pro ball.[26] She said that when the Cardinals hired her, she only had $14 in her bank account and had to borrow from her parents to get to Florida for spring training.[27]

Early in the 2014 season, Balkovec told MLB.com, "I still have a lot to prove to everyone in this organization and to everyone in the field, but hopefully I'm making a good first impression. I hope I can do a good enough job here to open the door for other women who want to be involved in strength and conditioning."[28]

The Cardinals dismissed questions about challenges Balkovec would present. "When you carry yourself the way Rachel does and you're professional about the way you go about your daily work, it's not a problem and it won't be a problem," said Oliver Marmol, who was managing the State College Spikes, the Cardinals affiliate in the Class A short-season New York-Penn League. He added:

> Rachel has taken things to another level by building a curriculum around strength and conditioning and what the players need to know for certain exercises. Now there's no excuse for the Latin guys to not be able to do an exercise the right way because they didn't understand. Rachel cares about these guys as people, so they take an interest in learning the language and being able to communicate with her and do everything the right way. The effort she's put in to teach them and to learn the language herself has been extraordinary.[29]

Cardinals head athletic trainer Greg Hauck also praised the hiring, saying the Cardinals had been impressed with Balkovec's knowledge and thinking. "She would do the program but would take things a step further." he said. "She started looking at how much the guys were running during games and a lot of other components, and no one had told her to do those things. She added onto her job duties, which was exciting to see."[30]

Hundreds of applications had poured in for the job, but "Rachel stood out amongst them all," said Hauck. "We took the best strength coach we interviewed, male or female."

Despite being the only woman in an all-male environment, Balkovec felt confident that her career as a former collegiate athlete would help garner the respect of the players. "If they're in a slump or on a roll, or if they're feeling great or if their bodies hurt, those are all things I experienced in my own career," she said. "And really, it just gives me a little street cred. I think the guys care more that I can throw a baseball than they do about what I can do in the weight room."

Just as she had as an intern in Johnson City, Balkovec went beyond her role as a strength and conditioning coach. She took on extra responsibilities such as accompanying players on grocery shopping trips, educating them about how to read nutritional labels, and helping them with their English. She would play the role of older sister and mom. The players eventually started affectionately calling her "Raquelita."[31]

HOUSTON AND LATIN AMERICA

After two years with the Cardinals, Balkovec moved to the Houston Astros as their Latin American Strength and Conditioning Coordinator in 2016, the first woman to hold such a job in affiliated baseball.[32] Bill Firkus, the Astros director of sports medicine and performance, said gender did not factor into Balkovec's hiring: "It was more we're looking for a certain type of person—open-minded, forward-thinking, incredibly skilled, passionate to get better every day, and she fit the bill."[33] Balkovec's increasing proficiency with Spanish, which she continued to learn on her own, caught the attention of assistant director of minor league operations Pete Putila. He commended Balkovec for her dedication to learning and her ability to foster team building and competition. "It was a unique challenge given that these players were from a different country speaking a different language," he said. "I mean, she really took control there. The kids had fun, too. She just always expected excellence and found ways to get that from the players"[34]

Allen Rowin, director of minor league operations for the Astros, who was responsible for hiring Balkovec, echoed that sentiment. "You could look in the weight room and not tell the difference from her and other strength coaches," he said. "She just happened to have

a ponytail. She was doing the same mechanics, using the same plan as everybody else. She blended in with the guys, throwing with rehab assignments, running, stretching. No difference."[35]

In 2018, Balkovec was promoted to strength and conditioning coach for the Corpus Christi Hooks, the Astros' Double-A affiliate in the Texas League. "I was so fortunate to be with the Astros 2016 through 2018—maybe unfortunate, but fortunate in some ways," she said at her introductory press conference as Tampa Tarpons manager in 2022, alluding to the Astros' big-league sign-stealing scandal in 2017. "I was seeing them on the forefront of technology, just getting Trackman and Rapsodo. I was just baptized with fire. As a strength coach, I was managing eight different technologies in 2018. It was extremely helpful."[36]

In addition to her primary role, Balkovec started collaborating with and learning from various hitting coaches within the organization.[37] One of them was Dillon Lawson, who would go on to play a pivotal part in advancing Balkovec's career trajectory. "Dillon took me under his wing, and I soon found myself partaking in hitting meetings, reading articles, and having extended conversations that helped fuel my interest in hitting," she told me. "Dillon also set me on my path to go back to school to earn my second master's degree, in addition to guiding me towards doing my own research on eye-tracking for hitters."[38]

Balkovec enrolled at Vrije University in Amsterdam to pursue that second master's, in human movement sciences. While there, she became an apprentice hitting coach for the Netherlands National Baseball and Softball programs.[40]

To fulfill her academic research obligations, Balkovec became a research and development intern at Driveline Baseball in Kent, Washington.[41] Although she mostly studied gaze tracking for hitters, one of her biggest contributions came in Driveline's motion capture lab. "We went from athletes throwing 5 to 7 mph lower to athletes [hitting personal records] in the lab," said Driveline sports science manager Anthony Brady of Balkovec's time in Kent. "Rachel was super adamant about setting the tone for the culture in the lab and getting everything out of the athletes."[42]

Balkovec received her second master's degree from Vrije University in 2019.

WEARING PINSTRIPES

On November 22, 2019, after having lived in 15 cities and three countries over 12 years, Balkovec became the first female hitting coach in affiliated professional baseball when she signed on with the New York Yankees as

Balkovec shattered a glass ceiling when she became the first woman to manage in afflated baseball, for the Tampa Tarpons.

a hitting coach for the organization's rookie-level Gulf Coast League team in Tampa.[43]

Lawson, who was then working for the Yankees, dismissed any suggestion that Balkovec was merely a symbolic appointment. "She's not a token hire. She never was a token hire. Whether she's male or female, it doesn't change the fact that she is a great coach," he said. "Not everyone will understand this, but you wish everyone could."[44]

The 2020 minor-league season was shut down during spring training because of the COVID-19 pandemic, so Balkovec went to Australia and became a hitting coach for the Sydney Blue Sox of the Australian Baseball League.[45] During her time with the Blue Sox, one of her players was Manny Ramirez. The Red Sox legend spoke highly of Balkovec. "Rachel has helped me a lot with training, lifting, hitting," he said. "She's smart, she's a woman of integrity, she knows what she wants and she's persistent. Rachel has a big future."[46]

The minor leagues resumed operations in 2021, and Balkovec was the first woman named to coach in the Futures Game.[47] The National Baseball Hall of Fame and Museum in Cooperstown asked for her game-worn cap, which was put on display.

On January 9, 2022, the Yankees named Balkovec manager of the Tampa Tarpons of the Class A Florida State League.[48] Another first was added to the list.

Balkovec told The Athletic that vice president of player development Kevin Reese had approached her in December 2021. "Reese said that you don't have to be a defensive specialist to be a manager right now," Balkovec said. "Let's open our minds to what a manager really is: a leader. When he described it like that, I immediately opened my mind to it. I think this is actually a better role for me than a hitting coach. I don't lose sleep over mechanics. I lose sleep over culture."[49]

Reese described the decision as a no-brainer. "The feedback was always positive on Rachel," he said. "Everybody was on board. This is about her qualifications and her ability to lead."[50]

Balkovec would soon garner acclaim from the likes of Yankees general manager Brian Cashman and manager Aaron Boone, commissioner Rob Manfred, and tennis legend Billie Jean King, who tweeted, "History made in baseball!"[51]

After that tweet, Balkovec joked, "Okay, I can die now. My career's over."[52]

At her introductory press conference as Tarpons manager, a Zoom call with 112 media correspondents online, Balkovec described her journey as "the American dream." She said the initial word that crossed her mind upon getting the job was "gratitude." As one might suspect, she reiterated her gratitude to her parents, saying they "raised me to be a competitive athlete, not a woman or a man, but just to be competitive and capable and aggressive." When asked about the sexist blowback that would likely follow her hiring, Balkovec said, "Three years ago, I was sleeping on a mattress that I had pulled out of a dumpster in Amsterdam. If you know yourself and you know where you came from, it doesn't really matter."

As the season began, Balkovec said her style would revolve around establishing elevated and clear expectations, embracing honesty and straightforwardness, and ensuring that every day holds significance. She told the University of New Mexico alumni publication *Mirage Magazine*, "My goal is really to know the names of the girlfriends, the dogs, the families of all the players. My goal is to develop them as young men and young people who have an immense amount of pressure on them. My goal is to support the coaches that are on the staff."[53]

Balkovec told ESPN that she spent the months leading up to her managerial debut meticulously learning the rule book, and she didn't shy away from saying she felt nervous. "I'm going to make mistakes, and they're going to go on Twitter," she said. "People are like, 'Do you struggle with imposter syndrome?' And I'm like, 'Every f---ing day.' You know why? Because I put myself in stressful situations. I've been nervous my whole life, in a good way. …If you're not nervous about what you're doing, then you're just comfortable."[54]

MANAGING THE TARPONS

Balkovec made her managerial debut on April 8, 2022, at Joker Marchant Stadium, home of the Lakeland Flying Tigers, a Detroit affiliate. Before the game, after signing numerous autographs, Balkovec said:

> It's been 10 years of just working to this point. … I was blatantly discriminated against back then. Some people say not to say that, but it's just part of what has happened, and I think it's important to say because it lets you know how much change has happened. So, blatant discrimination, that was 2010-ish, and now here we are 12 years later and I'm sitting here at a press conference as a manager.[55]

Though the spotlight was clearly on her, Balkovec said she didn't feel as though she were making history. "I feel like the Yankees are making history," she said.

As Balkovec—the visiting manager—ran onto to the field toward the first-base coaching box in the top of the second inning, a chant resonated throughout the crowd of nearly 3,000: "Let's go, Rachel!" That night, Balkovec would secure her inaugural victory as manager.

After the game, Jasson Dominguez, the Yankees' top prospect at the time, talked about how much the game meant to him. "It was an honor to play in the game and I feel very humbled," he said. "We just wanted to get that first win out of the way to give her some confidence in her new role and it was important to get that done today. I will never forget this day."

Balkovec was presented with the game ball following the last out. But she had to give up her Tarpons jersey and hat. They too were en route to the Hall of Fame for public display.[56]

Before departing from the stadium, Balkovec stood in the outfield and absorbed the surroundings. "On one level this is drawing young people to the game, female or male, but this moment transcends sports," she said. "They may not know about minor-league baseball, but they showed up for this moment. Sports always brings so many people together from different backgrounds and, in my case, a different gender. And once you're together in that same room, you realize you're all just human beings and you're going after the same thing."[57]

The Tarpons ended the year with a record of 61–67 (.477), finishing fifth in the six-team Florida State League West Division.[58] As of August 2024, four Tarpons from Balkovec's inaugural season have gone on to play in the major leagues, not counting the six big-leaguers she managed while they were on injury rehab assignments.[59]

In 2023, the Tarpons were 61–69 and finished last in their division.[60] In one of many signs of the changes in baseball, Balkovec was thrown out of a June game by a female umpire, Isabella Robb, herself a trailblazer, one of only two women umpiring in the minor leagues in 2023.[61] Balkovec's two-year record in Tampa: 122–136.

As that second season neared its conclusion, Balkovec reflected on her journey, describing it as a "whirlwind" that sometimes felt slow and at others seemed to fly by. She noted that her two years in Tampa had been as much about strengthening previous lessons on leadership as they'd been about gaining new insights:

> I had somebody ask me at the beginning of the year if I'm a player's manager, and I thought for a second and I said "No, I'm not." I think that my job at the lower levels is to really keep these guys accountable and keep them looking at what they can do to get better, and not taking their side as much. …Relentless accountability for the guys is really the best thing for them. Never feels good in the moment, probably not for me or for them. I don't like to always be (the) bad cop, but I think it's just what they might thank me for 10 years from now.[62]

PHOTO BY MIKE LOMOGLIO / COURTESY OF THE TAMPA TARPONS

Balkovec spent two full seasons managing the Tarpons before taking a position in the Miami Marlins front office in 2024.

A MOVE UP TO MIAMI

On January 9, 2024, the Associated Press reported that Balkovec would be leaving the Yankees organization to become the director of player development for the Miami Marlins, where new president of baseball operations Peter Bendix was reshaping the organization's front office.[63] Prior to bringing Balkovec on board, Bendix had hired former Philadelphia Phillies and San Francisco Giants manager Gabe Kapler as assistant general manager and Vinesh Kanthan, former assistant director of baseball operations for the Texas Rangers, as director of baseball operations.[64] In his report on Balkovec's hiring, which the organization did not announce until a week after the news broke, Jeff Passan of ESPN observed that Balkovec would have "arguably the second-most-taxing job in the organization behind Bendix's. Farm directors oversee more than 150 players and dozens of managers and coaches."[65]

"There's a lot of us kind of starting fresh and new," Balkovec told Kyle Sielaff and Stephen Strom of the Marlins Radio Network. "It's all kind of a really blank slate for us personally, of kind of getting a fresh perspective on what's going on inside the organization and where it could possibly go."[66]

Balkovec emphasized the importance of being in the moment, controlling the controllables, and setting small goals. For example, she imagined telling a player, "'Hey, 16-year-old Latin American player, your goal is to make it in the big leagues!' That can be seven years from now. That can get really easily lost and forgotten about, and you can lose motivation. But, if I give you a small goal, right now, to accomplish that's a part of that process, then you're going to be much more likely to see that right in front of your face and to really push for it."[67]

HANDLING CRITICISM

The interviews I have conducted with Balkovec in recent years, which would invariably become valuable learning experiences for me, have often centered around coping with criticism and navigating rejection. During a 2020 interview, I asked her how she manages when people make offensive remarks. She said:

I just feel bad for them. This is an unpopular opinion, but I do not believe that anyone bullies you; I believe you allow yourself to be bullied. Now, I would like to add, when you are an 11-year-old child in middle school, it is much more difficult to handle bullying. I was bullied all the way through high school, but luckily, when I was younger, my parents told me, "OK, you are

being bullied, now what are you going to do about it?" My parents did not go to the principal to aid in my defense. They told me to handle the situation, which is exactly what I did. I learned how to stand up for myself in the face of bullying. Now, this is obviously not the case in all situations. There are some situations no child should have to go through, I completely understand that. However, for most of your average run-of-the-mill bullying, we need to take it upon ourselves to make our kids tougher and we need to make adults tougher as well to handle such bullying.[68]

She said she's able to brush off any offensive criticism because it's happened before and will happen again. "I can either choose to let that into my head, or I can look at them and think, 'Wow, that's really sad. I hope you do not have a daughter, I hope you do not have a wife, I hope you do not have a sister and I hope you do not have a mother, because that is embarrassing.'"[69]

Balkovec even goes so far as to say she's "glad" for the discrimination she's endured over the years. "This is a little counterintuitive," she told GoLobos.com, "but I'm glad I was discriminated against. By the time I was full time, I had done multiple internships. I was super prepared. I'm glad my path was difficult, and it still serves me to this day." She says that within five minutes of her entering a room, her presence and confident bilingual communication make any lingering prejudice disappear. "The players I've worked with, whether they like me or not, whether they agree with what I'm saying or not, they do respect me," she said. "They recognize my passion, my hard work, and my expertise."[70]

Player development departments have significantly expanded in recent years, with teams now employing roles that were fringe or nonexistent a decade ago, such as performance science, behavioral science, and baseball innovation. Teams are increasingly open to hiring specialists who are not former players. With the coaching landscape at all levels of professional baseball now far more expansive, Balkovec and other women have been given opportunities to demonstrate that their skills and knowledge can help organizations thrive.

BEYOND MANAGING AND BEYOND BASEBALL

When Balkovec was managing the Tarpons, she told The Athletic that the role would be a stepping stone toward her ultimate aspiration of becoming a general manager:

When you think about bridging the gap between being a minor-league hitting coach and general manager—that's a pretty big gap. For a while I thought I needed to become a scout because, like, that's what GMs do. But I love the coaching aspect and developing personal relationships with people. And when you say relationships, that usually means one person, but I love orchestrating a group of human beings and putting them together to do really difficult tasks, which is hard to do.[71]

Beyond the diamond and outside of the executive offices, Balkovec aims to serve as an inspiration, especially to young women and fathers with daughters. "I want to be a visible idea for young women," she said. "I want to be out there. It's something I'm very passionate about."[72]

She talked about that during our telephone interview in 2020: "Hitting a baseball is the least of my concerns," she said. "I am more concerned with: Did I make a man grow into a better father? A better husband? Did I make an impact on how dads view their daughters? How did I positively impact the community? That is what matters to me, that is what makes me happy."[73]

Balkovec followed through on this sentiment during the height of the COVID-19 pandemic. In March 2020, she created a GoFundMe called "Humans for Humans During COVID," pledging to donate $5 of her own money daily while requesting a $10 minimum donation for every podcast and interview she did.[74] When asked about this by WBUR, Boston's NPR station, Balkovec said, "After we were sent home, I just kind of felt helpless, and I was like, 'Wait, I'm not helpless. I can do something.'"[75] She would end up raising over $6,000.[76]

After years of resilience and battle scars, Balkovec has emerged as a beacon of hope and inspiration on the baseball field and off, serving as a role model particularly for women in male-dominated fields, but also people from all walks of life. ∎

Notes

1. Elizabeth Merrill, "New York Yankees Minor League Manager Rachel Balkovec Has Worked Her Entire Life for This Moment," ESPN, April 8, 2022, https://www.espn.com/mlb/story/_/id/33691782/new-york-yankees-minor-league-manager-rachel-balkovec-worked-entire-life-moment.
2. Merrill.
3. Anna Katherine Clemmons, "Title IX Stories: Yankees' Class-A Manager Rachel Balkovec Never Gave up Quest," Fox Sports, June 22, 2022, https://www.foxsports.com/stories/mlb/tile-ix-stories-yankees-class-a-manager-rachel-balkovec-never-gave-up-quest; Barrett Snyder, "Cover Interview: Rachel Balkovec, New York Yankees," *Inside Pitch Magazine*, March/April 2022, https://www.abca.org/magazine/magazine/2022-2-March_April_Cover_Interview_Rachel_Balkovec.aspx; Leslie Linthicum, "Former Lobo catcher climbs the MLB ladder," *Mirage Magazine*, May 2, 2022, https://mirage.unm.edu/big-league/.
4. Snyder, "Cover Interview: Rachel Balkovec."
5. Clemmons, "Title IX Stories."
6. "2019–2020 Alumna of the Year: Rachel Balkovec '05," SKUTT Catholic, https://skuttcatholic.com/alumna-of-the-year-2020/.
7. Merrill, "New York Yankees Minor League Manager Rachel Balkovec."
8. Merrill.
9. Mac Engel, "How Erin Hartigan and Rachel Balkovec realized dreams with Bally Sports and NY Yankees," *Fort Worth Star-Telegram*, April 8, 2022, https://www.star-telegram.com/sports/spt-columns-blogs/mac-engel/article260196760.html.
10. Lindsay Berra, "Cards Have Pioneer in Female Strength Coach Balkovec," MLB.com, May 30, 2014, https://www.mlb.com/news/cards-have-pioneer-in-female-strength-coach-rachel-balkovec/c-77462528.
11. Merrill, "New York Yankees Minor League Manager Rachel Balkovec."
12. Engel, "How Erin Hartigan and Rachel Balkovec realized dreams."
13. "2019–2020 Alumna of the Year."
14. "Former Lobo Rachel Balkovec Makes History as First Female Minor League Manager," GoLobos.com, January 11, 2022, https://golobos.com/news/2022/01/10/former-lobo-rachel-balkovec-makes-history-as-first-female-minor-league-manager/; Merrill, "New York Yankees Minor League Manager Rachel Balkovec."
15. Snyder, "Cover Interview."
16. Snyder, "Cover Interview."
17. Tiona Donadio, "Rachel Balkovec Becomes First Female Minor League Manager," Game Haus, January 14, 2022, https://thegamehaus.com/mlb/rachel-balkovec-first-female-minor-league-manager/2022/01/14/; Rachel Holland, "LSU Grad Rachel Balkovec Named Minor League Baseball Manager," LSU Media Center, January 21, 2022, https://www.lsu.edu/mediacenter/news/2022/01/21balkovectarpons.rh.php; "About," RachelBalkovec.com, https://www.rachelbalkovec.com/about.
18. Holland, "LSU Grad Rachel Balkovec."
19. Alex Schroeder, "How Rachel Balkovec Made Baseball History," WBUR, May 22, 2020, https://www.wbur.org/onlyagame/2020/05/22/rachel-balkovec-yankees-coach-mlb.
20. Schroeder.
21. Berra, "Cards Have Pioneer."
22. Clemmons, "Title IX Stories."
23. Berra. "Cards Have Pioneer."
24. "First female Yankees hitting coach describes her long journey to the top," CBS News, March 7, 2020, https://www.cbsnews.com/news/rachel-balkovec-first-female-yankees-hitting-coach-describes-her-long-journey-to-the-top/.
25. Clemmons, "Title IX Stories."
26. Berra, "Cards Have Pioneer."
27. Ken Davidoff. "Rachel Balkovec is only just beginning with historic Yankees job," *New York Post*, January 14, 2022, https://nypost.com/2022/01/12/rachel-balkovec-is-only-just-beginning-with-yankees-job/.
28. Berra, "Cards Have Pioneer."
29. Berra.
30. Berra.
31. Berra.
32. Brian McTaggart, "Astros' strength coach blazing trail as female," MLB.com, February 27, 2016, https://www.mlb.com/news/astros-rachel-balkovec-breaking-down-barriers-c165143530; Nicole Brodeur, "How a West Seattle woman is making history with the New York Yankees," *Seattle Times*, January 7, 2020, https://www.seattletimes.com/seattle-news/i-have-to-do-this-west-seattle-woman-helps-major-league-baseball-players-to-keep-their-eyes-on-the-ball/.
33. McTaggart. "Astros' Strength Coach."
34. Merrill, "New York Yankees Minor League Manager."

35. Adam Winkler, "Astros executive who hired Rachel Balkovec says her skill set was always there," ABC13 Eyewitness News, January 14, 2022, https://abc13.com/first-female-manager-in-minors-rachel-balkovec-low-a-tampa-tarpons-new-york-yankees/11465008/.

36. Matt Young, "What Rachel Balkovec said about the Astros in her introductory press conference," Chron, January 13, 2022, https://www.chron.com/sports/astros/article/Rachel-Balkovec-Astros-Yankees-manager-first-woman-16770307.php.

37. Schroeder, "How Rachel Balkovec Made Baseball History."

38. Snyder, "Cover Interview."

39. Brodeur, "How a West Seattle woman is making history."

40. "Rachel Balkovec Becomes First Female Manager in Affiliated Pro Baseball," FloSoftball, January 12, 2022, https://www.flosoftball.com/articles/7334157-rachel-balkovec-becomes-first-female-manager-in-affiliated-pro-baseball.

41. Rob Terranova, "Yanks' Balkovec sees dual responsibility," MiLB.com, January 20, 2020, https://www.milb.com/news/q-a-with-new-york-yankees-hitting-instructor-rachel-balkovec-312444932.

42. Merrill, "New York Yankees Minor League Manager."

43. George A. King III, "Yankees hire Rachel Balkovec as minor league hitting coach," New York Post, November 23, 2019, https://nypost.com/2019/11/23/yankees-hire-rachel-balkovec-as-minor-league-hitting-coach/; Bryan Hoch, "Rachel Balkovec tabbed Low-A Skipper," MLB.com, January 12, 2022, https://www.mlb.com/news/rachel-balkovec-to-manage-yankees-low-a-team.

44. Merrill, "New York Yankees Minor League Manager."

45. "New York Yankees name Rachel Balkovec manager of the Tampa Tarpons," Yes Network, January 11, 2022, https://www.yesnetwork.com/news/new-york-yankees-name-rachel-balkovec-manager-of-the-tampa-tarpons.

46. Christian Nicolussi, "How Sydney's hitting coach smashed through US baseball's glass ceiling," Sydney Morning Herald, December 18, 2020, https://www.smh.com.au/sport/how-sydney-s-hitting-coach-smashed-through-us-baseball-s-glass-ceiling-20201217-p56ogp.html.

47. Michael Guzman. "Rachel Balkovec makes futures game history," MLB.com, July 11, 2021, https://www.mlb.com/news/rachel-balkovec-futures-game-history.

48. Nick Selbe, "Report: Yankees to Hire Rachel Balkovec as First-Ever Female Manager in Minor Leagues," Sports Illustrated, January 9, 2022, https://www.si.com/mlb/2022/01/10/yankees-hiring-rachel-balkovec-first-ever-woman-manager-minor-leagues.

49. Lindsey Adler, "How Yankees' Rachel Balkovec became baseball's first female manager: 'It's a credit to her," The Athletic, January 12, 2022, https://theathletic.com/3067563/2022/01/12/how-yankees-rachel-balkovec-became-baseballs-first-female-manager-its-a-credit-to-her/.

50. Linthicum, "Former Lobo Catcher Climbs the MLB Ladder."

51. Brendan Kuty, "Yankees introduce Rachel Balkovec as 1st woman manager: 7 takeaways," NJ.com, January 12, 2022, https://www.nj.com/yankees/2022/01/yankees-introduce-rachel-balkovec-as-1st-woman-manager-7-takeaways.html; Associated Press, "Rachel Balkovec looks forward to breaking barrier as hitting coach," Chicago Tribune, December 11, 2019, https://www.chicagotribune.com/sports/national-sports/sns-mlb-yankees-rachel-balkovec-hitting-coach-20191211-ic32fojcvvfzhez2qbd6lwwtx4-story.html; Olivia Wotherspoon, "Rachel Balkovec Becomes First-Ever Female Minor League Manager," The Owl Feed, February 1, 2022, https://theowlfeed.com/8878/sports/rachel-balkovec-becomes-first-ever-female-minor-league-manager/.

52. Adam Wells, "Rachel Balkovec Discusses Billie Jean King Interaction After Being Hired by Yankees," Bleacher Report, January 12, 2022, https://bleacherreport.com/articles/10023617-rachel-balkovec-discusses-billie-jean-king-interaction-after-being-hired-by-yankees.

53. Linthicum, "Former Lobo Catcher Climbs the MLB Ladder."

54. Merrill, "New York Yankees Minor League Manager."

55. Mark Didtler, "Rachel Balkovec cheered, wins debut managing Yanks affiliate," AP News, April 9, 2022, https://apnews.com/article/mlb-business-sports-baseball-lakeland-3fdb8e38d132d9aef2a2ea65dfaabfdc.

56. Didtler; Holly Cain. "Rachel Bakovec is managing just fine, thank you," OSDBSports, April 12, 2022, https://web.archive.org/web/20220412180606/https://www.osdbsports.com/editorials/rachel-bakovec-managing-just-fine-thank-you.

57. Cain.

58. "2022 Florida State League," Baseball Reference, https://www.baseball-reference.com/register/league.cgi?id=96464f9a.

59. "2022 Tampa Tarpons," Baseball Reference, https://www.baseball-reference.com/register/team.cgi?id=8b39a9c4.

60. "2023 Florida State League," Baseball Reference https://www.baseball-reference.com/register/league.cgi?id=5da9dd89.

61. Associated Press, "Yankees Minor League Manager Rachel Balkovec Ejected from Game by Female Umpire," Toronto Star, July 1, 2023, https://www.thestar.com/sports/baseball/milb/yankees-minor-league-manager-rachel-balkovec-ejected-from-game-by-female-umpire/article_e48dab77-c8e5-5a40-bac5-2346b149d53b.html.

62. Didtler, "Yankees minor league manager Rachel Balkovec wrapping up second season with Single-A Tampa," Local10.com, September 7, 2023, https://www.local10.com/sports/2023/09/07/yankees-minor-league-manager-rachel-balkovec-wrapping-up-second-season-with-single-a-tampa/.

63. Alanis Thames, "Miami Marlins in agreement to hire Rachel Balkovec as director of player development, AP source says," January 9, 2024, https://apnews.com/article/marlins-rachel-balkovec-05ee0f4743d1442ff8b5197a581442c3. Balkovec was not the first female farm director/director of player development to be hired by an MLB organization. The Astros hired Sara Goodrum, who had been hitting coordinator for the Milwaukee Brewers, as farm director in February 2022. Goodrum occupied that role in both 2022 and 2023.

64. Christina De Nicola, "Front-Office hires Kanthan, Kapler debut at WM," December 4, 2023, https://www.mlb.com/news/marlins-hire-vinesh-kanthan-as-director-of-baseball-operations.

65. Jeff Passan, "Marlins Hire Trailblazer Rachel Balkovec as Farm Director, Sources Say," ESPN, January 9, 2024, https://www.espn.com/mlb/story/_/id/39273180/marlins-hire-trailblazer-balkovec-farm-director-sources-say.

66. Laura Georgia, "As director of player development, Balkovec speaks on Marlins' culture and expectations," Fish on First, May 9, 2024, https://fishonfirst.com/news-rumors/miami-marlins/rachel-balkovec-player-development-culture/.

67. Georgia.

68. Rachel Balkovec, interview by Barrett Snyder.

69. Balkovec.

70. Linthicum, "Former Lobo Catcher Climbs the MLB Ladder."

71. Adler, "How Yankees' Rachel Balkovec."

72. Linthicum, "Former Lobo Catcher Climbs the MLB Ladder."

73. Rachel Balkovec, interview by Barrett Snyder.

74. Rachel Balkovec, "Humans for Humans During COVID," GoFundMe, Accessed August 25, 2024, https://www.gofundme.com/f/humans-for-humans-during-covid.

75. Schroeder, "How Rachel Balkovec Made Baseball History."

76. Balkovec, "Humans for Humans During COVID."

Gavy's Hall-Worthy 200

Rick Reiff

What more is there to say about Clifford Carlton "Gavy" "Cactus" Cravath, the enigmatic Deadball Era slugger relegated to the dustbin of baseball history by George Herman Ruth? How about this: He was likely the first player to hit 200 home runs in affiliated baseball. Babe Ruth was, of course, the first to 200 homers in the *majors* (and first to 300, 400, 500, 600 and 700), but Cravath, whose 20-year career was split almost evenly between the majors and minors, was almost certainly the first to reach 200 counting *all leagues*. His numbers are there in the record book—119 homers in the majors, 107 in the minors, and seven in the 1903 "independent" Pacific Coast League.

Yet this accomplishment has seldom been acknowledged—at least not for the past 100 years. In August 1920, *The Sporting News* asserted that Cravath's career home run total, which it reckoned at 218, "still holds out a challenge to the Babe."[1] (Babe met the challenge late in the 1923 season, just months after Cravath retired.)[2]

Cravath's 233 homers, 210 of them collected in the pre-1920 Deadball Era, should cement his status as the greatest home-run hitter before Ruth. It puts him well ahead of Roger Connor, the Hall of Fame nineteenth century slugger whose 138 big-league blasts are often cited as the pre-Ruth standard; adding his known minor league homers only gets Connor to 148.

And it begs the question, why the heck isn't Cravath in the Hall of Fame already? As with many things Gavy (nearly always spelled Gavvy by the press, but Cravath himself preferred a single "v") the question spurs debate.[3] Let's start with some facts in Cravath's favor.

- He dominated the home-run category as no player before him.

- He set the twentieth century single-season homer mark in the majors (24 in 1915), nearly matched the minors mark with 29 in 1911 (Ping Bodie had 30 in 1910), held the twentieth century's career homer mark before Ruth, and was the big bat on Philadelphia's first and only National League pennant winner in a 67-year span.

- He led the National League in home runs six times and the majors four times. Counting the American Association, he won eight home run titles in 10 seasons and missed making it 10 straight by just four homers.[4] From 1912 through 1919 he led all of major league baseball in home runs (116) and RBIs (665) and led the National League in total bases, slugging average, and on-base plus slugging average (OPS).

Even in Ruth's breakout year of 1919, an aging Cravath's performance was notable. His National League-leading 12 home runs were a distant second to Babe's record-shattering 29, but were compiled in only 214 at-bats. Applying Cravath's homer percentage to the same number of plate appearances as Ruth would've had the leaderboard at Ruth 29, Cravath 25, everyone else 10 or fewer.

As Ruth was en route to hitting an astronomical 54 homers in 1920, *The Sporting News* trumpeted Cravath as "the real champion" but conceded, "The Babe may in time make even Cravath's record look sick."[5] In the era of the lively ball, it didn't take long.

Yet Cravath also showed what he, too, could do with the live ball. As a 40-year-old playing manager for the Pacific Coast League's Salt Lake City Bees in 1921 and 41-year-old pinch hitter for the American Association's Minneapolis Millers in 1922, he posted modern-style power numbers: 22 home runs in 431 at-bats, a .316 batting average, and .527 slugging average.

Modern metrics also put Cravath in exclusive company. His ballpark-adjusted 151 OPS+ (meaning no Baker Bowl distortion, which will be addressed shortly) places him 38th all-time (tied with Honus Wagner and ahead of most Hall of Famers), and 14th among players from age 31 (ranking between Willie Mays and Hank Aaron). His OPS+ for 1912–19 leads all National Leaguers and trails only Ty Cobb, Ruth, Tris Speaker, and Joe Jackson. He twice led National League position players (excluding pitchers) in Wins Above Replacement (WAR). His Offensive Wins Above Replacement (oWAR) of 28.7 from 1912–17 is best in the league.

Baseball historian and statistical analyst Bill James has ranked Cravath as the third-greatest right fielder from age 32–36, after Ruth and Aaron.[6] So the question becomes, why isn't Cravath better appreciated?

Here are the main arguments made against him, which we'll address in turn:

- He spent too much time in the minors.

- His first big-league trial was a flop.

- He hit a lot of cheap homers at Baker Bowl.

- He seldom homered on the road.

- He bombed in his only World Series.

- He was a one-dimensional player: couldn't field, couldn't run.

SPENT TOO MUCH TIME IN THE MINORS

Cravath had a truncated major-league career. He didn't make it to the majors until he was 27 and initially failed to catch on, returning to the minors and not becoming a big-league regular until he was 31. His big-league numbers, including WAR of 33, are impressive for being compiled in the equivalent of only eight seasons, but fall short of the usual Hall of Fame standards. But Cravath's prolonged time in the minors is a reflection of how baseball operated in the early 1900s, not a verdict on his ability.

The minors weren't "minor league" as the term applies today. Stringent draft rules, the majors' Northeast

Gavy Cravath led the NL in home runs six times in seven seasons.

SABR / RUCKER ARCHIVE

US orientation, and competitive salaries kept many talented players in the minors for much or all of their careers. The Midwest-situated American Association, where Cravath thrived, was particularly strong, with rosters dominated by major leaguers on the way up or down.[7] The high stature of minor league ball was reflected in the iconic T206 series of tobacco cards, issued from 1909 to 1911. A fourth of the entire set, 134 cards, depicts minor leaguers—among them "Cravath, Minneapolis."[8]

"On the whole the leading clubs of the American Association could give battle on even terms to the second division teams of the majors," *Baseball Magazine* editor F.C. Lane wrote in 1914.[9] A newspaper story reporting on Cravath's 1912 signing with the Phillies observed that "outside of the major leagues the American Association boasts of the best twirlers in the land."[10]

If the Pacific Coast League, where Cravath spent five formative and productive seasons, had not yet earned its reputation as "the third major league," it was already a respected feeder of West Coast talent to the "eastern" leagues. Cravath's teammates on the Los Angeles Angels included past, present, and future major league stars in Dummy Hoy, Frank Chance, Hal Chase, and Fred Snodgrass.

Cravath's major league record is missing what was arguably his peak: 1910 and 1911, when at ages 29 and 30 he tore up the American Association. "No one can tell me that I wasn't hitting well enough for a berth in the majors at that time," Cravath recounted for *Baseball Magazine* in 1918. "I know I was. I was hitting then better than I can now…I finally managed to slug my way back into the Majors, but three years were gone."[11]

Big league teams wanted him, but draft rules bound him to Minneapolis. American Association clubs, Lane wrote, "have frequently, in pursuit of their own best business interests, found it advisable to smother talent which would have found a freer expression in the very highest circuits of the country, as in the case of Cravath."[12]

FIRST BIG-LEAGUE TRIAL WAS A FLOP

Cravath entered the majors in 1908, fresh from being chosen his PCL team's Most Valuable Player.[13] Fourteen months later he was back in the minors. In 94 games with the Boston Red Sox in 1908 he batted .256 with a single home run. In 22 games for the Chicago White Sox and Washington Nationals in the spring of 1909 he batted .161.

Even Cravath admirer Lane declared, "He was the property of three American League clubs in succession…failing to make good in every case." Nearly

90 years later Bill James rendered the same verdict: "He failed trials with Boston, Washington, and Chicago in the American League due to illness, injuries, and competition from other new acquisitions like Tris Speaker and Clyde Milan."[14] Cravath himself expressed disappointment with his performance, blaming it in part on not being played regularly.[15]

But look again: If his wasn't a stellar debut, in the context of the Deadball Era it was still a solid rookie showing. Cravath's 1908 batting average was 17 points higher than the league average. He hit 11 triples to go with the one homer. His .737 OPS was a significant 139 points above the league average and second-highest on the Red Sox. Despite playing only part-time, he compiled 1.7 WAR, fourth-best among Boston non-pitchers.

His brief stint with Chicago, often described as a "slow start," contained hidden gems: 19 walks in 19 games, a robust .406 on-base percentage, and one of only four home runs the White Sox would hit all year. "That dreadful and historic bat of Cravath's is still pulling the Sox out of tight places," the *Los Angeles Herald* reported in early May. "It isn't so much the hitting he is doing as the opponents' fear of what he might do. Consequently, the pitchers keep passing him…"[16]

The newspaper expressed disbelief when White Sox owner Charles Comiskey shipped him to Washington in a multi-player trade: "That Cravy, stick marvel that he is, should be let go by Comiskey, when the Windy City papers have been filled with wonderful accounts of his timely hitting and steadiness, and one scribe even went so far as to remark that 'Cravath can hold center garden for the rest of his life if he desires,' comes as a shock to his friends and admirers in Los Angeles…Cravath may give Comiskey cause for regret that he let him go, for the stocky slugger seems ripe for sensational performance."[17]

It's debatable whether Cravath's return to the minors after a 15-day, three-game stop in Washington was even a demotion. The Nationals were on their way to 110 losses and manager Joe Cantillon was on his way out. But Cantillon owned a piece of the Minneapolis Millers, which were operated by his brother Mike. In a blatant but legal conflict of interest, Joe sent Washington players to Minneapolis to help Mike assemble an American Association powerhouse. The next season, Joe took over as the Millers manager and won three straight championships.[18]

"When I went to Washington the club was in sad shape," Cravath told Lane. "[Joe Cantillon] told me from the first that he intended to take me to Minneapolis with him."[19]

Cravath's 1909 AA season was solid, 1910 and 1911 were spectacular. He led the league in homers, doubles, hits, and total bases both seasons. Cravath, a right-handed batter, is said to have honed an opposite-field stroke to take advantage of his home Nicollet Park's short right field and high fence—a configuration uncannily similar to that of Baker Bowl, which he was soon to master.[20]

In the 1912 pre-season several big-league teams vied for Cravath, including the White Sox, apparently undeterred by his supposedly disappointing 1909 audition.[21] The ensuing skirmish required the intervention of the National Commission, which seized upon an apparent clerical error to free Cravath from his Millers contract and award him to the Phillies.[22]

This time he was in the majors to stay.

CHEAP HOMERS IN BAKER BOWL

A disproportionate 78% of Cravath's major league homers, including all 19 of his major league-leading 1914 clouts, were hit in his "cigar box" home ballpark.[23] But was Cravath lucky or was he opportunistic? From 1912 through 1919 he hit a fifth of the Baker Bowl homers with less than a twentieth of the plate appearances. Cravath hit 60% as many homers as all visiting teams put together. About half of his shots went over Baker Bowl's 40-foot right-field wall, a mere 279½ feet down the line and about 320 feet in the power alley.[24] That was an inviting target for left-handed batters but required opposite-field power from Cravath.

He bristled at the critics: "If I could drop a lot of home runs over that fence there was nothing to prevent a good many other sluggers who have been on the club the past many years from doing the same," Cravath said. He added, "That right-field fence isn't always a friend…I have hit that fence a good many times with a long drive that would have kept on going for a triple or a home run."[25]

SELDOM HOMERED ON THE ROAD

This is a corollary to the above argument: Take away Baker Bowl, you take away Cravath's power. Indeed, he only hit 26 road homers. But that figure, paltry as it looks, typifies sluggers of the 1910s (Ruth excepted). Cravath's percentage of road homers to plate appearances slightly trails Joe Jackson and Ty Cobb, roughly matches Frank Schulte, and exceeds Home Run Baker, Heinie Zimmerman, Larry Doyle and teammates Fred Luderus and Sherry Magee.

And note that Cobb hit 46 inside-the-park homers, a whopping 39% of his career total; Cravath only hit four. Perhaps big parks benefited the fleet-footed Ty as much as a small park helped Gavy.

BOMBED IN HIS ONLY WORLD SERIES

One postseason shouldn't define a career. But the 1915 World Series was indeed a disappointment for the record-setting home run champ. Cravath in 16 at-bats managed only two hits and no homers and struck out six times as the Phillies fell to the Boston Red Sox in five games. In the first inning of the final contest he came to bat with the bases loaded and none out and grounded into a pitcher-to-catcher-to-first double play. (Later accounts would even claim that Cravath pulled a "boner" by bunting on a full count, a description unsupported by contemporaneous newspaper stories.)[26]

Cravath's struggles—reporters' creative epithets for him included "fat baboon," "rich-hued lemon,"[27] and "a plain bust"[28]—were contrasted with the stellar all-around play of Boston outfielders Harry Hooper and Duffy Lewis, who between them hit three homers in Baker Bowl.[29] Phillies manager Pat Moran came to Cravath's defense, telling the *Washington Times* that his slugger "was all crippled up, and I know lots of ball players that would not have even attempted to play with their legs in the condition Gavvy's [*sic*] are."[30]

Still Cravath displayed his power, but this time in the wrong ballpark: the new, cavernous Braves Field, where the Red Sox moved their World Series home games because it had more seats than Fenway Park. "Cravath got three blows that in Philadelphia would have been home runs," Grantland Rice wrote.[31] William A. Phelon seconded the observation: "Cravath, single-handed, would have won the series at almost any other ballyard in the land, for three of his gigantic flies were pulled down by the Boston outfielders so far from home that they were sure home runs on other grounds."[32] By contrast, Hooper and Lewis' homers didn't even make it out of Baker Bowl—they landed in the temporary outfield seats.[33]

Nor was Cravath entirely unproductive: His hits were a double and a triple and he drove in the go-ahead run in the Phillies' lone victory. The Red Sox respected the right-handed-batting Cravath to the end, keeping their brilliant young southpaw Babe Ruth off the mound.[34]

A ONE-DIMENSIONAL PLAYER

Cravath was slow. He admitted as much.[35] But he wasn't Ernie-Lombardi slow–he averaged almost 10 triples and 10 stolen bases a year. In his early PCL days he might even have been fast, as evidenced by 183 stolen bases over five seasons. A simple explanation for

his lack of speed is that by the time he got to Philadelphia he was 31, already aging in baseball years.

In the field he wasn't Dick-Stuart bad. He threw well, three times leading National League outfielders in assists. In 1913 *Baseball Magazine* described him as "an earnest and industrious worker" in the field.[36] But most contemporary accounts disparage his fielding.[37] That aligns with his -9.5 Defensive WAR (dWAR).

Yet how much should those shortcomings count against him? The Hall of Fame includes other sluggers who didn't run or field well—Ralph Kiner, Harmon Killebrew, Jim Thome, and "Big Papi" David Ortiz to name a few. They're honored for what they *could* do, not for what they *couldn't*.

But unlike them, Cravath played before his time—a long-ball hitter in a low-scoring era that lionized speed and defense and measured offense almost exclusively by batting average. Today he's lost in time—too ancient to interest most baseball fans, captured only in a few black-and-white photographs and tethered to shoulder-shrugging dead-ball stats.

Historians and statisticians have tools to rectify misperceptions. The more we study Cravath, the better his chance to someday make the Hall.

CONCLUSION

Even though advanced metrics were many years away, some peers intuited that Cravath's value wasn't being accurately gauged. Prescient articles in *Baseball Magazine* featured Cravath as Exhibit A for why the game needed a better offensive statistic than batting average. "Jake Daubert, reckoned on any sane basis, is not equal to that of Cactus Cravath by a very wide margin. In fact, the two are not in the same class," Lane wrote in 1916. "And yet, according to the present system, Daubert is the better batter of the two. It is grotesqueries such as this that bring the whole foundation of baseball statistics into disrepute."[38]

Lane, anticipating Bill James' Runs Created formula, proffered a system that gave weighted run values to singles, doubles, triples, and homers and used it to show that Cravath was 42% more productive than Daubert in 1915, even though Daubert had out-hit Cravath .301 to .285.[39] (Lane's formula holds up well: More than a century later, Baseball Reference's Runs Created per Game measure, (RC/G), gives Cravath a 52% advantage).

John J. Ward wrote in 1918 that Cravath "has suffered more than any other player now in baseball from the absurdity of a system which gives a batter as much credit for a scratch single as for a home run with three men on bases…Long considered by the pitchers the most dangerous hitter in his circuit, he has never yet received the recognition which is his due or the proper rewards to which his talents have entitled him."[40]

Ward said that in a "system built upon total bases" the .280-hitting Cravath topped Edd Roush, Zack Wheat, Heinie Groh and every other .300-hitting National Leaguer in 1917.[41] Ward's "system" would later have a name: slugging average.

Cravath argued his case colorfully: "Short singles are like left-hand jabs in the boxing ring, but a home run is a knock-out punch…Some players steal bases with hook slides and speed. I steal bases with my bat."[42]

But it took Ruth to make home runs the coin of the baseball realm. The game moved on from Cravath and Cravath moved on from baseball. He returned home to Laguna Beach, California, invested in real estate, enjoyed fishing and lawn bowling, and, despite the lack of a law degree, spent decades as the elected justice of the peace. When he died in 1963 at age 82 some locals were surprised to learn that Judge Cravath had once been a baseball star.[43]

The Hall of Fame has no plaque for Cravath, but it does have a file on him that includes a questionnaire he filled out many years after his last game. One of the questions was, "If you had it all to do over, would you play professional baseball?" Cravath's terse response knocked it out of the park: "At present prices yes."[44] ∎

Acknowledgments

Thanks to Baseball Reference's databases and their Stathead research engine, which were used extensively for statistics in this article. Also thanks to William Victor, who crunched some of the numbers. And thanks to SABR's online newspaper archives, the Library of Congress' digitized newspapers, and the Giamatti Research Center of the National Baseball Hall of Fame and Museum, and the Laguna Beach Historical Society for most of the news and magazine citations.

Notes

1. "Here's the Real 'Champion,'" *The Sporting News*, August 19, 1920, 3. The article credited Cravath with seven more home runs at that point in his career than does Baseball Reference.
2. According to Baseball Reference, Ruth hit his 234th professional home run on September 13, 1923. Cravath's career total was 233.
3. Sportswriters seem to have universally preferred "Gavvy," but it is well documented that Cravath always spelled his nickname "Gavy," including in his signature as a judge in Orange County.
4. Baseball Reference. Cravath was one shy of the National League home run crown in 1916 and three short in 1912.
5. "Here's the Real 'Champion,'" *The Sporting News*.
6. Bill James, *The New Bill James Historical Abstract* (New York: The Free Press, 2001), 807.
7. Baseball-Reference. One-time major leaguers comprise roughly three-fourths of 1910 American Association rosters.
8. "1909–11 White Border T206 Guide," Throwback Sports Cards, https://www.throwbacksportscards.com/1909-11-t206-tobacco-baseball-card-set.
9. F.C. Lane, "Cactus Cravath, the Man Who Started Late," *Baseball Magazine*, June, 1914, 32.
10. "Western Phenom Signs with Phils," 1912, unidentified newspaper clip in the Gavvy Cravath player file, Giamatti Research Center, National Baseball Hall of Fame and Museum, Cooperstown, NY.
11. "Cactus" Cravath, "What the Batting Records Have Cost Me," *Baseball Magazine*, July, 1918.
12. Lane, "Cactus Cravath," 32
13. Although some references, including obits, state that Cravath won the PCL MVP Award, the award was not first given until 1927.
14. Bill James, *The New Bill James Historical Abstract*, 807.
15. Lane, "Cactus Cravath," 28.
16. A.E. Dunning, "Timely Topics," *Los Angeles Herald*, May 4, 1909, 4.
17. A.E. Dunning, "Timely Topics," *Los Angeles Herald*, May 17, 1909, 6.
18. Terry Bohn, "Joe Cantillon," Society for American Baseball Research, https://sabr.org/bioproj/person/joe-cantillon/.
19. Lane, "Cactus Cravath," 28.
20. Bill Swank, "Gavvy Cravath", Society for American Baseball Research, 2021, https://sabr.org/bioproj/person/gavvy-cravath/.
21. Ernest J. Lanigan, "Gavvy Might Break Home Run Mark If Played More," undated newspaper clipping, Gavvy Cravath player file, Giamatti Research Center; "Outfielder Cravath Is Awarded to Phillies," undated newspaper clipping, Gavvy Cravath player file, Giamatti Research Center.
22. "Outfielder Cravath Is Awarded to Phillies."
23. "Baker Bowl was often described as 'tiny' and frequently laughed at as a 'cigar box' or 'band box.'" *Lost Ballparks*, Lawrence S. Ritter, 1992, 10.
24. Accounts vary of Baker Bowl's precise dimensions in the 1910s, but there is agreement that the distances to right field and right-center field were short and the fence/wall was high.
25. Cactus Cravath, "The Secret of Home Run Hitting," *Baseball Magazine*, July, 1917.
26. In December 1915, *Baseball Magazine*'s Wm. A. Phelon described the play as a bunt. In the December 2, 1926, *The Sporting News*' Jim Nasium (pen name of Edgar Forrest Wolfe) said it was a bunt and one of the "historical boners of baseball." *The Sporting News* even mentioned the episode in its June 8, 1963, obituary of Cravath, adding that it was manager Pat Moran who called for the surprise play. But not a single game-day story examined for this article mentioned a bunt. It was described as "an easy grounder" by the *New York Tribune*, "a bounder" by the *New York Evening World* and *Washington* (DC) *Evening Star*, "Cravath rolled to Foster" by the *Richmond Times Dispatch*, "a flabby little hopper" by the *New York Sun*, and "hit to the pitcher" by the *Washington Times*.
27. Wm. A. Phelon, "How I Picked the Loser," *Baseball Magazine*, December, 1915.
28. William B. Hanna, "Red Sox Earn 1915 Baseball Championship," *The* (New York) *Sun*, October 14, 1915, 10.
29. Phelon, "How I Picked the Loser."
30. Pat Moran, "Manager of Phillies Admits He is Disappointed," *Washington Times*, October 14, 1915, 13.
31. Grantland Rice, *Philadelphia Evening Public Ledger*, October 14, 1915, 11.
32. Phelon, "How I Picked the Loser."
33. Phelon, "How I Picked the Loser."
34. Swank, 2021.
35. "You know, I am not much of a base runner. They call me leaden footed, and I admit it." F.C. Lane, 1914, 108.
36. "The All-American Baseball Club," *Baseball Magazine*, December, 1913.
37. One of many examples: "His fielding and his base running have never been above mediocrity." F.C. Lane, 1914, 116.
38. F.C. Lane, "Why the System of Batting Averages Should Be Changed," *Baseball Magazine*, March, 1916.
39. Lane, "Batting Averages," 1916.
40. John J. Ward, "The Proposed Reform in Batting Records," *Baseball Magazine*, July, 1918.
41. Ward.
42. Lane, "Cactus Cravath," 31.
43. Swank, 2021.
44. Gavvy Cravath player file, Giamatti Research Center. The center said the undated questionnaire is from the early 1960s.

Closing the Gap

The MVP Cases for Lew Fonseca, Joe Cronin, and Hack Wilson

John Racanelli

On May 7, 1929, the American League announced it had abolished the "League Award," the most valuable player honor that it had awarded annually since 1922, ostensibly because "it tended to create ill-feeling among the players."[1] The National League followed suit on June 8, eliminating its League Award, which had been given annually since 1924, citing similar reasons.[2] James Long of the *Pittsburgh Sun-Telegraph* heralded the move, writing, "'The most valuable player' stuff was the bunk and never did anything but harm the game, inasmuch as it gave the favored player an exaggerated idea of his importance and created petty jealousies on the team."[3]

The leagues' dubious public justifications sparked skepticism, and speculation swirled that the magnates had grown weary of the players who finished high in the MVP voting holding out for higher salaries.[4] The leagues were also able to save the $1,000 cash payout (approximately $18,000 today) that accompanied each award. The AL gave no award in 1929. The NL stopped after giving Chicago Cubs second baseman Rogers Hornsby his second MVP that year.[5]

The Baseball Writers Association of America (BBWAA) took over voting in 1931 and has chosen a Most Valuable Player for each league ever since, which leaves an awkward gap between the end of the league awards and the current incarnation of the award: Three MVP seasons are unfairly ignored. Following each of those seasons, however, polling was completed by the sportswriters and a record of the voting results was published contemporaneously.[6] Accordingly, crowning the consensus Most Valuable Player for each of these three league-seasons—Lew Fonseca, Joe Cronin, and Hack Wilson—is reasonably straightforward.

THE CHALMERS AWARD

The idea of a most valuable player award originally grew from a promotion sponsored by the Chalmers-Detroit Automobile Company, which offered a new car to the player who posted the highest batting average in 1910.[7] Owner Hugh Chalmers, "an enthusiastic baseball booster," was perhaps hoping to simply hand the car over to hometown Tiger Ty Cobb, who had won the past three batting titles.[8]

The 1910 AL batting race, however, ended in controversy (and a lawsuit!) as manager Jack O'Connor and the St. Louis Browns were accused of purposely allowing Cleveland's Napoleon Lajoie seven bunt hits in a season-ending doubleheader to wrest the batting crown from Cobb.[9] Ultimately, Chalmers ended up giving away two cars—one each to Cobb and Lajoie—after league president Ban Johnson declared that Cobb had actually won the batting title over Lajoie, .384944 to .384084.[10]

In 1911, Chalmers announced a modified scheme by which his company would give a car "to each of two players, one in the National League and one in the American League, who do the most to help their respective teams."[11] Connie Mack telegraphed Chalmers praising the plan to reward "the most valuable ball player in each league," perhaps unintentionally coining the term for the leaguewide honor.[12] Chalmers thereafter tasked a committee of baseball writers to determine the winner for each league.[13] The Chalmers Company awarded cars to a pair of players through the 1914 season, then abruptly ended the contest, claiming that the plan all along had been to run the promotion for five years.[14]

THE LOST YEARS

When the American League revived the idea to select a most valuable player in 1922—accompanied by a $1,000 cash reward—the owners imposed two conditions: (1) no player-managers were eligible because of the influence they might impose on game action; and (2) no repeat winners.[15] The initial plan called for a commission of newspaper men in each league city and a chairman "not actively connected with baseball" to select a player on the basis of "all-around ability, faithfulness, and freedom from accident, sickness, etc."[16] The National League considered establishing an MVP award of its own in 1922 but did not make the award official until 1924, without any restrictions imposed on player-managers or repeat winners.[17]

Despite the American League's decision to discontinue the MVP selection in 1929, the Associated Press assembled a committee that included a baseball writer from each of the eight league cities to vote. The polling was conducted in precisely the same manner as in previous years: a first-place vote was worth eight points, a second-place vote seven points, and so on. *The Sporting News* also named Most Valuable Players in those years using a similar slate of writers: Al Simmons was crowned the 1929 American League MVP, Joe Cronin was christened 1930 American League MVP, and Bill Terry was named 1930 National League MVP. The transparent nature of the processes undertaken by the Associated Press and *The Sporting News* makes it possible to determine the consensus MVP for each of these years.

1929 AMERICAN LEAGUE MVP: LEW FONSECA (CLEVELAND)

Lew Fonseca was a man of many talents: licensed dentist, accomplished singer, ping-pong aficionado and "expert card manipulator."[18] Following four seasons with the Cincinnati Reds and one with the Philadelphia Phillies from 1921–25, Fonseca found himself with the Newark Bears in the International League in 1926. After batting .381 with 21 home runs for Newark, Fonseca was traded to the Cleveland Indians.

Playing at all four infield positions for Cleveland in 1928, Fonseca garnered enough support to place 22nd in MVP voting, despite having only appeared in 75 games. Fonseca was installed as Cleveland's first baseman the following season and flourished, leading the AL with a .369 batting average and setting career marks in hits (209), runs (97), doubles (44), triples (15), runs batted in (103), and stolen bases (19).

SABR / RUCKER ARCHIVE

Lew Fonseca
1929 American League MVP

Following the 1929 season, the Associated Press committee crowned Fonseca as American League MVP with 46 points.[19] Cleveland's general manager, Billy Evans, celebrated Fonseca's win by giving him a check for $1,000 to replace the reward the AL had discontinued.[20] (The subsequent *Sporting News* vote placed Fonseca in a third-place tie with 31 points.)[21] The complete results are shown In Table 1.

Table 1. 1929 American League Most Valuable Player Voting Results

Place	Player	Team	AP	TSN	Total
1	Lew Fonseca	Cleveland	46	31	77
2	Heinie Manush	St. Louis	26	31	57
3	Al Simmons	Philadelphia	16	40	56
4	Tony Lazzeri	New York	22	33	55
5	Charlie Gehringer	Detroit	25	19	44
6	Jimmy Dykes	Philadelphia	31	8	39
7	Joe Judge	Washington	24	9	33
8	Jimmie Foxx	Philadelphia	15	8	23
9	Babe Ruth	New York	19	–	19
9	Willie Kamm	Chicago	8	11	19
9	Earl Averill	Cleveland	6	13	19
12	Marty McManus	Detroit	9	3	12
13	Mickey Cochrane	Philadelphia	8	–	8
13	Carl Reynolds	Chicago	6	2	8
13	Jack Rothrock	Boston	3	5	8
16	Oscar Melillo	St. Louis	7	–	7
16	Tommy Thomas	Chicago	7	–	7
16	Wes Ferrell	Cleveland	–	7	7
19	Bill Dickey	New York	–	6	6
20	Russ Scarritt	Boston	4	1	5
20	Red Kress	St. Louis	–	5	5
22	Art Shires	Chicago	–	4	4
22	Dale Alexander	Detroit	–	4	4
22	Harry Rice	Detroit	–	4	4
22	Goose Goslin	Washington	–	4	4
22	Phil Todt	Boston	–	4	4
27	Lu Blue	St. Louis	3	–	3
27	Sam Jones	Washington	–	3	3
27	Sam Rice	Washington	–	3	3
30	Milt Gaston	Boston	2	–	2
30	Moe Berg	Chicago	–	2	2
32	Joe Cronin	Washington	1	–	1

Fonseca had received two points in the 1928 Most Valuable Player voting, but never received another vote for the remainder of his career.

1930 AMERICAN LEAGUE MVP: JOE CRONIN (WASHINGTON)

Nineteen-year-old shortstop Joe Cronin smacked his first big-league hit for the Pittsburgh Pirates on August 4,

1926. In September, he took over as starting second baseman and things looked bright for the youngster. However, personnel changes prior to the 1927 season conspired to keep Cronin on the bench and he appeared in just 12 games for the Pirates, despite being with the club for the entire season. He was sold to the American Association Kansas City Blues on April 1, 1928 and played half a season there before Washington purchased his contract in July. Cronin claimed the starting shortstop job in 1929 and had a nice season, which included an MVP vote following the campaign.

Cronin blossomed in 1930, batting a career-high .346, leading the league with 154 games played, and setting career highs in runs (127), hits (203), runs batted in (126), stolen bases (17), and total bases (301). Washington improved from 71–81 and a fifth-place finish in 1929 to 94–60 and second place in 1930.

Following the season, the appointed committee of baseball scribes chose Cronin as the American League MVP as he garnered one vote for first place, four votes for second place, and one each for fourth, fifth, and sixth.[22] (The subsequent *Sporting News* vote also placed Cronin first with 52 points.)[23] The complete results are shown in Table 2, below.

Cronin collected MVP votes in seven subsequent campaigns, finishing as high as fifth. However, this 1930 Most Valuable Player Award would be the only one of his Hall of Fame career.

Table 2. 1930 American League Most Valuable Player Voting Results

Place	Player	Team	AP	TSN	Total
1	Joe Cronin	Washington	48	52	100
2	Al Simmons	Philadelphia	39	46	85
3	Lou Gehrig	New York	39	29	68
4	Charlie Gehringer	Detroit	36	31	67
5	Ted Lyons	Chicago	26	30	56
6	Wes Ferrell	Cleveland	25	29	54
7	Eddie Morgan	Cleveland	15	6	21
8	Mickey Cochrane	Philadelphia	13	7	20
9	Lefty Grove	Philadelphia	8	9	17
10	Babe Ruth	New York	7	9	16
11	Goose Goslin	St. Louis	6	8	14
12	Danny MacFayden	Boston	7	5	12
13	Tom Oliver	Boston	2	7	9
14	Lefty Stewart	St. Louis	4	4	8
14	Tony Lazzeri	New York	–	8	8
16	Red Kress	St. Louis	–	6	6
17	Carl Reynolds	Chicago	5	–	5
17	Milt Gaston	Boston	4	1	5
19	Oscar Melillo	St. Louis	2	–	2
19	Lu Blue	St. Louis	2	–	2
21	Earl Webb	Boston	–	1	1

Joe Cronin
1930 American League MVP

Hack Wilson
1930 National League MVP

1930 NATIONAL LEAGUE MVP: HACK WILSON (CHICAGO)

Lewis Robert "Hack" Wilson was famously "built like a beer keg and not unfamiliar with its contents."[24] Following a relatively undistinguished start to his major-league career with the New York Giants, Wilson was sent by John McGraw to the American Association Toledo Mud Hens in 1925. He was left unprotected, and the Chicago Cubs selected him in the 1925 major league draft. As Chicago's center fielder from 1926–29, Wilson led the NL in home runs three times and finished third once.

In 1930, Wilson appeared in 155 games for the Cubs and set career highs for runs (146), hits (208), home runs (56), runs batted in (191), base on balls (105), batting average (.356), on-base average (.454), slugging percentage (.723), and total bases (423), and his OPS of 1.177 is still a single-season Cubs record. The 191 runs batted in remain a major-league record, perhaps belonging in the conversation about unbreakable marks (see Table 3, opposite).

Wilson received Most Valuable Player votes in five other seasons, finishing as high as fifth in 1926. This 1930 MVP Award would be the only one of his Hall of Fame career.

HONORING LEW, JOE, AND HACK

While hitters love to find gaps, baseball historians prefer to close them. Official recognition of the Most Valuable

Table 3. 1930 National League Most Valuable Player Voting Results

Place	Player	Team	AP	TSN	Total
1	Hack Wilson	Chicago	70	41	111
2	Frank Frisch	St. Louis	64	43	107
3	Bill Terry	New York	58	47	105
4	Chuck Klein	Philadelphia	33	24	57
5	Babe Herman	Brooklyn	35	17	52
6	Glenn Wright	Brooklyn	27	11	38
7	Paul Waner	Pittsburgh	14	17	31
8	Kiki Cuyler	Chicago	27	–	27
9	Al Lopez	Brooklyn	12	12	24
10	Walter Berger	Boston	8	14	22
11	Elwood English	Chicago	13	8	21
12	Rabbit Maranville	Boston	9	11	20
13	Fred Lindstrom	New York	17	–	17
14	Gabby Hartnett	Chicago	10	4	14
15	Travis Jackson	New York	7	6	13
16	Burleigh Grimes	St. Louis	9	2	11
17	Charley Gelbert	St. Louis	2	8	10
18	Pie Traynor	Pittsburgh	3	6	9
18	Red Lucas	Cincinnati	–	9	9
20	Gus Mancuso	St. Louis	6	–	6
20	Pat Malone	Chicago	6	–	6
22	Taylor Douthit	St. Louis	4	–	4
22	George Grantham	Pittsburgh	2	2	4
24	Adam Comorosky	Pittsburgh	–	3	3
25	Ray Kremer	Pittsburgh	2	–	2
25	Tony Cuccinello	Cincinnati	–	2	2
27	Dazzy Vance	Brooklyn	1	–	1
27	Harry Heilmann	Cincinnati	1	–	1
27	Joe Stripp	Cincinnati	–	1	1

Player campaigns of Fonseca, Cronin, and Wilson would provide an uninterrupted line of MVP awards reaching back to the 1920s for each league. This awkward gap could be closed.

At its core, the only true difference in American League MVP voting between 1928 and the 1929–30 seasons was the league's withdrawal of the $1,000 cash reward. Same for the National League in 1930—the *only* season since 1924 in which a league MVP is not recognized.

American League MVP voting was handled in the same manner in 1929 and 1930 as it was done for the officially recognized league awards through 1928 (one writer representing each of the eight AL cities casting a ballot of eight players for a maximum total of 64). There were several baseball writers who voted in 1929 and/or 1930 who cast MVP votes before and after, as shown in Table 4, below.

Similarly, the National League vote for 1930 was handled in the exact same manner as it had been in 1924–29 (one writer representing each of the eight NL cities casting a ballot of 10 players for a maximum total of 80). Again, there were several voters in 1930 who participated in the MVP selection process both before and after (see Table 5, below).

The Sporting News voting committees for 1929 and 1930 are shown below. The published list of voters for 1930 was combined, which tends to indicate that the writers for two-team cities participated in both the AL

Table 4. American League Most Valuable Player Voting Committees (1928–32)

City	1928	1929	1930	1931	1932
Boston	Paul Shannon	Paul Shannon	Burton Whitman	Burton Whitman	Melville Webb
Chicago	Harry Neily	John Hoffman	Harry Neily	John Hoffman	Irving Vaughan
Cleveland	Ed Bang	Gordon Cobbledick	Ed Bang	Stuart Bell	Ed Bang
Detroit	Harry Salsinger	Harry Salsinger	Harry Salsinger	Harry Bullion	Harry Salsinger
New York	William Hanna	Ford Frick	Will Wedge	Charles Segar	William Slocum
Philadelphia	James Isaminger	William Dooly	Stoney McLinn	John Nolan	James Isaminger
St. Louis	J. Edward Wray	Sid Keener	Herman Wecke	James Gould	J. Edward Wray
Washington	Denman Thompson	John Keller	Denman Thompson	John Keller	Frank Young

Table 5. National League Most Valuable Player Voting Committees (1928, 1930–32)

City	1928	1930	1931	1932
Boston	Nick Flatley	Paul Shannon	James O'Leary	Paul Shannon
Brooklyn	Tom Meany	Garry Schumacher	Thomas Holmes	Thomas Holmes
Chicago	Irving Vaughan	Irving Vaughan	Ed Burns	Wayne Otto
Cincinnati	Jack Ryder	Tom Swope	Frank Grayson	Tom Swope
New York	Bozeman Bulger	Fred Lieb	Daniel Daniel	George Phair
Philadelphia	Steve Grauley	Harry Robert	Edwin Pollock	Stoney McLinn
Pittsburgh	Ed Ballinger	Charles Doyle	Charles Doyle	Ed Ballinger
St. Louis	James Gould	Martin Haley	J. Roy Stockton	Martin Haley

Although Joe Cronin's MVP award was "unofficial" at the time, it is included in his Hall of Fame plaque in Cooperstown.

Hack Wilson's 191 RBIs in 1930 remains the single-season record in MLB.

and NL voting. There was considerable overlap between this group and writers involved with the Associated Press MVP selection committees held earlier in each year (Table 6).

Table 6. *The Sporting News* Most Valuable Player Voting Committees (1929–30)

City	1929	1930
Boston	Paul Shannon	Burt Whitman
Brooklyn	N/A	Tommy Holmes
Chicago	Harry Neily	Irving Vaughan
Cincinnati	N/A	Tom Swope
Cleveland	Ed Bang	Ed Bang
Detroit	Harry Salsinger	Sam Greene
New York	William Hanna	Joe Vila
Philadelphia	James Isaminger	James Isaminger
Pittsburgh	N/A	Ralph Davis
St. Louis	John Wray	Herman Wecke
Washington	Denman Thompson	Denman Thompson

Starting in 1931, the BBWAA began voting for league MVPs, adopting the system previously used to select the National League winners: 10 points for first place, nine points for second place, and so on, for a maximum of 80.[25] Nevertheless, the Most Valuable Player selections for 1931 through 1934 were deemed "unofficial" in contemporary reporting.[26] When the 1935 MVP awards were announced for Hank Greenberg of Detroit in the AL and Gabby Hartnett of Chicago in the NL, however, the selections no longer included the "unofficial" modifier.[27] The BBWAA used this system for MVP voting through 1937. In 1938, the voting system was expanded to include three writers from each city in each league and the ballot enlarged to 14, for a maximum vote total of 336.

Baseball and fans alike should recognize and celebrate these Most Valuable Player campaigns, especially considering that the MVPs for Fonseca, Cronin, and Wilson would be the only such award for each man. Indeed, the plaque honoring Cronin at the National Baseball Hall of Fame in Cooperstown prominently heralds his selection as the American League Most Valuable Player in 1930! It is time to close the gap. ■

Acknowledgments

The author would like to extend special thanks to Mark Armour, Ryan Fagan, Steve Gietschier, Bill Deane, and Adam Darowski for their kind direction and encouragement.

Sources

In addition to the sources cited in the endnotes, the author also utilized:

Armour, Mark, "Joe Cronin," Society for American Baseball Research, https://sabr.org/bioproj/person/joe-cronin/.

Baseball Reference (which now recognizes these MVP campaigns).

Gabcik, John, "Lew Fonseca," Society for American Baseball Research, https://sabr.org/bioproj/person/lew-fonseca/.

Retrosheet.

Notes

1. "A.L. Abandons Most Valuable Player Award," *Decatur* (IL) *Herald*, May 7, 1929, 12. AL MVP Award winners: 1922: George Sisler, St. Louis; 1923: Babe Ruth, New York; 1924: Walter Johnson (Washington); 1925: Roger Peckinpaugh, Washington; 1926: George Burns, Cleveland; 1927: Lou Gehrig, New York; 1928: Mickey Cochrane, Philadelphia.

2. "National No Longer Will Give Awards," *Rochester Democrat and Chronicle*, June 8, 1929, 17. NL MVP Award winners: 1924: Dazzy Vance, Brooklyn; 1925: Rogers Hornsby, St. Louis; 1926: Bob O'Farrell, St. Louis; 1927: Paul Waner, Pittsburgh; 1928: Jim Bottomley, St. Louis; 1929: Hornsby, Chicago.

3. James Long, "Sports Comment," *Pittsburgh Sun-Telegraph*, May 7, 1929, 20.

4. Murray Robinson, "As You Like It," *Brooklyn Standard Union*, May 7, 1929, 14.

5. The National League had no rule preventing a player from winning multiple awards. Hornsby had also been voted NL MVP in 1925 with St. Louis.

6. The Associated Press and *The Sporting News* held separate votes in 1929 for the American League and in 1930 for the American League and National League.

7. "Auto for Best Batsman," *The New York Times*, March 1, 1910, 10.

8. "Baseball for Hugh Chalmers," *Detroit Free Press*, March 2, 1910, 14.

9. *O'Connor v. St. Louis American League Baseball Co.*, 181 S.W. 1167, 193 Mo.App. 167 (Mo. App. 1916).

10. "Chalmers Felicitates Cobb," *Chicago Tribune*, October 16, 1910, 22; "Cobb Wins Title and Auto," *Chicago Tribune*, October 16, 1910, 22. Some simple math seems to indicate that the 196 hits in 509 at-bats credited to Cobb at the time resulted in a .385069 batting average and Lajoie's 227 hits in 591 at-bats would have been .384095. Regardless, baseball historians have thoroughly reexamined these records and Baseball Reference now lists Lajoie with a .383 batting average (227 hits in 592 at-bats) and Cobb with a .382 batting average (194 hits in 508 at-bats.) Both are credited with the batting title on the website.

11. "Mack Approves Chalmers' Plan," *Altoona* (PA) *Times*, February 14, 1911, 9.

12. "Mack Approves Chalmers' Plan." At least as far back as 1875, the concept of most valuable player to *his ballclub* was recognized with the first documented use tied to a silver trophy given to Deacon White by a wealthy supporter engraved with the caption "Won by Jim White as most valuable player to Boston team, 1875." Peter Morris, *A Game of Inches* (Chicago: Ivan R. Dee, 2010), 541, citing Bill Deane, Award Voting, 5–6.

13. "Hugh Chalmers Would Stimulate Batting Averages," *Lansing State Journal*, February 3, 1911, 8.

14. "No More Free Autos for the Ball Players," *Pittsburgh Press*, December 27, 1914, 22. Winners of the Chalmers Award: 1911: Ty Cobb, Detroit (AL), Frank Schulte, Chicago (NL); 1912: Tris Speaker, Boston (AL), Larry Doyle, New York (NL); 1913: Walter Johnson, Washington (AL), Jake Daubert, Brooklyn (NL); 1914: Eddie Collins, Philadelphia (AL), Johnny Evers, Boston (NL).

15. "League Offers $1000 Reward for Player," *Baltimore Sun*, February 9, 1922, 11. Ty Cobb was ineligible for consideration as the Tigers' player-manager in 1922, despite batting .401/.462/.565 in 613 plate appearances.

16. "League Offers $1000 Reward for Player."

17. "Older League Meeting Ends in Love Feast," *Freeport* (IL) *Journal-Standard*, February 15, 1922, 8.

18. Mark Dukes, "AL Batting Champ Earned $1000 Raise," *Cedar Rapids Gazette*, April 9, 1989, 32.

19. Alan Gould, "Lew Fonseca is Named Most Valuable Player in A.L. by Sport Scribes," *Appleton* (WI) *Post-Crescent*, October 16, 1929, 12.

20. "Lew Fonseca Gets $12,000 Check in 1930," *Stockton Daily Evening Record*, December 16, 1929, 25.

21. "Simmons 'Most Valuable' Player in American League," *Joplin* (MO) *Globe*, December 25, 1929, 10.

22. "Joe Cronin Beats out Simmons and Gehrig," *Boston Globe*, October 10, 1930, 25.

23. "Cronin and Terry Named as Most Valuable Players," *The Sporting News*, November 27, 1930, 5.

24. Ron Coons, "A Tale of Two Sluggers," *Louisville Courier-Journal*, August 7, 1977, C-4.

25. "Writers to Pick Valuable Player," *Detroit Free Press*, April 14, 1931, 28; "Flash Best," *Cincinnati Enquirer*, October 21, 1931, 14.

26. "Previous Winners of American Loop Title of 'Valuable' Player," *Rock Island* (IL) *Argus*, October 28, 1931; "1932 Sport Champions," *Staunton* (VA) *Daily News Leader*, December 30, 1932, 6; "Sport Champions of 1933," *Eugene Guard*, December 31, 1933, 8; "Champions of the Sports World During 1934," *Oakland Tribune*, December 31, 1934, 10.

27. "International Amateur and Professional Sports Champions of 1935," *Hackensack Record*, December 31, 1935, 15.

28. Bill Terry's Hall of Fame plaque also includes a reference to his 1930 *Sporting News* Most Valuable Player Award.

The Pitcher's Cycle

Definition and Achievers (1893–2023)

Herm Krabbenhoft

One of baseball's highest-regarded feats is the cycle: "A single, double, triple, and home run (not necessarily in that order) hit by a player in the same game."[1] In the history of major league baseball (1876–2023) there have been 351 documented regular-season cycles, including seven in the Negro Leagues.[2] The distribution of the starting defensive positions of the players who achieved these cycles is provided in Table 1.

No starting pitcher has ever achieved the feat.[3] With the notable exception of Shohei Ohtani, pitchers have rarely batted since 1973 in the AL and since 2022 in the NL. Thus, the feat of achieving a cycle is limited to non-pitchers, and the cycle has become a de facto "Batter's Cycle" (BC). What about pitchers? How about a cycle *exclusively* for pitchers?

The three principal goals of the research described in this article are:

1) Devise a viable definition for a Pitcher's Cycle that is equivalent to the Batter's Cycle.

2) Compile a list of all Pitcher's Cycles from 1893 forward.

3) Highlight the special features and characteristics of the various Pitcher's Cycles.

To pursue the first objective, I looked up various definitions for the word "cycle." I wanted to adhere to the basic definition of a cycle, "a sequence of a recurring succession of events or phenomena," and create an equivalent to the batter's cycle: a series of pitching achievements commensurate to a batter collecting the series of types of safe hit.[4] A batter's primary objective is to get on base, which he can achieve *entirely by himself* by getting a safe hit, of which there are the four types. A pitcher's primary objective is to retire the batter, which he can do *entirely by himself* by striking out the batter, who occupies one of the nine positions in the batting order.[5]

Since a regulation baseball game consists of nine innings, a seemingly reasonable cycle would require the pitcher to strike out at least one batter in each inning. However, this definition has a couple issues. First, not all games last nine innings. Some are shortened due to weather, some go into extra innings, and some forego the bottom of the ninth because the home team is ahead. This variability would lead to different categories of Pitcher's Cycles, such as a six-inning PC or a seven-inning PC. Second, a player could achieve a PC by striking out a few players multiple times. While striking out at least one batter in each inning of a regulation nine-inning game is a noteworthy accomplishment, it doesn't merit the same level of regard accorded to the BC.

Since there are nine different players in the batting lineup, a reasonable cycle would be for the pitcher to strike out each of the opposing batters at least once in a game. One difficulty with this idea is that a player could be replaced before the pitcher had a chance to face him. To address this circumstance, the concept can be modified slightly: the pitcher must strike out at least one batter *from each of the nine recurring batting slots*. This would still require the hurler to fan at least nine different batters in the same game. And since, in a regulation nine-inning game, the batting order recurs at least three times, adherence to the basic definition of a cycle is achieved. Furthermore, in striking out at least one player from each of the nine batting slots, the pitcher achieves a complete set (series) of strikeout victims.

Thus, my definition of a Pitcher's Cycle: "The series of at least one player from each of the nine repeating batting slots (not necessarily in order) struck out by one pitcher in the same game."

My definition of a Pitcher's Cycle essentially paraphrases *The Dickson Baseball Dictionary* definition of a Batter's Cycle.[6] Similarly, while

Table 1. Distribution of Cycles According to the Achiever's Starting Field Position (1876–2023)

P	C	1B	2B	3B	SS	LF	CF	RF	DH
ZERO	17	52	39	37	38	53	54	53	8

a batter *hits* for his cycle, a pitcher *hurls* for his cycle. A batter collects specific *hits* for his cycle while a pitcher collects specific *strikeouts* for his cycle. While the Pitcher's Cycle requires a player to pitch at least three innings, it does not require the player to be a starting pitcher. Moreover, just like there is no limit to the number of plate appearances it takes a player to achieve the Batter's Cycle, there is no limit to the number of innings it takes a player to achieve the Pitcher's Cycle.[7]

With a viable definition of a Pitcher's Cycle in place, the next step was identifying the players who accomplished the feat. The 1893 season was chosen as the starting point because that was the first year for the current 60'6" distance between the pitcher's rubber and home plate.

RESEARCH PROCEDURE

Since a player needs a minimum of nine strikeouts to accomplish the Pitcher's Cycle, I started by generating a list of pitchers who amassed at least 9 strikeouts in an "ML" game. "ML" is enclosed in quotation marks to indicate that only the National, American, and Federal Leagues were considered for the research described in this article. My research on Pitcher's Cycles achieved in the Negro Leagues has been initiated and the results will be disseminated as soon as possible.

For the 1893–1900 period, I utilized the game-by-game pitching statistics provided in the ICI (Information Concepts Incorporated) sheets, digitized versions of which were graciously provided to me by Retrosheet's Dave Smith. For the 1901–2023 period, I used Baseball Reference's indispensable Stathead search engine. I queried for pitchers with nine or more strikeouts, then examined the box score and play-by-play to ascertain the batting order of the victims.

There are 87 games from the 1901–1915 period for which the box scores omit strikeout information about the batters. Fortunately, Jonathan Frankel has done some phenomenal research on strikeouts for the late nineteenth and early twentieth centuries. He graciously provided information that filled many of the gaps.[8] Nonetheless, 54 games remain for which it has not yet been determined whether the pitcher achieved a Pitcher's Cycle. See Supplement A (available on the SABR website) for pertinent information for these 54 games. Finally, John Rickert graciously wrote a computer program using the Retrosheet database to confirm the validity of my methodology for the 1901–2023 seasons.[9]

RESULTS

From 1893 to 2023, there were (at least) 483 Pitcher's Cycles by 276 different players, along with 316 Batter's Cycles by 279 different players.[10] Despite a difference of 167, the two sums are in the same ballpark and have the same order of magnitude. Table 2 provides a decade-by-decade comparison and Figure 1 provides a graphical comparison of the corresponding cumulative numbers.

Table 2 shows that the bulk of the 167-cycle difference has occurred in the last few decades; starting in 1990 and picking up speed in 2010. Thus, while the number of Batter's Cycles was greater than the number of Pitcher's Cycles for nearly every decade up to

Table 2. Decade-By-Decade Comparison of Pitcher's Cycles (PC) and Batter's Cycles (BC)

Decade	# BC (Total)		# PC Total		Difference Total	
1893–1900	8	(8)	0	(0)	-8	(-8)
1901–09	11	(19)	8	(8)	-3	(-11)
1910–19	11	(30)	12	(20)	+1	(-10)
1920–29	25	(55)	3	(23)	-22	(-32)
1930–39	29	(84)	9	(32)	-20	(-52)
1940–49	29	(113)	9	(41)	-20	(-72)
1950–59	11	(124)	19	(60)	+8	(-64)
1960–69	14	(138)	37	(97)	+23	(-41)
1970–79	29	(167)	45	(142)	+16	(-25)
1980–89	27	(194)	30	(172)	+3	(-22)
1990–99	24	(218)	54	(226)	+30	(+8)
2000–09	46	(264)	66	(292)	+20	(+28)
2010–19	38	(302)	125	(417)	+87	(+115)
2020–23	14	(316)	66	(483)	+52	(+167)

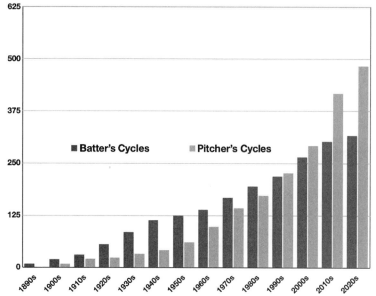

Figure 1. Decade-By-Decade Comparison of the Cumulative Numbers of Pitcher's Cycles and Batter's Cycles

the 1940s, the situation has been reversed since the 1950s. The total number of Pitcher's Cycles surpassed the total number of Batter's Cycles during the 1990s. From 1949 to 2019, home runs increased by 81.3% while strikeouts increased by 139.9%.[11] Pitchers are throwing harder and batters are focused on exit velocity and launch angles. These changes unavoidably lead to more strikeouts and more Pitcher's Cycles.

Because the Pitcher's Cycle is a new concept, it features several aspects that merit exposition, such as a team-by-team summary of PCs, the chronology of the career leaders, and postseason PCs. These topics and others are covered in the Appendix and Supplement, available on the SABR website.[12] The remainder of this article will focus on these four topics:

1. Relief Pitcher's Cycles

2. Perfect Pitcher's Cycles

3. Super Pitcher's Cycles

4. The only major-league player with both a Batter's Cycle and a Pitcher's Cycle

1. RELIEF PITCHER'S CYCLES

As seen in Table 3, Six of the players who achieved a Pitcher's Cycle did so in relief. Also, as described in Appendix G, Jesse Barnes earned a relief PC in the 1921 World Series.

Rube Marquard took over for Christy Mathewson after the first inning. Big Six pitched an uneventful first inning, but in the bottom of the frame, the Giants scored 13 runs. "Having the game on ice, [manager John] McGraw made several changes in his lineup. He took Mathewson out of the box, so as to save him for another game and he put Marquard in the box."[13] Marquard carved out his Pitcher's Cycle as the Giants emerged victorious, 19–5. Mathewson was credited with the win and Marquard was retroactively credited with a save.[14]

Gene Conley essentially pitched a complete game that he did not start. Starter Seth Morehead got rocked by the Cubs in the first frame, allowing a single to leadoff batter Tony Taylor, hitting the next batter, George Altman, walking the third batter, Lee Walls, and surrendering a bases-clearing double to clean-up hitter Ernie Banks. Conley came in from the bullpen at this point. The fireman got next batter, Bobby Thomson, to fly out, but then yielded an RBI triple to John Goryl before striking out Alvin Dark and Cal Neeman. Conley pitched rest of game, striking out 11 and blanking the Cubs for nine innings (a full-route pseudo-shutout).[15] Unfortunately, the Phillies were unable to overcome the first-inning deficit, losing 4–3. Morehead was charged with the loss. "Gene Conley pitched nine shutout innings for the Philadelphia Phillies today," wrote the Associated Press, "but had nothing to show for his efforts except self-satisfaction. In all, he fanned 11, two shy of the club record held by Ray Benge, Robin Roberts, and Jack Sanford, and whiffed every Cub in the starting lineup at least once. Conley, now figured to move into the Phils starting rotation, was obviously pleased with his performance. 'I'm ready now,' he said after the game. 'This is just what I needed. I'm ready for whatever the skipper (Eddie Sawyer) wants me to do, starting or relieving.'"[16]

Dave Hillman, who started for the Cubs in Conley's relief Pitcher's Cycle, achieved his own relief PC just a few weeks later. In an "It's-déjà-vu-all-over-again" twist, Seth Morehead, who had been traded from the Phillies to the Cubs on May 12, was once again the starting pitcher. Morehead walked Dodgers leadoff batter Junior Gilliam and gave up a single to Charlie Neal before he struck out Don Demeter. He then intentionally walked Gil Hodges immediately before Rip Repulski smashed a bases-clearing double. After walking Dick Gray, he was replaced by Hillman. Hillman threw a wild pitch to Johnny Roseboro, then walked him intentionally. Hillman then got things under control by striking out pinch hitter Duke Snider and opposing pitcher Stan Williams. Hillman pitched brilliantly for 7⅔ innings to complete the bottom of the eighth. In the top of the ninth, the Cubs rallied for a pair of runs to take a 7–5 lead. In the bottom of the ninth, Hillman walked Snider to lead off the inning. Don Elston was then summoned from the bullpen and

Table 3. Relief Hurlers Who Accomplished a Pitcher's Cycle

Pitcher	Team	Date (Game)	OPP	IP	SO	Result[2]
Rube Marquard	NYG*	1911-05-13	STL	8.0	14	ND-S (W)
Gene Conley	PHI*	1959-05-02	CHC	9.0	11	ND-GF (L)
Dave Hillman	CHC	1959-05-28	LAD*	7.2	11	W
Dick Radatz	BOS	1963-06-11	DET*	8.2	11	BS; W
Randy Johnson	ARI	2001-07-18	SDP*	7.0	16	W
Tyler Alexander	DET*	2020-08-02[1]	CIN	3.2	10	ND (L)

NOTES
1. An asterisk in the Team or OPP column indicates the game was played in that city.
2. In the Result column, ND means "No Decision," S means "Save," GF means "Game Finished," BS means "Blown Save."

retired the next three batters to secure the triumph for Chicago. Elston was rewarded (retroactively) with a save and Hillman was awarded the W, a nice complement to his second Pitcher's Cycle. He earned the first as a starting pitcher in 1958.

Dick Radatz earned his Pitcher's Cycle in an ideal payback manner. Radatz, nicknamed "The Monster," achieved his PC in a duel of relief pitchers at Tiger Stadium on June 11, 1963. Going into the bottom of the seventh, the BoSox clung to a 3–2 lead. Southpaw Wilbur Wood was on the hump for the Red Sox. Don Wert led off with a single and Dick McAuliffe sacrificed him to second. With Tigers starter Jim Bunning due up, Detroit manager Bob Scheffing called on the right-handed Bill Freehan to pinch hit. Boston Manager Johnny Pesky countered by calling on the Monster, a right-hander. Scheffing went to his bench again, summoning left-swinging Whitey Herzog to bat for Freehan. Radatz proceeded to strike out Herzog before passing Jake Wood. That brought up Bubba Phillips, a right-handed batter, and more managerial chess. Scheffing called on the left-handed batting Bill Bruton to pinch-hit for Phillips. Pesky stood pat with Radatz. Bruton delivered a single to knock in Wert with the tying run, which was officially charged to Wood. Radatz induced a groundout from Al Kaline to end the inning. While Radatz was not charged with Wert's run, he was retroactively charged with a blown save. The game remained knotted going into the top of the 15th inning, at which point the Red Sox took a 7–3 lead. In the last of the 15th, the Monster struck out pinch-hitter Frank Kostro and got Jake Wood to pop out, bringing up Bill Bruton. As it had happened, Bruton's number-two spot was the only strikeout Radatz needed. He simultaneously secured the victory and the PC: a Walk-off Strikeout Pitcher's Cycle.

Randy Johnson got his record-breaking eighth NL Pitcher's Cycle in a bizarre relief role against the Padres on July 19, 2001. The night before, Arizona's starting pitcher, Curt Schilling, had set down the first six batters in order. The D-backs had pushed across a run to provide a 1–0 lead going into the top of the third. With the bases empty and nobody out, Schilling was in the batter's box. The count was 0-and-2. "Transformer Explosion Suspends Padres Game" was the headline in the next day's newspaper story.[17] After a delay of over an hour, the backup lighting was deemed inadequate and the game was suspended, to be completed the next day as the first game of a "doubleheader." Upon resumption the next day, Brian Anderson replaced Schilling in the batter's box; he struck out looking and the strikeout was charged to Schilling. Johnson replaced Anderson in the Arizona lineup and nearly tossed a perfect game. He walked just one batter and gave up one hit, a harmless single. He struck out 16. After the game, Johnson said, "By no means do I go out and try to strike people out. It's probably one of the hardest things to do, especially against major league hitters. But I got in a groove. [Catcher] Damian [Miller] made some big blocks when I threw my breaking ball in the dirt."[18] Diamondbacks manager Bob Brenly jokingly added, "He may be the best long man, huh."

Tyler Alexander established an amazing relief-pitcher record in the first game of a doubleheader at Comerica Park. With each game scheduled for seven innings because of the COVID-19 pandemic, Alexander entered in the top of third with the Reds leading his Tigers, 3–0. Nick Castellanos had just hit a homer off starting pitcher Rony Garcia. Alexander struck out the next three batters in succession: Mike Moustakas (five pitches, swinging), Eugenio Suarez (three pitches, looking), and Jesse Winker (three pitches, swinging). In the top of the fourth, Alexander struck out the side: Nick Senzel (four pitches, swinging), Josh VanMeter (three pitches, looking), and Freddy Galvis (eight pitches, swinging). Alexander did it again in the fifth: Tucker Barnhart (four pitches, looking), Shogo Akiyama (four pitches, looking), and Castellanos (five pitches, swinging). The *Detroit Free Press* wrote, "Nine men up. Nine men down [via strikeouts]. It tied an American League record, set by the Tigers' Doug Fister against the Royals on September 27, 2012. Alexander's reaction—somewhere between 'meh' and 'whatever'—was perhaps as bewildering as his pitches. 'I don't know about special,' he said. 'I normally don't try to strike people out. But I would say that after about the fifth strikeout I was trying to strike people out. I don't know about special. We were just trying to get outs and keep us in it. It's surprising, I guess,' he said. 'I normally do throw a lot of strikes, and when I miss, I miss over the plate. I made a big focus on missing down. I didn't have very many bad misses and the mistakes I made were in the dirt so it gave me a chance for them to swing at it.' Alexander wasn't aware of the record until it was announced in the [virtually empty] stadium after he struck out Castellanos to end the fifth inning."[19] In the top of the sixth, Alexander terminated his string of strikeouts by hitting Moustakas.

2. PERFECT PITCHER'S CYCLES

When a pitcher strikes out nine batters in succession,

he automatically achieves a Pitcher's Cycle, as just described. Such a feat is herewith dubbed a Perfect Pitcher's Cycle.[20] Table 4 shows the 13 documented Perfect Pitcher's Cycles. The nineteenth and twentieth centuries saw one each. So far there have been 11 in the twenty-first century. Nice snippets about each of the Perfect Pitcher's Cycles are available in an article on MLB.com.[21] For four (or five) of the players, the Perfect Pitcher's Cycle was the only PC they achieved in their big-league careers. Mickey Welch and Pablo López achieved their Perfect Pitcher Cycles at the beginning of the game, while Tom Seaver ended the game with his. For Welch's 1884 Perfect Pitcher's Cycle, the distance from the front of the pitcher's box to home plate was only 50 feet.

3. SUPER PITCHER'S CYCLES

As mentioned previously, striking out at least one batter in each inning of a nine-inning game is a noteworthy accomplishment, though it doesn't quite measure up to the Batter's Cycle. However, combining that achievement with a Pitcher's Cycle affords an impressive feat herewith termed a "Super Pitcher's Cycle."[22] To earn credit for a Super Pitcher's Cycle, the player must strike out at least one batter in each of nine consecutive innings and at least one batter from each of the nine batting slots. A complete game is not required, so he could be removed after striking out a batter in the ninth inning or enter with an out already recorded in the first. The Super Pitcher's Cycle has been achieved 31 times by 23 players. Tables 5a and 5b present the pertinent details for the players who achieved a Super Pitcher's Cycle.

Four of those pitchers did not hurl complete games: Johnny Allen (1934), Mike Flanagan (1978), Nolan Ryan (1986), and Randy Johnson (2001). Allen struck out Eric McNair for the second out in the ninth inning, but injured his arm in the process and had to leave the game. Flanagan was replaced by Don Stanhouse to start the 10th inning with the score tied, 2–2. Ryan was relieved in the 10th inning with two runners on and one out in a scoreless game. Johnson was replaced to begin the 10th inning with the score tied, 1–1. Five players achieved multiple Super Pitcher's Cycles: Sandy Koufax (2), Tom Seaver (2), Ryan (4), Roger Clemens (3), and Pedro Martinez (2). Bill Hallahan achieved the first Super PC (1931). It was the only PC in his career. Vince Velasquez earned the most recent Super PC in 2015. Perhaps the most phenomenal Super PC was accomplished by Nolan Ryan. The Express struck out at least one batter in each of the 11 innings he pitched en route to a 19-K Super PC performance. In spite of this stellar complete-game effort, he lost the game, 1–0. Finally, as described in Appendix G, Bob Gibson accomplished a Super Pitcher's Cycle in Game 1 of the 1968 World Series.

4. THE ONLY PLAYER WITH BOTH A BATTER'S CYCLE AND A PITCHER'S CYCLE: SHOHEI OHTANI

Shohei Ohtani has achieved one Batter's Cycle (thus far) in his major-league career, on June 13, 2019, at Tropicana Field versus the Tampa Bay Rays. Batting third as the Angels' designated hitter, Ohtani slugged a three-run homer off Ryan Yarborough in the first inning, doubled off him in the third, and tripled off him in the fifth. He singled off Hunter Wood in the seventh. Fittingly, the Angels won the game, 5–3, thanks in part to the four runs Ohtani produced. In the batting cage before his final at bat, Ohtani expressed to infielder David Fletcher that more than anything he wanted to increase the Angels' tenuous two-run lead. "I went and saw him in the cage and said, 'all you need is a single,'" Fletcher said. "He was like, 'No, I want another homer.' I don't think he was trying to hit a single. He was definitely trying to hit another homer if you watch the at bat. But I'm glad he got the single."[23]

After the game Ohtani said through a translator, "You need some power to hit the home run, some speed to accomplish a triple. To be able to do

Table 4. Players Who Achieved a Perfect Pitcher's Cycle

| Pitcher (Team) | Year | IP | Strikeouts | | | Total | PCs Career |
			Before	Streak	After		
Mickey Welch	1884	* 9.0 *	0	* 9	5	14	1+?
Tom Seaver (NYM)	1970	* 9.0 *	9	10 *	0	19	5
Jake Peavy (SDP)	2007	7.0	1	9	6	16	2
Ricky Nolasco (FLA)	2009	7.2	3	9	4	16	1
Aaron Harang (LAD)	2012	6.1	0	9	4	13	1
Doug Fister (DET)	2012	7.2	1	9	0	10	1
Max Scherzer (WAS)	2015	* 9.0 *	8	9	0	17	9
Tyler Alexander (DET)	2020	3.2	0	9	1	10	1
Jacob deGrom (NYM)	2021	6.0	1	9	4	14	8
Aaron Nola (PHI)	2021	5.1	0	10	2	12	4
Pablo López (MIA)	2021	6.0	0	* 9	0	9	2
Corbin Burnes (MIL)	2021	8.0	0	10	5	15	2
Andrew Heaney (TEX)	2023	5.0	1	9	0	10	2

NOTES: In the IP column, entries bracketed with asterisks indicate a complete game. In the Streak column, an asterisk preceding the entry indicates that the streak started with the first batter of the game; an asterisk succeeding the entry indicates that the streak ended with the last batter of the game.

Table 5a—Players with a Super Pitcher's Cycle (1901–91)

Pitcher	Team	Year	IP	SO	Result
Bill Hallahan	STL*	1931	* 9.0 *	13	W
Johnny Allen	NYY*	1934	8.2	12	W
Bob Feller	CLE	1946	* 9.0 *	14	W
Dick Drott	CHC*	1957	* 9.0 *	15	W
Stan Williams	LAD*	1961	* 9.0 *	12	W
Sandy Koufax	LAD*	1961	* 13.0 *	15	W
Sandy Koufax	LAD*	1965	* 9.0 *	14	W
Mike Cuellar	HOU	1966	* 9.0 *	12	W
Tom Seaver	NYM*	1970	* 9.0 *	19	W
Gaylord Perry	SFG	1970	* 9.0 *	14	W
Bill Stoneman	MON*	1971	* 9.0 *	14	W
Tom Seaver	NYM	1973	* 9.0 *	16	W
Nolan Ryan	CAL*	1974	* 11.0 *	19	L
Ron Guidry	NYY*	1978	* 9.0 *	18	W
Mike Flanagan	BAL*	1978	* 9 *	13	ND (W)
Roger Clemens	BOS*	1986	* 9.0 *	20	W
Nolan Ryan	HOU*	1986	9.1	14	ND (W)
Nolan Ryan	TEX	1990	* 9.0 *	14	W
Nolan Ryan	TEX	1991	* 9.0 *	16	W

NOTE: In the IP column, entries bracketed with asterisks indicate a complete game.

Table 5b—Players with a Super Pitcher's Cycle (1992–2023)

Pitcher	Team	Year	IP	SO	Result
Roger Clemens	BOS	1996	* 9.0 *	20	W
Kerry Wood	CHC*	1998	* 9.0 *	20	W
Roger Clemens	TOR*	1998	* 9.0 *	18	W
Pedro Martinez	BOS*	1999	* 9.0 *	16	W
Pedro Martinez	BOS	2000	* 9.0 *	17	L
Randy Johnson	ARI*	2001	9.0	20	W
Curt Schilling	ARI	2003	* 9.0 *	14	W
Roy Halladay	TOR*	2005	* 9.0 *	10	W
Brandon Morrow	TOR*	2010	* 9.0 *	17	W
Clayton Kershaw	LAD*	2015	* 9.0 *	15	W
Max Scherzer	WAS	2015	* 9.0 *	17	W
Vince Velazquez	PHI*	2016	* 9.0 *	16	W

that at the major league level is going to lead to a lot of confidence. The important thing now is to try to continue this tomorrow." He then added, "I wasn't necessarily trying to hit a single. I was just trying to get on base, whether it was a base on balls or any other way because it was still a close game."[24] Responding to a postgame question about being the first Japanese player to hit for the cycle, Ohtani said, "Simply very happy to accomplish this. There's been so many great Japanese players that have come before me. Being the first one to accomplish it [makes me] really happy and makes for a lot of confidence down the road."[25]

Ohtani has achieved two Pitcher's Cycles (thus far) in his major-league career. The first came on April 20, 2022, at Minute Maid Park against the Houston Astros. Ohtani struck out a dozen over six innings. In the first, he fanned leadoff batter Jeremy Pena (slot one) and Michael Brantley (two). In the second he whiffed clean-up hitter Yordan Alvarez (four). He struck out the side in the third and fourth: Niko Goodrum (seven), Jason Castro (eight), and Jose Siri (nine), Pena, Brantley, and Alex Bregman (three). Alvarez flied out in the fifth, snapping Ohtani's string of six consecutive strikeouts. Ohtani then resumed his strikeout clinic by fanning Kyle Tucker (five) and Yuri Gurriel (six), giving him the Pitcher's Cycle. Also of significance, Ohtani had retired each of the first 15 batters; he was hurling a perfect game. In the sixth, he fanned leadoff batter Goodrum for his 12th strikeout, but

Castro lined a single to center, breaking up the perfecto. Ohtani closed out the frame with a popout, a walk, and a groundout. "Ohtani threw 81 pitches [55 strikes] on a night [Angels manager Joe] Maddon had said he would be limited to 85. But, Maddon said after the game that he would not have pulled him with a perfect game intact regardless of the pitch count. 'There's no number,' Maddon said. 'He was going to pitch a perfect game. I'm not going to get in the way of a player's greatness—ever.' Ohtani was asked if he was thinking about the perfect game. 'I was aware of it, but I knew the pitch count was getting up there, and I was thinking I wouldn't be able to finish it,' he said. Ohtani was also the designated hitter, batting leadoff for the Angels. Facing Jake Odorizzi, he started the game by drawing a base on balls, and, as the Angels proceeded to bat around, he also clouted a two-RBI double off Blake Taylor. In the third, facing Cristian Javier, he lined out to third base. In the top of the sixth, again squaring off against Javier, he bunted for a single. After leaving the mound, Ohtani flied out to left in the bottom of the eighth. The final result was a 6–0 triumph for the Angels, with Ohtani as the winning pitcher. "Ohtani was asked if it was his top performance in the majors. 'It could be,' he said with a smile in Japanese through a translator." He had achieved the Pitcher's Cycle and was halfway to a Batter's Cycle.

Ohtani's second PC came on May 3, 2023, at Busch Stadium. He hurled the first five innings, striking out 13 Cardinals. In the bottom of the first, he fanned leadoff batter Lars Nootbaar (slot one), Paul Goldschmidt (two), and Wilson Contreras (five). He also gave up a homer to Nolan Gorman. Ohtani whiffed three batters in the second: Dylan Carlson (seven), Brendan Donovan (eight), and Tommy Edman (nine). In the third inning he atoned for the homer he yielded by striking out Gorman (three) and Nootbaar. In the fourth, Ohtani struck out Alec Burleson (six) and Donovan, but he was touched for three runs on two doubles and another home run (by Carlson). In the fifth, he struck out three: Nootbaar (for the third time), Goldschmidt (for the second time), and Nolan Arenado (four), giving him the Pitcher's Cycle. At the end of five innings, the Angels trailed, 4–3. Ohtani had thrown 97 pitches while striking out 13 batters. His 13th strikeout was the 500th of his career, putting him in select company: in major-league history, only he and Babe Ruth have accumulated 500 strikeouts and 100 home runs.[27]

Wrote Rhett Bollinger, "Ohtani had a strange start outside of his strikeout total, however, as he allowed four extra-base hits, walked a batter, hit another and threw two wild pitches. So while it was special for Ohtani to reach yet another milestone, he was frustrated he only made it through five frames. 'I gave up a couple homers and I wanted to get through six or seven innings, minimum,' Ohtani said through interpreter Ippei Mizuhara. 'So more than the strikeouts, I'm just disappointed I couldn't pitch deeper in the game.'"[28] Ohtani made three plate appearances as the pitcher. He singled in the first, then again in the third, driving in a run to give the Angels a 2–1 lead. He popped out in the fifth. Ohtani had two plate appearances as the DH. He grounded out in the seventh and doubled in the ninth, eventually coming around to score the go-ahead run.

SUMMARY

A viable definition of a Pitcher's Cycle has been devised to characterize a feat commensurate with the Batter's Cycle. From 1893 to 2023, there were 483 Pitcher's Cycles, achieved by 276 different pitchers. At present, Randy Johnson holds the career records for the most Pitcher's Cycles in the major leagues (21) and the National League (11). He shares the American League record (10) with Chris Sale. Because of the huge increase in strikeouts during the past few decades, Pitcher's Cycles have become more frequent than Batter's Cycles, perhaps dimming the luster of the PC. From 1893 to 1949 (57 seasons), there were 113 BCs and 41 PCs, a difference of negative 72. From 1950 to 1999 (50 seasons), the corresponding numbers were 105 and 185, a difference of *positive* 80. From 2000 to 2023 (only 24 seasons), the corresponding numbers are 98 and 257, a difference of positive 159. Of the 13 Perfect Pitcher's Cycles, 11 were achieved since 2007. Super Pitcher's Cycles have been accomplished 31 times by 23 pitchers; Nolan Ryan holds the record with four Super PCs. Shohei Ohtani is the only player in history with both a Batter's Cycle and a Pitcher's Cycle.

DISCUSSION

The most important question is whether the Pitcher's Cycle, as defined here, is as noteworthy a feat as the Batter's Cycle. Table 6 lists some typical single-game batter's feats, along with (in my opinion) commensurate feats for pitchers.[29]

Based on the information provided in Table 6, I contend that the answer is a resounding *yes*! The Pitcher's Cycle is a noteworthy feat, just as the Batter's Cycle is. Significantly, the Pitcher's Cycle and the Batter's Cycle are accomplishments achieved—*entirely by the player himself*—via *skill*. However, it would be fair to describe both the Pitcher's Cycle and the Batter's Cycle as quirky or fluky.

With regard to skill, achieving the Batter's Cycle requires the batter to employ each of the three keystone skills of offense: collecting four hits in a game requires hitting for average, collecting three extra-base hits requires hitting for power, and hitting a double and a triple requires speed. However, the requirement of collecting *each* of the four types of hits in one game imparts quirkiness and/or flukiness to the Batter's Cycle. A player can use expertise to specifically try for a single by bunting or employing the Willie Keeler approach of hitting 'em where they ain't. Similarly, a player can swing for the fences to purposely try for a home run. However, doubles and especially triples are not likely to be achieved by a player trying to specifically hit them on purpose. Thus, while each individual type of base hit requires skill, assembling the complete series involves some luck. To wit, when Rod Carew achieved his Batter's Cycle on May 20, 1970, he told reporters, "Lots of luck. That's it, lots of luck."[30] At least two players, Kelly Gruber and Jeff Frye, eschewed a sure extra-base hit by "skillfully" stopping at first base complete the Batter's Cycle with a single.[31]

Achieving the Pitcher's Cycle also requires skill. Strikeouts are valued especially because they preclude balls in play that could result in an error or an out that allows an existing base runner to advance. There are different types of hitters, such as free swingers, go-with-the-pitch hitters, high-ball hitters, and so on. As with the Batter's Cycle, while skill is needed to strike out any one batter, striking out at least one batter from each batting slot requires some luck. To illustrate this, let's consider these two games:

- **September 21, 1954,** (2nd) at Fenway Park: Frank Sullivan of the Boston Red Sox emerged with a 4–3 victory over the Philadelphia Athletics. He surrendered eight hits and issued three walks in 8⅓ innings before being relieved. He allowed

Table 6. Single-Game Feats for Batters and Pitchers (Since 1893)

Batter's Feat (#)	Achievers (Year)	Pitcher's Feat (#)	Achievers (Year)
Most Hits		Most Strikeouts	
(A) 9-Inning Game (7)	(A) Rennie Stennett (1975)	(A) 9-Inning Game (20)	(A) Roger Clemens (1986, 1996);
(B) >9-Inning Game (9)	(B) Johnny Burnett (1932)	(B) >9-Inning Game (21)	Kerry Wood (1998); Randy Johnson (2001);
			Max Scherzer (2016); (B) Tom Cheney (1962)
Most Doubles (4)	50 Players: First—Frank Bonner (1894) Last—Jarren Duran (2023)	?	
Most Triples (4)	Bill Joyce (1897)	?	
Most Home Runs (4)	16 Players: First—Bobby Lowe (1894) Last—J.D. Martinez (2017)	?	
Most Cycles (3)	Bob Meusel (1921, 1922, 1928) Babe Herman (1931, 1931, 1933) Adrian Beltre (2008, 2012, 2015) Trea Turner (2017, 2019, 2021) Christian Yelich (2018, 2018, 2022)	Most Cycles (21)	Randy Johnson [1992 (2), 1993 (2), 1995 (1), 1997 (3), 1998 (2), 1999 (2), 2000 (2), 2001 (4), 2003 (1), 2004 (2)]
Most Consecutive Hits (7)	Cesar Gutierrez (1970) Rennie Stennett (1975)	Most Consecutive Strikeouts (10)	Tom Seaver (1970) Aaron Nola (2021) Corbin Burnes (2021)
Total Cycles (316)	279 players	Total Cycles (483)	276 players

NOTE: Randy Johnson struck out 20 batters in 9 innings on May 8, 2001, and was then replaced at the start of the 10th inning. Johnson did not pitch in the 10th inning. The game eventually took 11 innings.

two earned runs on solo homers by Jim Finigan and Bill Renna. He struck out nine batters, one from each slot, earning the Pitcher's Cycle. After the game, Sullivan said, "I wasn't pitching right. My back is killing me. I hope I didn't hurt myself."

- **May 11, 2016**, at Nationals Park: Max Scherzer of the Washington Nationals emerged with a 3–2 victory over the Detroit Tigers. He threw a complete game, walking none and scattering six hits. Both runs were earned, coming on solo homers by Jose Iglesias and J.D. Martinez. Scherzer struck out 20 batters, at least one in each inning, but, he did *not* earn the Pitcher's Cycle. He failed to strike out Victor Martinez, the clean-up hitter, who went 3-for-4 with three singles and a groundout. After the game Scherzer said, "There's something [special] about 20. Tonight was an emotional game, facing a former team and all those guys I have so much respect for. And so to have a game like this against that caliber of hitter on their side, it really puts a feather in my cap." Going into the ninth inning, Scherzer had already set down 18 batters on strikes, giving him the chance to tie Tom Cheney's single-game record of 21 strikeouts. "It crossed my mind," said Scherzer. "I was thinking of all the different

scenarios in an 0–2 count that I could do to be able to get that last strikeout." Instead, James McCann ended the game by grounding into a 5–4 force out. Nonetheless, Scherzer's 20 K's equaled the record for strikeouts in a nine-inning game, shared by Roger Clemens (1986 and 1996), Kerry Wood (1998), and Randy Johnson (2001). "That's some serious company," said Scherzer. "It won't sink in right now, but it's an amazing accomplishment. Had to go through some tough, tough hitters there with Miggy [Miguel Cabrera], J.D., and Victor, and all those guys over there. Those guys are unbelievable and they gave me a heck of time tonight."[33]

While Scherzer turned in a phenomenally skillful performance, he was not fortunate enough to achieve the Pitcher's Cycle. It would have marked the fourth PC of his career (he currently has eight). Sullivan turned in an acceptably skillful performance while fortunately accomplishing his first and only PC.

The first use of the word "cycle" to describe a player collecting a single, double, triple, and home run in one game was in 1921; *after* 70 cycles had already been achieved: "George Sisler on August 13 [1921] hit the cycle by getting on [via] a single, double, triple, and home run, and by getting an extra double in the same game."[34] Furthermore, as Mike Huber and Allison Davidson subsequently reported, the term did not again appear in print over the next 10 years, during which time another 22 cycles were achieved. According to Huber and Davidson, "By 1938, it seems that the phrase ["hitting for the cycle"] to describe this rare event was indeed commonplace."[35] So while nowadays regarded as a prestigious feat, the Batter's Cycle had an induction period of roughly 60 years. The Pitcher's Cycle, if also eventually deemed a prestigious feat by baseball fans, might follow a similar course. ■

Acknowledgments

With grateful appreciation, I heartily thank all the people who have contributed to Baseball Reference and Retrosheet, thereby making their websites phenomenal baseball-research-enabling vehicles. Special thanks are gratefully extended to John Rickert for graciously writing a computer program using the Retrosheet database to generate a complete list of players who achieved the Pitcher's Cycle during the 1901–2023 period, thereby confirming my hands-on research and ensuring that the players who achieved the Pitcher's Cycle were identified. It is a pleasure to again thank Jonathan Frankel for providing his superb strikeout research to me. I thank Dave Smith (Retrosheet) for kindly providing digitized versions of the ICI sheets for the 1893–1900 seasons. I also thank Rick Schabowski for providing game accounts in the *Milwaukee Journal* and the Milwaukee Sentinel for the Milwaukee-vs-Detroit game on July 03, 1901. I thank Cliff Blau for providing me with "batters struck out" details from the *New York Evening Telegram* for two 1899 games. I thank Matt Spitz for coining the term "Perfect Pitcher's Cycle." I thank Patrick Todgham for dubbing the term "Super Pitcher's Cycle." I thank Pete Palmer for his guidance on strikeouts statistics and the "large lead rule" (note 14). I thank Kevin Johnson and Tom Thress for providing the pertinent information the seven players from the Negro Leagues who achieved Batter's Cycles. I thank Steve Hirdt, Jeff Robbins, and Gary Stone, for especially helpful discussions.

Dedication

I enthusiastically and appreciatively dedicate this article to Dixie Tourangeau, my friend and baseball research colleague. Thanks so much for all the superb research help you've provided to me over the past so-many years and for all of the good times we've enjoyed at Fenway and the various SABR Convention ballparks.

Notes

1. Paul Dickson, *The Dickson Baseball Dictionary* (New York: W.W. Norton & Company, 2009), 237.
2. (a) "Hit for the Cycle," Baseball Almanac, accessed October 3, 2023, https://www.baseball-almanac.com/hitting/Major_League_Baseball_Players_to_hit_for_the_cycle.shtml.
(b) According Retrosheet's list of cycles, https://www.retrosheet.org/cycles_chron.htm, George Hall hit for the cycle on June 19, 1876.
(c) Baseball Almanac's list includes a postseason cycle by Brock Holt, on October 8, 2018, which gives the grand total of 344 cycles.
(d) According to information provided by Tom Thress of Retrosheet and Kevin Johnson of Seamheads, seven verified cycles were achieved in the Negro Leagues. According to Johnson, another 12 "known" Negro

League cycles are awaiting corroboration by balanced box scores. Email exchanges with Kevin Johnson and Tom Thress, July 04-07, 2024; discussion with Kevin Johnson, August 10, 2024.
3. Jimmy Ryan of the White Stockings completed his July 28, 1888, cycle as a pitcher after having started the game as Chicago's center fielder. Ryan, who was the leadoff hitter for the White Stockings, singled to open the game in the first inning. He followed with a triple in the top of the second inning. In the bottom of the second, with the Wolverines leading, 7–4, Ryan switched positions with Chicago's starting hurler, Mark Baldwin; the bases were loaded with two outs. Ryan struck out the first batter he faced, Count Campau, to retire the side. Ryan remained on the mound for the rest of the game. In the fourth inning, Ryan walloped a 2-run homer. In the fifth frame he added another triple to his batting line. In the seventh, he reached on a fielding error by the left fielder ("a rattling liner that was too hot for Twitchell's hands"). In what turned out to be his final plate appearance, in the eighth, Ryan clouted a double, giving him the cycle. Thus, for the entire game, Ryan collected a single and a triple while he was Chicago's center fielder, and a homer, triple, and double while he was a relief pitcher. His pitching line was 7.1 innings, 10 runs allowed on 9 hits (including one homer), four strikeouts, two walks, one hit batter, and two wild pitches. The White Stockings emerged victorious, 21–17. Complete details of Ryan's accomplishments are given in the following newspaper accounts: (a) "Home Runs All Around," *Chicago Tribune*, July 29, 1888, 14; (b) "They Hit the Ball Hard," *The* (Chicago) *Inter Ocean*, July 29, 1888, 2; (c) "Sluggers Outslugged," *Detroit Free Press*, July 29, 1888, 4; (d) "Was Waterloo Thus?," *Detroit News*, July 29, 1888, 8.
4. "Cycle Definition & Meaning," Merriam-Webster, accessed August 26, 2024, https://www.merriam-webster.com/dictionary/cycle.
5. Although the catcher must hold on to the third strike to actually retire the batter, the pitcher alone is credited with a strikeout.
6. Dickson, 237.
7. Thus, accomplishing the Pitcher's Cycle by hurling in extra innings is fully acceptable. For example, two of the players who have hit for the Batter's Cycle since 1893 achieved their cycle-clinching hit in the 14th inning. George Brett (double in his seventh plate appearance on May 28, 1979) and Jay Buhner (triple in his seventh plate appearance on June 23, 1993).
8. Jonathan Frankel, email exchanges, September 4–October 5, 2023, and January 2–4, 2024.
9. John Rickert, email exchanges, October 12–November 21, 2023.
10. A chronological register of the 483 Pitcher's Cycles is provided on a decade-by-decade basis in Supplement B (available on the SABR website).
11. Herm Krabbenhoft, "Going Downtown with a Golden Sombrero—Combining Baseball's Best and Worst True Outcomes," *Baseball Research Journal*, Volume 52, Number 2, 55.
12. APPENDICES:
(available on the SABR website at https://sabr.org/journal/article/the-pitchers-cycle-definition-and-achievers-1893-2023/)
Appendix A: Each Franchise's First and Most-Recent Pitcher's Cycle
Appendix B: Franchise-Record Holders
Appendix C: The Chronology of the Career Leaders
Appendix D: The All-Time Top-10
Appendix E: Extra-Inning Pitcher's Cycles
Appendix F: Pitcher's Cycles in Consecutive Games
Appendix G: Postseason Pitcher's Cycles
In addition, the Supplement for this article (also on the SABR website) provides the following:
Supplement A: Pitchers With Nine or More Strikeouts in a Game and Incomplete "Batters Struck Out" Statistics
Supplement B: Chronological Register of Players Who Achieved a Pitcher's Cycle (1893–2023)
Supplement C: Alphabetical Register of Players Who Achieved a Pitcher's Cycle (1893–2023)
Supplement D: Team-by-Team Registers of Players Who Achieved Pitcher's Cycles

13. (a) "Did Anyone See Bresnahan's Goat?," *The* (New York) *World*, Evening Edition, May 13, 1911, 1. (b) "Giants In Run Cataclysm," *The* (New York) *Sun*, May 14, 1911, 13. (c) "Bang! Slam! Went Giants," *New York Daily Tribune*, May 14, 1911, 10.

14. That Mathewson is credited with being the winning pitcher is a consequence of "the large lead rule." Pete Palmer, email correspondence, November 2, 2023: "If you leave the game with a large lead, you can get the win because the manager is saving you for the next game. I don't know when that practice was in effect. There were no [official] rules for 'winning' and 'losing' pitchers until 1950." See also: (a) Frank Vacarro, "Origin of the Modern Pitching Win," *Baseball Research Journal* (Volume 42, Number 1, Spring 2013) 50; (b) Frank J. Williams, "All the Record Books Are Wrong," *The National Pastime*, 2013, 50; (c) Joe Wayman, "The Matty-Alex Tie," *Baseball Research Journal* (Number 24, 2013), 25.

15. Allen Lewis, "Cubs' 4 in 1st Defeat Phils Despite Relief by Conley," *Philadelphia Inquirer*, May 03, 1959, S1.

16. "Gene Conley Ready To Take Over As Starter For Phils," *Danville* (Virginia) *Register*, D1.

17. "Transformer explosion suspends Padres game," *The* (Palm Springs, California) *Desert Sun*, July 19, 2001, D4.

18. Richard Obert, "Big Unit K's 16 to finish suspended game," *Arizona Republic*, July 20, 2001, D1.

19. Carlos Monarrez, "Swift Wiffs," *Detroit Free Press*, August 03, 2020, B1.

20. The origin of "Perfect Pitcher's Cycle" is as follows: I attended the September 10, 2023, Giants-Rockies game at Oracle Park with three friends. I cheered for every Colorado batter Keaton Winn struck out. While I was scoring the game, I explained my Pitcher's Cycle research to my friends and was carefully charting each K that Winn achieved. When Winn struck out Austin Wynns to end the fifth inning, I enthusiastically exclaimed that Winn just needed to K two more batting slots, two and six, to accomplish the Pitcher's Cycle. A couple of Giants fans seated in front of me asked what I was talking about. I gave a brief account of my research project and, to provide some perspective, I mentioned that Nolan Ryan had 12 Pitcher's Cycles and that Randy Johnson had 18 through the 2001 season, the most recent season I had completed at the time. I also mentioned that there were 13 pitchers who had struck out at least 9 batters in a row and that, therefore, they had automatically achieved the Pitcher's Cycle. One of them responded matter-of-factly, "So they had perfect cycles." I replied, "Yeah! That's cool! A Perfect Pitcher's Cycle! What a neat way to express that! I got his name—Matt Spitz—and said I would give him credit for coming up with the term. Thanks, Matt! As it turned out, Winn did not strike out the second-slot batter, Ezequiel Tovar),in the sixth. Similarly, Winn did not have the opportunity to strike out the sixth-slot batter, Hunter Goodman, as the Giants brought in a relief pitcher in the seventh inning.

21. Matt Kelly and Sarah Langs, "Most Consecutive Strikeouts by a Pitcher," MLB.com, April 10, 2023, accessed October 30, 2023, https://www.mlb.com/news/most-consecutive-strikeouts-by-pitcher-in-game#:~:text=Thanks%20to%20a%20David%20Bote,record%20with%2010%20consecutive%20strikeouts. For additional information about Mickey Welch's Perfect Pitcher's Cycle, see: (a) Harry Simmons, "An Overlooked Feat," *The Sporting News*, October 23, 1941, 6; (b) George Buckley, "Why Did Mickey Smile?" *Baseball Research Journal* (Volume 11, 1982), 127.

22. The origin of the "Super Pitcher's Cycle" is as follows: At a hot stove league discussion on December 3, 2023, at the Cambridge Common & Lizard Lounge in Cambridge, MA, the topic of Pitcher's Cycles came up, along with the feat of a pitcher striking at least one batter in each inning of a nine-inning game. I mentioned that while there were nearly 500 PCs, there were only 30-some instances where the PC player also struck out at least one batter in each inning (of a nine-inning game). Patrick Todgham then said, "Those should be called 'Super Pitcher's Cycles.'" I agreed and said I would give him credit for the term. Thanks, Patrick!

23. Maria Torres, "A night to remember for Ohtani," *Los Angeles Times*, June 14, 2019, D1.

24. "Angels' Ohtani first Japanese player to hit for cycle," Associated Press, June 13, 2019, accessed November 5, 2023, https://spectrumlocalnews.com/nc/triad/ap-top-news/2019/06/14/angels-ohtani-first-japanese-player-to-hit-for-cycle0.

25. J. Scott Shaffer, "June 13, 2019: Shohei Ohtani becomes first Japanese player to hit for cycle," SABR Games Project, accessed November 5, 2023, https://sabr.org/gamesproj/game/june-13-2019-shohei-ohtani-becomes-first-japanese-player-to-hit-for-the-cycle/.

26. Kristie Rieken, "'Virtuoso' Ohtani Mows Down Astros," *Los Angeles Times*, April 21, 2022, B10.

27. Lynn Worthy, "Gallegos coughs up late lead, Cards lose," *St. Louis Post Dispatch*, May 4, 2023, page B1.

28. Rhett Bollinger, "Make room for Shohei! Ohtani joins Babe in another club," MLB.com, May 3, 2023, accessed October 23, 2023, https://www.mlb.com/news/shohei-ohtani-joins-babe-ruth-in-500-strikeout-100-home-run-club?game_pk=718320.

29. Stathead.com. Other sources consulted: (a) Seymour Siwoff, *The Elias Book of Baseball Records* (New York: W.W. Norton & Company, 2009), 237; (b) *The Major League Baseball Ultimate Book of Baseball Records* (Toronto, Ontario, Canada: Fenn/McClelland & Stewart, 2013), 132; (c) Lyle Spatz, Editor, *The SABR Baseball List & Record Book* (New York: Scribner, 2007), 191; (d) Joseph Dittmar, *Baseball Records Registry* (Jefferson, North Carolina: McFarland & Company, Inc., Publishers, 1997); (e) Joseph L. Reichler, Revised by Ken Samelson, *The Great All-Time Baseball Record Book* (New York: Macmillan Publishing Company, 1993), 181; (f) David Nemec, *Great Baseball Feats, Facts, & Firsts* (New York: NAL Penguin,Inc., 1987), 237.

30. (a) "Royals' Metro in Awe as Carew Keeps Hitting," (Saint Cloud, Minnesota) *Daily Times*, May 21, 1970, 29; (b) Tom Briere, "Twins Win 7th Straight," (Minneapolis) *Star-Tribune*, May 21, 1970, 31. See also: Herm Krabbenhoft, "From Kralick to Lopez and Carew to Polanco—Interesting Aspects of the Pitcher's Cycles and Batter's Cycles Achieved by Minnesota Twins Players," *The National Pastime*, 2024, 60.

31. Herm Krabbenhoft, "When You Come to a Fork in the Road," *Baseball Research Journal* (Volume 47, Number 1, Spring 2018) 72.

32. Hy Hurwitz, "Hy and Inside," *Boston Globe*, September 22, 1954, 8.

33. Ian Quillen, "Nats top Tigers 3-2," *The Park City Daily News* (Bowling Green, KY), May 12, 2016, C8.

34. (a) Herm Krabbenhoft, "Quasi-Cycles—Better Than Cycles?," *Baseball Research Journal* (Volume 46, Number 2, Fall 2017) 107; (b) Chuck McGill, email correspondence, June 1, 2017; (c) From the *Tennessean* (Nashville, Tennessee, August 21,1921, 12) was the following news item: "George Sisler on August 13 hit the cycle by getting on a single, double, triple, and home run, and by getting an extra double in the same game." (d) *The Dickson Baseball Dictionary* cites a 1933 *Washington Post* article as the first to use the term "cycle": Paul Dickson, *The Dickson Baseball Dictionary* (New York: W,W, Norton & Company, New York, 2009) 237. (e) In this issue, John Racanelli reports an earlier date: June 10, 1920. John Racanelli, "Desperately Seeking Singles," *Baseball Research Journal* 53, no. 2, (2024) 46.

35. Michael Huber and Allison Davidson, "Origin of the Phrase 'Hitting for the Cycle' and An Approach to How Cycles Occur," *Baseball Research Journal* (Volume 47, Number 1, Spring 2018) 112.

Desperately Seeking Singles

The Palpable Heartache of Near-Miss Cycles

John Racanelli

"With the bases full Foley caught the sphere fair on the end of his ash and away it went over the left field fence for a home run."[1] This first-inning grand slam on May 25, 1882, by Buffalo Bisons outfielder Charles "Curry" Foley sparked a 20–1 rout over the rival Cleveland Blues. Along the way, Foley also slugged a triple in the second inning, a double in the fifth, and a single in the third. However, no one at Riverside Park in Buffalo that afternoon was likely aware of the historic baseball curiosity that had occurred—Foley had just hit for the first cycle in major-league history.

A BASEBALL CURIOSITY

A cycle consists of at least one single, double, triple, and home run hit by a player in a single game. A "natural" cycle requires that the hits occur in order from single to home run, while a reverse natural cycle calls for the opposite. That a cycle is simply a specific collection of hits by a player during an arbitrary span of at-bats does not make the feat any less fascinating, however.

On June 10, 1920, Akron Buckeyes (International League) infielder Bill Webb was noted to be "the first player to hit for the cycle this season...Bill clouting two singles, a double, a triple, and a round tripper off Toronto hurling," perhaps becoming the earliest professional player to have his accomplishment reported.[2] Interestingly, use of the words "this season" in this article implies that hitting for the cycle was recognized prior to 1920 in some circles, though this author has yet to unearth earlier references.

Two months later on August 8, Browns first baseman George Sisler hit for the cycle against the Washington Nationals at Sportsman Park in St. Louis. Sisler had "delivered all kinds of hits, a single, double, triple and home run," but the feat was not contemporaneously celebrated by name.[3] In fact, when Bobby Veach and George J. Burns each hit for cycles on September 17, the *Brooklyn Daily Eagle* reported that Veach was "the first player in his league to hit for the cycle" that season, evidently unaware Sisler had turned the trick several weeks earlier.[4] In 1921, the *York Daily Record* reported that the Yankees' Bob Meusel had hit for the cycle on May 7 and noted that Sisler, Veach, and Burns had each hit for the cycle the previous season.[5]

When Browns second baseman Oscar Melillo and Giants outfielder Mel Ott hit for cycles in the same week in 1929, the *Hartford Courant* declared that "both men thereby entered their names in that classic list of sluggers who have 'hit the cycle.'"[6] As of 1930, recognition of the achievement was still not universal, however. When Giants infielder Freddie Lindstrom hit for the cycle at Pittsburgh on May 8, the papers noted the feat.[7] There was no mention of a cycle in the papers, however, when Cubs center fielder Hack Wilson or Cardinals left fielder Chick Hafey hit for the cycle on June 23 or August 21, respectively. In 1934, *The Sporting News* listed cycles as American League highlights for the previous season (but did not publish a corresponding list of the four cycles in the National League in 1933).[8]

On June 29, 1935, Cardinals left fielder Joe Medwick hit for the cycle at Cincinnati, the only cycle in either the AL or NL that season, but a pair of amateur ballplayers—Ethel Higgins and Eve Jocha—each hit for the cycle *in the same game* as the Mansfield (Ohio) Red Birds shellacked the Ashland club 26–8 on August 18, 1935.[9] In 1937, a sports page trivia question asked readers to name the last major league player to have hit for the cycle.[10] However, the purported answer (Joe Medwick, 1935) was incorrect. Giants first baseman Sam Leslie had completed a cycle on May 24, 1936—a seemingly tacit acknowledgment that cataloging the accomplishment was still very much in flux.

When Cardinal Johnny Mize hit for the cycle on July 13, 1940, an article in the *St. Louis Post-Dispatch* the following morning noted the achievement without defining the feat, although each hit and the inning in which it occurred was detailed.[11] When Yankees catcher Buddy Rosar hit for the cycle less than a week later, at least one newspaper mentioned the feat in a subheading without providing any further details; while another story defined hitting for the cycle for readers "in lay terms."[12]

Coincidentally, Rosar might have been the first player to admit on the record the requisite knowledge he had hit for the cycle and was proud of the achievement.[13] The cycle was well on its way to becoming a generally accepted term in the baseball lexicon.

CYCLES AND NEAR-MISS CYCLES

Baseball Almanac appears to have the most complete list of cycles—344 in all—spanning from Curry Foley in 1882 to Jose Altuve in 2023; see Table 1.[14] Six players have completed three cycles in their careers: John Reilly (1883, 1883, 1890); Babe Herman (1931, 1931, 1933); Bob Meusel (1921, 1922, 1928); Adrian Beltre (2008, 2012, 2015); Christian Yelich (2018, 2018, 2022);

and Trea Turner (2017, 2019, 2021). No one has hit a fourth cycle—yet.

Utilizing Baseball Reference's Stathead feature to search 1901 through 2023, we find at least 6146 attempts at a cycle have fallen a home run short, 15,659 have fallen a triple short, and 2058 have failed to register the necessary double (See Table 2).[15] But presumably the most frustrating near-miss is when a player falls a measly single short of completing the cycle. Not surprisingly, the odds of missing a cycle by a particular hit correlate well with the frequency of that type of hit.[16]

There have been at least 520 occurrences of a player falling a single short of the cycle starting with

Table 1: Cycles (1880–2023)

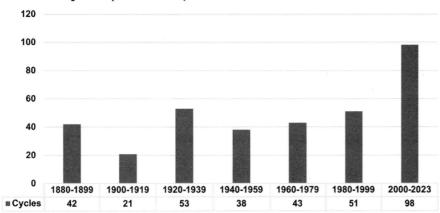

	1880-1899	1900-1919	1920-1939	1940-1959	1960-1979	1980-1999	2000-2023
Cycles	42	21	53	38	43	51	98

Table 2: Near-Miss Cycles (1901–2023)

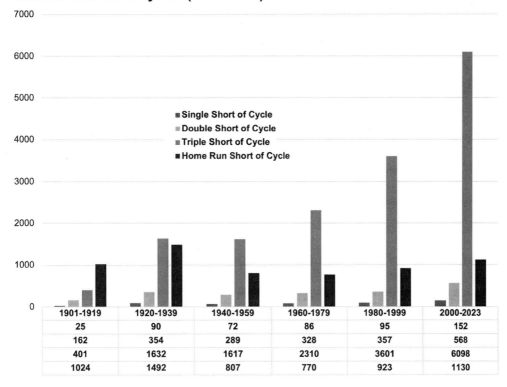

Legend:
- Single Short of Cycle
- Double Short of Cycle
- Triple Short of Cycle
- Home Run Short of Cycle

1901-1919	1920-1939	1940-1959	1960-1979	1980-1999	2000-2023
25	90	72	86	95	152
162	354	289	328	357	568
401	1632	1617	2310	3601	6098
1024	1492	807	770	923	1130

Boston American's outfielder Chick Stahl on August 20, 1901[17]. There have been 41 players who had multiple games in which they fell a single short of the cycle (See Table 3). Ten players have fallen a single shy of the cycle three separate times each and six of those players never hit for the cycle in their (otherwise illustrious) careers.

Frank Robinson and Gregg Jefferies each had three single-shy near-miss cycles but were otherwise able to add a cycle to their respective baseball resumes. When Robinson fell a single short on May 6, 1956, the *Cincinnati Enquirer* noted that he "just missed hitting for the cycle" after being robbed of a single by Granny Hamner in the sixth.[18] Robinson eventually hit for the

Table 3. Players with Multiple Single-Shy Games, but no Cycles in Major League Career (1901–2023)

	Player	Team (Year)	Team (Year)	Team (Year)
1	Henry Aaron	Milwaukee Braves (1957)	Milwaukee Braves (1958)	Milwaukee Braves (1962)
2	Ellis Burks	Boston Red Sox (1988)	Colorado Rockies (1994)	Colorado Rockies (1996)
3	Brian Giles	Pittsburgh Pirates (2000)	Pittsburgh Pirates (2001)	San Diego Padres (2004)
4	Magglio Ordóñez	Chicago White Sox (2000)	Detroit Tigers (2008)	Detroit Tigers (2010)
5	Babe Ruth	New York Yankees (1923)	New York Yankees (1930)	New York Yankees (1931)
6	Manny Trillo	Chicago Cubs (1976)	Chicago Cubs (1977)	Philadelphia Phillies (1980)
7	Moises Alou	Montreal Expos (1993)	Chicago Cubs (2004)	
8	Barry Bonds	Pittsburgh Pirates (1988)	San Francisco Giants (2000)	
9	Bruce Campbell	Cleveland Indians (1937)	Cleveland Indians (1938)	
10	Robinson Canó	New York Yankees (2005)	New York Yankees (2011)	
11	Joe Carter	Cleveland Indians (1986)	Toronto Blue Jays (1992)	
12	Yoenis Céspedes	Oakland Athletics (2014)	New York Mets (2017)	
13	José Cruz	Toronto Blue Jays (2001)	Toronto Blue Jays (2002)	
14	Dom DiMaggio	Boston Red Sox (1941)	Boston Red Sox (1948)	
15	Del Ennis	Philadelphia Phillies (1950)	Philadelphia Phillies (1952)	
16	Steve Finley	San Diego Padres (1997)	Arizona Diamondbacks (1999)	
17	Nomar Garciaparra	Boston Red Sox (1997)	Boston Red Sox (2003)	
18	Alex Gordon	Kansas City Royals (2007)	Kansas City Royals (2011)	
19	Ken Harrelson	Boston Red Sox (1967)	Boston Red Sox (1968)	
20	Grady Hatton	Cincinnati Reds (1947)	Cincinnati Reds (1949)	
21	Raúl Ibañez	Kansas City Royals (2002)	Seattle Mariners (2007)	
22	Travis Jackson	New York Giants (1929)	New York Giants (1929)	
23	Al Kaline	Detroit Tigers (1956)	Detroit Tigers (1971)	
24	Chet Laabs	St. Louis Browns (1939)	St. Louis Browns (1941)	
25	Roger Maris	Kansas City Athletics (1958)	New York Yankees (1961)	
26	Eddie Mathews	Milwaukee Braves (1960)	Milwaukee Braves (1960)	
27	Hal McRae	Kansas City Royals (1977)	Kansas City Royals (1979)	
28	Chris Owings	Arizona Diamondbacks (2014)	Arizona Diamondbacks (2014)	
29	Dave Parker	Pittsburgh Pirates (1975)	Pittsburgh Pirates (1977)	
30	Josh Reddick	Houston Astros (2017)	Houston Astros (2017)	
31	Edd Roush	Cincinnati Reds (1924)	New York Giants (1929)	
32	Mike Schmidt	Philadelphia Phillies (1977)	Philadelphia Phillies (1988)	
33	Marcus Semien	Oakland Athletics (2019)	Toronto Blue Jays (2021)	
34	Gary Sheffield	Florida Marlins (1994)	Los Angeles Dodgers (2000)	
35	Al Simmons	Philadelphia Athletics (1925)	Philadelphia Athletics (1929)	
36	Ian Stewart	Colorado Rockies (2009)	Colorado Rockies (2010)	
37	Chris Taylor	Los Angeles Dodgers (2016)	Los Angeles Dodgers (2018)	
38	Mark Trumbo	Los Angeles Angels of Anaheim (2011)	Los Angeles Angels of Anaheim (2012)	
39	Larry Walker	Montreal Expos (1992)	Colorado Rockies (1996)	
40	Lou Whitaker	Detroit Tigers (1983)	Detroit Tigers (1989)	
41	Ken Williams	St. Louis Browns (1920)	St. Louis Browns (1923)	

cycle on May 2, 1959, and came close two additional times, once each for Cincinnati (1964) and Baltimore (1969). Jefferies came up a single short on three different occasions for the Mets in 1988 (in back-to-back weeks, during his first 11 major league starts) and 1989. His first near-miss cycle on August 29 featured his first career triple and home run. "I'd be lying if I said I wasn't thinking about hitting for the cycle," he said after the game.[19] Jefferies later hit for the cycle with the Phillies on August 25, 1995.

Lou Gehrig came within a single of completing cycles in 1927, 1929, and 1930 but was eventually able to close the deal twice, hitting for the cycle on June 25, 1934, and August 1, 1937. When Joe Cronin of the Washington Nationals hit for the cycle on September 2, 1929, the *Evening Star* was more impressed with Cronin's 12 total bases on five hits, "thought to be the best made in the American League at least in the past two or three seasons."[20] Cronin came close to cycles for Washington in 1930, 1931, and 1932, but fell a single short each time. Cronin hit for his second cycle on August 2, 1940, as a member of the Red Sox.

OH, SO CLOSE

Of the six players who came within a single of hitting for the cycle three times without ever having hit for the cycle, two of those players finished their respective playing careers as the all-time home run leader (one surpassing the other); three others hit at least 280 career home runs; and the final player finished his career with just 61 home runs, with nearly 5% of his career home runs and 10% of his career triples occurring in that trio of games in which he fell a single shy of the cycle.

BABE RUTH (THREE CHANCES FOR SINGLE)

On July 2, 1923, Yankees outfielder Babe Ruth hit a home run, triple, and double in his first four at-bats, the first three requirements for a reverse natural cycle.[21] When he came to bat in the seventh, Ruth hit a ball off Nationals twirler Bonnie Hollingsworth that was caught down the right-field line. Ruth was replaced in right field by Elmer Smith following the Yankees' half-inning.

On July 18, 1930, Ruth again came within a single of hitting for the cycle but fell short in five at-bats as the Yankees lost to the Browns in St. Louis. The papers noted that Ruth "gave his rivals something of a lesson in long distance clouting" with a home run, triple and double, yet there was no mention he had fallen a single shy of the cycle.

On May 21, 1931, Ruth again began the day with the three toughest hits of a reverse natural cycle having

collected a home run, triple, and double in his first three at-bats against Willis Hudlin at Cleveland's League Park. However, Ruth flew out and grounded out in his final two at-bats that afternoon as the Yankees held on for the 7–6 win. No contemporaneous notations regarding how close Ruth came to hitting for the cycle on this occasion has been found.

Babe Ruth had three career chances to hit a single to complete the cycle but had no such luck. (Ruth also had nine games in which he fell a double short of the cycle, 41 games where he was a triple short, and seven games in which he was a home run short of a cycle.)

ELLIS BURKS (THREE CHANCES FOR SINGLE)

On July 17, 1988, Red Sox center fielder Ellis Burks hit a home run, triple, and double through the first four innings against the Royals at Fenway Park. A lineout and strikeout in his last two at-bats prevented him from completing the reverse natural cycle, however.

As a member of the Rockies, Burks had a triple and double in his first two at-bats against the Cardinals on May 3, 1994, but he reached first on an error by third baseman Todd Zeile in the fourth inning and was walked intentionally in the sixth. He hit a home run off Willie Smith in the eighth, but never got another plate appearance in the game. After the game, Burks was optimistic about the team, "If we can hold guys to three or four runs a game, especially with this lineup, we're going to win a lot," but his near-miss cycle was not mentioned.[22]

Burks started his game on August 24, 1996, at Coors Field with a reverse natural cycle in his first three at-bats against the Pirates. In the sixth Burks drove in Walt Weiss with a flyout. Unfortunately, he did not get another at-bat in the game. His near miss was noted the next morning, however, "Burks narrowly missed hitting for the cycle. He had a homer, triple, and double in his first three at-bats, then sent a drive to the center-field wall for a sacrifice fly."[23]

Ellis Burks had three career chances to hit a single to complete the cycle, but was denied. (Burks also had one game in which he fell a double short of the cycle, 25 games where he was a triple short, and one game in which he was a home run short of a cycle.)

HENRY AARON (TWO CHANCES FOR SINGLE*)

In a game against the Pirates at Forbes Field on May 3, 1957, Braves outfielder Henry Aaron knocked a double, home run, and triple in six at-bats as Milwaukee pulled off an extra-inning win against Pittsburgh. Aaron's triple came off Roy Face in the top of the eleventh and he scored the go-ahead run on a Bobby Thomson single. The Braves held on to win 8–7. Aaron's near-miss cycle was not mentioned the next day's papers—but the cycle hit by a Pennsylvania high school sophomore named Neubiser was.[24]

In a game at home on September 12, 1958, Aaron had a double, home run, and triple in his first four at-bats against the Cardinals, but never got another at-bat as the Braves shut out St. Louis, 6–0.

On May 3, 1962, the Braves visited the Philadelphia Phillies and Aaron began the evening contest with a reverse natural cycle in his first three at-bats. Facing Bobby Locke in the top of the eighth, Aaron struck out swinging. Aaron had one final at-bat in the top of the ninth as Milwaukee had their last chance to erase a two-run deficit to the Phillies. Facing Jack Baldschun, Aaron hit a home run to left field that scored Mack Jones to tie the game.

Henry Aaron had two career chances to hit a single to complete the cycle but was unable to complete the deal. (Aaron also had one game in which he fell a double short of the cycle, 29 games where he was a triple short, and seven games in which he was a home run short of a cycle.)

* Aaron's performance on May 3, 1962, qualifies as a quasi-cycle (four extra base hits in a game, with at least one of each of the three types of extra base hits).[25]

BRIAN GILES (TWO CHANCES FOR SINGLE)

On August 15, 2000, Brian Giles and the Pittsburgh Pirates visited the Houston Astros at Enron Field. In his first three at-bats against Jose Lima, Giles had a reverse natural cycle going. In the top of the eighth, however, southpaw rookie Wayne Franklin hit Giles with a pitch and Giles never got another plate appearance.

On August 9, 2001, Giles hit a home run, double, and triple in his first three at-bats against Dodgers pitcher Chan Ho Park at PNC Park. Alberto Reyes got Giles to chase in the bottom of the seventh, the strikeout having been Giles' final at-bat of the game. Pirates Manager Lloyd McClendon commented after the game, "I know everybody in the park wanted a single, but I was rooting for another home run."[26]

Then with the Padres in 2004, Giles hit a triple in his first at-bat, drew a walk in the third, hit a home run in the fifth, and was walked intentionally by Antonio Alfonseca in the seventh inning on August 18 against Atlanta in San Diego. In his final at-bat Giles smacked a double that ended the game when Mark Loretta was thrown out at home. Giles' near-miss cycle was not noted that next day, but the cycle hit by Mark Teixeira on August 17 was still newsworthy.[27]

Brian Giles had two career chances (one of which resulted in his having been plunked) to hit a single to complete the cycle but missed out. (Giles also had two games in which he fell a double short of the cycle, 13 games where he was a triple short, and four games in which he was a home run short of a cycle.)

MAGGLIO ORDÓÑEZ (ONE CHANCE FOR SINGLE)

On April 23, 2000, Magglio Ordóñez hit a three-run home run in the first inning against Detroit's Dave Borkowski. He had a double in his next at-bat and then was caught looking in the third. Ordóñez hit a leadoff triple in the bottom of the sixth and had one more chance to complete his cycle. However, Ordóñez whiffed against Matt Anderson in the bottom of the eighth. Ordóñez was aware how close he was, "yeah, everybody told me. I was looking for that base hit."[28]

While playing for the Tigers in 2008, Ordóñez grounded out in his first at-bat against the Twins at the Metrodome on September 6. In his next three at-bats Ordóñez socked a double, triple, and home run but never got another chance at the plate.

On June 3, 2010, Ordóñez began his day with a popout in the bottom of the first against Cleveland at Comerica Park. He followed with a triple, groundout, and double, and ended his offensive day with a home run off Tony Sipp in the bottom of the seventh. Detroit won the game 12–6. His near-miss cycle was mentioned the following morning, but the postgame conversation still concerned Armando Galarraga's near perfect game the night before. Tigers manager Jim Leyland commented, "I was a little concerned about so much emotion spent last night because of the situation that maybe we would be a little flat today, but we weren't."[29]

Magglio Ordóñez had one career chance to hit a single to complete the cycle but did not manage the feat. (Ordóñez never had a game in which he fell a double short of the cycle, had 26 games where he was a triple short, and three games in which he was a home run short of a cycle.)

MANNY TRILLO (ZERO CHANCES FOR SINGLE)

On July 10, 1976, Cubs second baseman Manny Trillo smashed a double in the first and a home run in the third off Giants pitcher Jim Barr at Wrigley Field. He flew out to right field in the sixth and tripled in the eighth. (All three of Trillo's hits scored Pete LaCock.) Trillo did not get another at-bat, however, as the Cubs beat San Francisco, 8–6.

On May 5, 1977, Trillo had a home run and double in his first two at-bats off Astros hurler Floyd Bannister. He struck out in the bottom of the fifth against Joe Niekro and then tripled off Joe Sambito in the seventh.

Manny Trillo only hit 61 home runs in the major leagues, yet came within a single of the cycle three separate times.

The Cubs hung on to win, 8–7, but Trillo never had an opportunity to complete his cycle.

Playing at second base for the Phillies at Veterans Stadium on July 14, 1980, Trillo had a double and home run in his first two at-bats against Pittsburgh's Rick Rhoden but flew out in his next two at-bats. In the bottom of the eighth, Trillo laced a triple to right field off Grant Jackson but did not get another at-bat in the game.

Trillo, who compiled 61 home runs and 33 triples in his 17-year major league career, never had a chance to hit a single to complete a cycle. He never otherwise hit for the cycle and was never a double short of the cycle. Trillo had four games in which he was a triple short of the cycle and two games in which he was a home run shy.

Trillo was unaware how close he had come to a cycle those three times: "I missed by a single three times? Man, that's the easiest one!"[30]

NEAR-MISS CYCLE CURIOSITIES

There is a palpable delight in the hearts of many baseball fans when a player hits for the cycle—regardless of the arbitrary nature of the feat—because it is a decidedly rare occurrence. Near-miss cycles are much more common, but the excitement exists only for that player's final at-bats with the potential to complete the cycle.

No pitcher has hit for the cycle, but three have come within a single of doing so: Grover Alexander, Chicago Cubs (1925), Bill Sherdel, St. Louis Cardinals (1926), and Steve Sundra, St. Louis Browns (1942). Three hitters each came up a single shy of the cycle on consecutive days in 1988: Chet Lemon, Detroit

Tigers (June 17), Chris Sabo, Cincinnati Reds (June 18), and Andre Dawson, Chicago Cubs (June 19). Ken Griffey (Cincinnati Reds) and Ken Griffey Jr. (Seattle Mariners) each had one game where they fell a single short of the cycle (1977 and 1998, respectively), but neither hit for the cycle in their respective careers.

Regardless, near-miss cycles are appropriate occasions for passing lament—especially when the player was (desperately) seeking a single. ∎

Sources

www.baseball-reference.com
www.retrosheet.org

Appendices

Appendices available on the SABR website: https://sabr.org/journal/article/desperately-seeking-singles-the-palpable-heartache-of-near-miss-cycles/.
- Near-Miss Cycle Career Leaders (1901–2023).
- A-4: Online list of Near-Miss Cycles (1901–2023).

Notes

1. "A Great Game," *Buffalo Courier Express*, May 26, 1882, 4.
2. "Eight Akron Players are Still Hitting Above .300 Mark—Bill Webb is Leading," *Akron Evening Times*, June 19, 1920, 10. The author has not yet found any earlier mention of a baseball player hitting for the cycle or any etymological context. (Searches prior to this specific article mostly concerned motorcycle or bicycle collisions.)
3. "Big League Stuff," *Indiana Daily Times* (Indianapolis), August 9, 1920, 6.
4. "Features of the Week on the Diamond," *Brooklyn Daily Eagle*, September 26, 1920, 63.
5. "Heilmann is Hitting for .521 Percentage," *York* (Pennsylvania) *Daily Record*, May 14, 1921, 7; Herm Krabbenhoft, "Quasi-Cycles: Better Than Cycles?," *Baseball Research Journal*, Fall 2017; Michael Huber and Allison Davidson, "Origin of the Phrase 'Hitting for the Cycle' and An Approach to How Cycles Occur," *Baseball Research Journal*, Spring 2018 (these previous *Baseball Research Journal* articles suggest that the term "cycle" dated back at least as far as 1921).
6. "Melillo and Mel Ott Hit for Cycle in Big Leagues," *Hartford Courant*, June 9, 1929, 43.
7. "Gets Five Hits," *Reading* (Pennsylvania) *Times*, May 9, 1930, 23.
8. Henry Edwards, "High Spots of 1933 in American League," *The Sporting News*, January 11, 1934, 2. Players who hit for the cycle in 1933: AL—Mickey Cochrane (Philadelphia), Pinky Higgins (Philadelphia), Jimmie Foxx (Philadelphia), and Earl Averill (Cleveland); NL—Pepper Martin (St. Louis), Chuck Klein (Philadelphia), Arky Vaughan (Pittsburgh), and Babe Herman (Chicago).
9. "Higgins, Jocha hit for Cycle," *News-Journal* (Mansfield, Ohio), August 19, 1935, 8.
10. "How Much Do You Know?," *Republican and Herald* (Pottsville, Pennsylvania), April 6, 1937, 8.
11. "Mize Hits for Cycle," *St. Louis Post-Dispatch*, July 14, 1940, 35.
12. "Yanks Batter Smith, Indians by 15–6 Score," *Journal and Courier* (Lafayette, Indiana), July 20, 1940, "Buddy Rosar Hits for Cycle" listed in subheading; "Yankees Club Tribe, 15–6; Cycle for Rosar," *Daily News* (New York, New York), July 20, 1940, 136.
13. Frederick Lieb, "Buddy Rosar, Being Fitted for Bill Dickey's Big Shoes, Proves Shining Example of Yanks' Polishing System," *The Sporting News*, January 2, 1941, 3.
14. Baseball Almanac, "MLB Players to Hit for the Cycle," www.baseball-almanac.com/hitting/Major_League_Baseball_Players_to_hit_for_the_cycle.shtml, accessed December 20, 2023. Retrosheet also lists 344 cycles but includes a disputed cycle for George Hall on June 14, 1876,

and omits Freddie Freeman's August 18, 2021, cycle for unknown reasons. Using Baseball Reference's Stathead search feature, the author found 300 cycles beginning with Fred Clarke's on July 23, 1901. However, Harry Davis's cycle from July 10, 1901, was not included in the Baseball Reference search results. Additionally, there are four Negro League cycles listed on Retrosheet (but not found on the Baseball Almanac list) that have been included by the author in Table 1—Bonnie Serrell, Kansas City Monarchs (1944); Hank Thompson, Kansas City Monarchs (1947); Jim Pendleton, Chicago American Giants (1948); and Willard Brown, Kansas City Monarchs (1948).

15. For purposes of this article, Baseball Reference searches were used to calculate the occurrences of those games in which players fell one type of hit short of completing a cycle. Generally, the Baseball Reference Stathead feature has searchable box scores going back to 1901. Accordingly, this article considers games played from July 23, 1901 through the present, with the caveat that additional occurrences before and after this date certainly exist and may be discovered later as detailed box scores and game accounts are uncovered and/or digitized.

16. Andy, "Missing the Cycle," BR Bullpen, https://www.baseball-reference.com/blog/archives/101.html, accessed July 8, 2024.

17. Near-miss cycles from the Negro Leagues for the 1940-1948 season have not been included in the calculations due to the author's inability to find an automated manner in which to query the box scores for those games.

18. "Lou Smith's Notes," *The Cincinnati Enquirer*, May 7, 1956, 46.

19. "Rookie Jefferies Makes His Mark," *The Ithaca* (New York) *Journal*, August 30, 1988, 11.

20. John Keller, "Cronin's Hitting Sets Mark for Griffs: Jones Must Battle to Annex Medal," *Evening Star* (Washington, DC). September 3, 1929, 33.

21. "No Change in Batting Lead," *Santa Cruz* (California) *Evening News*, July 19, 1930, 8.

22. Mike Eisenbath, "Rockies Rain HRs On Cards," *St. Louis Post-Dispatch*, May 4, 1994, 27.

23. "Bombers, Thompson Beat Bucs," *The Daily Sentinel* (Grand Junction, Colorado), August 25, 1996, 31.

24. "Meyersdale, Rockwood Continue Streak; Witt Hurls No Hitter," *The Daily American* (Somerset, Pennsylvania), May 4, 1957, 7.

25. Herm Krabbenhoft, "Quasi-Cycles: Better Than Cycles?," *Baseball Research Journal*, Fall 2017

26. Paul Meyer, "Giles, Wilson Help Pirates Finish Off L.A.," *Pittsburgh Post-Gazette*, August 10, 2001, 46.

27. "Who's Hot," *Cincinnati Enquirer*, August 19, 2004, 40.

28. Jimmy Greenfield, "No Brawling, Just a Sox Mauling," *Chicago Tribune*, April 24, 2000, 25.

29. Vince Ellis, "Focused Tigers Deliver 17 Hits," *Detroit Free Press*, June 4, 2010, 19.

30. Manny Trillo, interview with author January 13, 2024.

The Single's Slow Fade

The Diminishing Role of the Single Since the Deadball Era

James Musso

Major League Baseball implemented a package of rule changes for the 2023 season designed to address complaints that the game had become tedious to watch.[1] Those complaints centered on pace of play and lack of action, with fans and media noting fewer balls in play and stolen bases and more strikeouts and home runs.[2] Some underlying reasons for these developments have been identified as ballparks that encourage slugging; an increase in the number of pitchers used during a game; the increased use of defensive shifts; and players' widespread participation in offseason training programs that emphasize higher launch angles for hitters and higher velocity and spin rates for pitchers.[3]

As a result of the new rules, the average length of a game was reduced by 24 minutes to 2:42—a level last attained in 1985—and 2:39 if only counting nine-inning games. The number of stolen bases was the highest since 1987, and the league batting average for left-handed hitters rose 11 points to .247.[4] Beyond that, the evidence of progress is murky, especially with regard to the level of action on the field (strikeouts remain very high).

Many observers, including MLB itself, believe the game has yet to be played in a way that achieves its potential as a pastime rooted in the American psyche.[5] Each time a batter steps into the box, this pastime, at its best, tells an engaging tale about a man, first fighting off projectiles with only a wooden club, then embarking on an exciting journey down treacherous basepaths, all in the hope that he will overcome whatever obstacles block his way and finally return home. What would such a game look like?

It would display a variety of skills, each of which would be necessary, in varying degrees, to win.[6] There would be contact hitters who excelled at advancing baserunners. There would be fast singles and triples hitters who could beat out grounders, take the extra base, and hit for average. There would be agile and athletic players capable of making great defensive plays. And yes, there would be some slow-footed, muscle-bound sluggers, too. There would be oversized power pitchers, of course, but they would be complemented by junkballers and control specialists capable of pitching more than five innings.

All of this is, of course, an ideal, an aspiration that will never be fulfilled. But we need to know if we're headed in the right direction. We need to know how close we are. There's always the eye test, of course, based on the belief that fans will know it when they see it. But the eye test isn't as reliable when one is looking for something that hasn't been seen much over the course of history. This paper proposes the use of a simple metric, the singles proportion, as an effective tool for understanding how the game of baseball is being played today and, indeed, how the game was being played at any particular point in its history.[7] The Live Ball Era was baseball's most transformative period of the twentieth century. This paper concludes that the period beginning in 2016 and continuing through the 2023 season may turn out to be just as transformative, but in a way that takes us further from our ideal, unless Major League Baseball can reverse the tide.[8]

1. THE SINGLES PROPORTION

1.1 Definition and Uses

Few observers of Major League Baseball think about singles, at least not much, not anymore. One reason for this is the single's diminishing role in the game. We can measure this by looking at singles as a proportion of on-base events (hits, walks, and hit-by-pitches) in the American and National Leagues over the course of the leagues' existence.[9] This singles proportion (or singles prop for short) tells us more about how runs were scored in a given time frame than about how many runs were scored. It tells us something about the importance of singles relative to other on-base events.[10] When we look at it over the course of many years, it can even be a useful and interesting way to divide the history of major-league baseball into distinct eras. (See section 2.)

1.2 Behavior Over Time

For our purposes, it is enough for now to simply show the decline of the single since 1919, the end of the Deadball Era, when, on average, significantly fewer balls were used per game, compared to the 120 or so balls per game today. The baseballs were often soft from overuse, disfigured by scuff marks, and dark with dirt, tobacco juice, spit, and myriad other foreign substances. Thus, pitches were difficult to see and moved in unpredictable ways toward home plate. When a pitch was hit, the ball didn't travel as far.[11] Teams scraped for runs by bunting, executing the hit-and-run, and stealing bases. This small-ball style of play produced a meager 3.92 runs per game between 1901 and 1919. And singles were a whopping 58% of all on-base events. Singles would never again be as prominent as they were in the Deadball Era.

To see what happened with singles after modern baseball's infancy, we plotted the singles prop along with the home-run prop from 1920 through 2023 (Figures 1 and 2). In each plot, the line connecting the data points for each season has been divided into the same eight segments, labeled A through H, each of which represents a distinct trend in the singles proportion. Segments in darkly shaded boxes represent periods in which the singles prop (or the home-run prop) was in a down cycle, while segments in lightly shaded boxes represent periods in which those props were in an up cycle. Section 2 discusses these periods from a historical perspective. In the singles proportion plot (Figure 1) the horizontal line at .501 represents the mean singles proportion for the entire period shown, 1920–2023. In the home-run proportion plot (Figure 2) the horizontal line at .068 represents the mean home-run proportion for the entire period shown, 1920–2023. The discussion following Figure 1 will focus first on the singles prop.

Several facts are evident from the singles proportion plot:

- Since the Deadball Era, about half of all on-base events have been singles.

- The singles prop has experienced numerous rises and falls during the last 104 seasons.

- The long-term trend of the singles prop is downward.

- The singles prop has been at historically low levels since 2016.

1.3 Explanations for Long-term Downward Trend

The downward trend of the singles prop tells us that, relative to other on-base events, batters today rely less on the single to reach base than they ever have. It tells us that singles don't contribute to run production as much as they once did. Babe Ruth started it all back in 1920 when a confluence of circumstances allowed him to hit an astounding 54 home runs. It was a demonstration for the fans that baseball with more home runs was more fun to watch. His popularity was a demonstration for the owners that baseball with more home runs was more profitable. And it was a demonstration for the teams that more home runs could make a valuable contribution to winning games.[12]

As the game was being transformed, baseball observers began to look at data and think seriously about the relative importance of events like singles and home runs in helping to produce runs.[13] The analysis of baseball data took a giant leap starting in the 1970s, when the processing speed of computers and then the emergence of the World Wide Web allowed an ever-broader range of baseball observers to use ever-more-advanced statistical methods to study ever-larger volumes of data.[14] Over the decades and through all the technological advances, baseball analysts never retreated from what is now universally accepted regarding the importance of hitting for power. The first half of the story is that there came to be a broad, data-based recognition, starting with baseball analysts and writers and eventually spreading to major-league front offices, that runs are most efficiently produced with extra-base hits, especially home runs.[15]

The equally important second part of the story was the realization that at any level of development, many players who aren't already considered power hitters can become power hitters with the proper training.[16]

This evolution in thinking influenced player acquisition, minor-league instruction, offseason training, and player compensation.[17] Power hitters were rewarded with large contracts, and it gradually became more common for players to spend their offseasons with professional trainers to increase their launch angles, strength, and bat speed.[18] The new approach to building a winner gradually influenced even college, high school, and youth baseball programs. In recent years, slugging has become even more valued at the major-league level because improvements in pitching (both velocity and command of breaking pitches), data-driven defensive shifts, and changes in the way pitchers are utilized during a game (more pitchers giving maximum effort for shorter stints) make it even more difficult for hitters to string enough singles together to generate runs.[19]

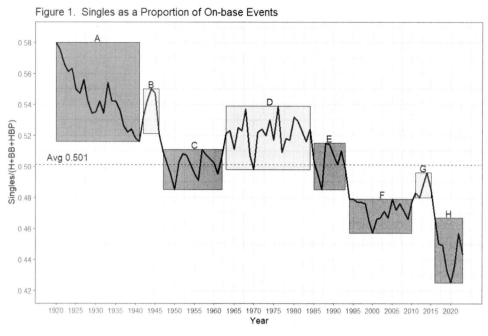

Figure 1. Singles as a Proportion of On-base Events

Figure 2. Home Runs as a Proportion of On-base Events

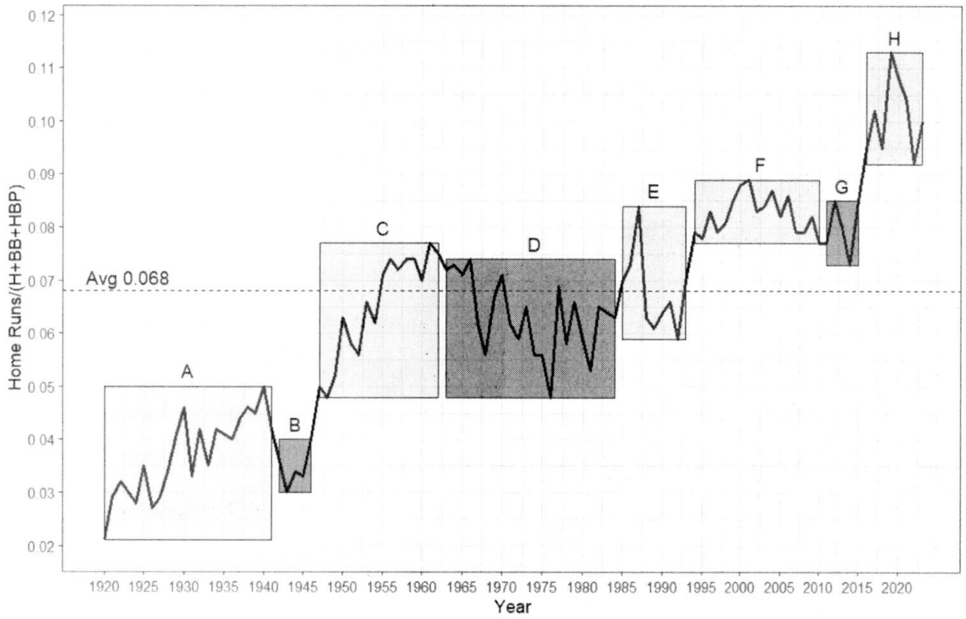

1.4 Effects of Long-term Downward Trend

There were consequences to the decisions now being made by front offices. Teams became willing to sacrifice some contact hitting, speed, and defense for the sake of additional slugging, particularly at certain positions.[20] The term "singles hitter" and "slap hitter" were commonly used by baseball observers and writers until fairly recently to describe players whose offensive contributions consisted largely of hitting singles. Such players also tended to be better baserunners, defenders, and bunters, and better at executing the hit-and-run and hitting behind baserunners. (See Appendix B and Table 4. Appendices can be found online at SABR.org.)

They made contact more frequently. This combination of skills was once considered a necessary piece of any well-rounded team. The term is rarely used now because so few players fit that description.

Players who were traditionally considered singles hitters generally had a singles prop around .600 or higher (see Appendix B for the post-1919 career singles prop leaders). In the 1976 season, when the league singles prop was .539, there were 37 such players in the majors who qualified for the batting title, including future Hall of Famers Lou Brock, Robin Yount, and George Brett. In 2019, when the league singles prop was .433, there were only six qualifying players at .600

or above, the most notable being Tim Anderson and Elvis Andrus.[21]

1.5 Relationship to Other Game Events

The impact of emphasizing slugging at the expense of other skills can also be seen by comparing the singles prop with the home-run prop. It's probably not surprising to see an inverse relationship between them; when one goes up, the other tends to go down. But in this case the negative correlation is very high. We computed the correlation coefficients for each on-base event proportion as well as stolen bases per game (SB/G), strikeouts per game (SO/G), sacrifice hits per game (SH/G), runs per game (R/G), hits per game (H/G), and batting average (BA) to better understand the relationships between the singles prop and other metrics (Tables 1 and 2). The underlying data are from the 1920 through 2023 seasons.[22]

Table 1 shows all positive correlation coefficients (for metrics that tend to move in the same direction), while Table 2 shows all negative correlation coefficients (for metrics that tend to move in opposite directions). The strongest correlations, with absolute values greater than 0.75, appear in light gray-bordered cells to help them stand out, as these are the most meaningful.

The easiest way to read these tables is to read down a particular metric's column to identify the other metrics with which it is most correlated (indicated by

Table 1. Positive Correlation Matrix of On-base Event Proportions and Other Metrics

	1B prop	2B prop	3B prop	HR prop	BB prop	HBP prop	SB/G	SO/G	SH/G	R/G	H/G	BA	Year
1B prop			0.82						0.80		0.45	0.46	
2B prop				0.34		0.57	0.36	0.41		0.55	0.33	0.30	0.47
3B prop	0.82								0.92	0.29	0.70	0.72	
HR prop		0.34			0.34	0.79	0.19	0.93					0.89
BB prop				0.34				0.21					0.24
HBP prop		0.57		0.79			0.27	0.87		0.06			0.81
SB/G		0.36		0.19		0.27		0.32		0.01	0.01	0.04	0.47
SO/G		0.41		0.93	0.21	0.87	0.32						0.96
SH/G	0.80		0.92							0.26	0.68	0.72	
R/G		0.55	0.29			0.06	0.01		0.26		0.80	0.79	
H/G	0.45	0.33	0.70				0.01		0.68	0.80		0.99	
BA	0.46	0.30	0.72			0.04		0.72	0.79	0.99			
Year		0.47		0.89	0.24	0.81	0.47	0.96					

Table 2. Negative Correlation Matrix of On-Base Event Proportions and Other Metrics

	1B prop	2B prop	3B prop	HR prop	BB prop	HBP prop	SB/G	SO/G	SH/G	R/G	H/G	BA	Year
1B prop		-0.44		-0.93	-0.47	-0.77	-0.10	-0.86		-0.14			-0.85
2B prop	-0.44		-0.21		-0.44				-0.19				
3B prop		-0.21		-0.87	-0.50	-0.66	-0.30	-0.89					-0.93
HR prop	-0.93		-0.87						-0.84	-0.01	-0.54	-0.55	
BB prop	-0.47	-0.44	-0.50			-0.04	-0.26		-0.51	-0.27	-0.57	-0.56	
HBP prop	-0.77		-0.66		-0.04				-0.56		-0.37	-0.36	
SB/G	-0.10		-0.30		-0.26				-0.15				
SO/G	-0.86		-0.89						-0.83	-0.17	-0.63	-0.64	
SH/G		-0.19		-0.84	-0.51	-0.56	-0.15	-0.83					-0.84
R/G	-0.14			-0.01	-0.27			-0.17					-0.14
H/G				-0.54	-0.57	-0.37		-0.63					-0.56
BA				-0.55	-0.56	-0.36		-0.64					-0.57
Year	-0.85		-0.93						-0.84	-0.14	-0.56	-0.57	

Source: Data from "Major League Batting Year-By-Year Batting Totals," Baseball Reference, https://www.baseball-reference.com/leagues/majors/bat.shtml.

the positive and negative coefficients with the largest absolute values in tables 1 and 2). Several observations can then be made:

1) The singles prop, the triples prop, and sacrifice hits per game are strongly correlated with each other, which means they have a strong tendency to move together in the same direction.

2) The home-run prop, strikeouts per game, and the hit-by-pitch prop also have a strong tendency to move together in the same direction.

3) There is a very strong negative correlation between the singles prop and the home-run prop. Historically, they've moved in opposite directions. If home runs become a more important part of offense, singles become a less important part.

4) Both the singles prop and the home-run prop are very weakly correlated with runs per game, demonstrating what we stated earlier: The singles prop tells us more about how runs were scored than how many runs were scored.

5) The "Year" column in these tables treats the year as a number (e.g., the year 2020 equals the number 2,020). If the correlation between a statistic and the year number is high (strong) and positive, we're saying that statistic tends to increase over time. The tables reveal two strong long-term trends over the last century of baseball history, since the Deadball Era ended. The singles prop has fallen since 1919, while the home-run prop and strikeouts per game have risen over the same period.[23]

6) Hits and batting average have sometimes been used as a kind of proxy for the singles prop; that is, they've been used to try to describe how runs are being scored. But neither is strongly correlated with the singles proportion. To the contrary, hits and batting average tell us more about how many runs were scored. The singles prop, together with the home-run prop, is the single best way to measure how runs are being scored.

In sum, the computed correlations in Table 1 and Table 2 show how the singles prop is related to other game events and their metrics. These relationships are what give the singles prop its powerful ability to tell a story not just about singles in particular, but about how runs in general are being scored, indeed, about how the game is being played.

1.6 The End Result

The single has fallen to its lowest levels since the Deadball Era. Singles won't disappear, of course.[24] But they're largely an afterthought, a fortuitous byproduct of a failed home run, and today's game looks noticeably different. Teams look for different types of players and utilize a different offensive approach. These changes have brought more home runs and strikeouts, and fewer singles and triples, reducing the amount of action on the field itself.[25] The singles prop is the single best measure of on-field action simply because singles lead to more on-field action (baserunning, fielding, and throwing) than any other batting event.

2. A CLOSER LOOK AT THE HISTORY OF THE SINGLES PROPORTION

2.1 Introduction

Having seen what a depressed singles prop tells us about how the game is being played today, let's further test the efficacy of the singles prop as a metric by examining more closely its movements in the context of specific historical events. The task of explaining changes in the singles prop over the past century is a daunting one. We now know, for example, that any change in the baseball manufacturing process, no matter how trivial, and regardless of whether those involved are even aware of the change, has the potential to alter not only how many runs are scored, but how those runs are produced. This makes it difficult to attribute any change in the singles prop to one cause. Reality is always more complicated than the generalizations of historians. The truth is that changes in the singles prop over time are likely the net effect of multiple factors, some offsetting each other, some compounding each other, and some not even known to us.

Having said that, let's take a stab at it anyway because it's the only way we, as humans, can make sense of a complicated world. We need to see whether the singles prop is as informative about baseball's past as it is about its present. To do this, we aren't going to offer an explanation every time our plot of singles props (Figure 1, top) changes direction. Instead, we identified eight segments of the plot based on significant changes in trend. We labeled these segments A through H. We applied these same segments to the subsequent plot of home-run props (Figure 2) for ease of comparison.

For each segment or period, we'll identify some of the events driving changes in either the singles prop or home-run prop. In some cases, we'll identify an important event even though its impact on the singles prop or home-run prop is not clear. The events we identified ended up falling into one of seven categories: (1) equipment, (2) league policies and rules, (3) stadium architecture and field conditions, (4) statistical records or players, (5) talent pool, (6) run/hit prevention strategies, and (7) player training and instruction.[26] The events themselves are summarized in Table 3 in Appendix A, and discussed in some detail in the remainder of this section.

2.2 The Live Ball Era (1920–41)

The Singles Prop's Lengthy Decline (Segment A)

Segment A shows a dramatic rate of decline in the singles prop from 1920, when it was .580, through 1941 when it was .516. These years coincide with what is customarily referred to as the Live Ball Era. It might have been more accurate to name it the Clean New Ball Era. Spitballs and "emery" balls were banned at its outset, and umpires were directed to frequently replace scuffed, dirty, and discolored balls with clean new white ones.[27]

Once batters could see the ball better and unnatural breaking pitches were abolished, the walk and home-run props began trending up at the same time the singles prop started heading down. The team owners refrained from interfering for a decade, realizing that home runs were increasing the popularity of the game in the wake of the 1919 Black Sox Scandal. Their hands-off approach eventually gave way in reaction to the startling rise in home runs during 1929 and 1930. In 1931, the cushioned-cork center, which added ground rubber to the previous cork-only center, was introduced into baseballs to deaden them.[28] But this was but a brief interruption as the home-run prop soon resumed its upward trajectory. Runs per game remained relatively steady throughout this period, averaging 4.85, nearly a full run above the run rate during the Deadball Era.

The increase in home runs would not have been possible but for the emergence of concrete and steel stadiums, most of which had outfield fences that batters could reach more easily. In addition, the newer parks tended to move the fans further away from the field, creating more foul territory. This had the effect of making it easier for batters to make outs, thus making it more difficult to get hits. In short, the modern stadiums helped devalue the sequential offense (stringing multiple base hits together to produce runs) and boosted the value of power-oriented offense (reach base and wait there until a teammate hits a home run).

The first wave of modern parks opened between 1909 and 1923 and hung around until the early 1950s, when a second wave of parks was built. Yet the singles prop continued dropping throughout the Live Ball Era and even after. According to Bill James, "Almost every change in ballparks between 1930 and 1968 took hits out of the league. ...There is no change in ballparks that I am aware of between 1930 and 1968 that significantly favored batting averages. Some changes favored home-run hitters, but none or almost none favored singles hitters."[29]

Clean new balls, homer-friendly dimensions, and larger foul territory all made sequential hitting less efficient and slugging (particularly home runs) more efficient at generating runs, even though home runs came with a lot of strikeouts. Also contributing to this new reality were improvements in fielding gloves. During the 1920s, gloves with a full-sized deep pocket between the thumb and index finger emerged. Fielders could now reach balls they previously couldn't, and being able to catch a ball in the pocket lessened the impact on their fingers and palms.[30] Better fielding added to the difficulty of stringing together hits to produce runs. Small-ball strategies aimed at advancing baserunners made less sense now, as did filling roster spots with speedy contact hitters.

No player took greater advantage of modern stadiums, clean new balls, and improvements in fielding than Babe Ruth. He and his home-run records demonstrated for other players what was possible in the new playing conditions of the Live Ball Era. Both current and prospective players could now see with their own eyes that it was possible to have a powerful uppercut swing and still hit the ball consistently, or at least consistently enough. This effect likely grew throughout the Live Ball Era as players who adopted Ruth's approach to hitting in their youth gradually entered the league.[31]

2.3 World War II Upheaval (1942–46)

Replacement Players Play with a Replacement Ball (Segment B)

It took over 20 years for the singles prop to drop from .580 to .516 in 1941. But it only took three seasons during World War II to rise back up to .550 in 1944. Meanwhile, the proportion of extra-base hits fell enough to sink offensive levels back to 4.07 runs per game between 1942 and 1946. Scoring runs hadn't been that difficult since the Deadball Era.

World War II impacted the singles prop in two ways: It diminished the talent pool and it changed the materials used to manufacture baseballs. Rubber, an important ingredient of a baseball's core as well as a component of tanks and planes, was banned in items not essential to the war effort. The redesigned ball was made of less elastic materials. The dead ball, and with it, small ball, were back.[32] More importantly, Ted Williams, Joe DiMaggio, Stan Musial, and most of the rest of the best players were in military service. More than 500 major leaguers had their careers interrupted for a greater cause.[33] James estimates that only 40% of major-league players during this period were of major-league quality.[34]

2.4 Postwar Stability (1947–62)
The Singles Proportion Dives into a Period of Sameness (Segment C)

As soon as the war ended and the talent pool was replenished by returning veterans, and eventually newly integrated African Americans, the singles prop resumed the dramatic descent that had begun in the Live Ball Era. It declined every season from 1944 (.550) to 1950 (.485), the largest uninterrupted drop in baseball history until 2020. Then, for the first time, the singles prop appeared to establish a state of equilibrium, hovering above and then below the all-time average of .501 in a cycle that repeated itself three and a half times between 1947 and 1962.

The inverse relationship between the singles prop and the home-run prop holds up least well during this period. While the singles prop remained stable, the home-run prop, aided by the decision by both leagues to shrink the strike zone for the 1950 season, resumed its relentless trek upward from the Live Ball Era. Home runs as a proportion of on-base events increased steadily and significantly throughout this postwar period, from .048 in 1948 to .077 in 1961.[35] The level of offense was not changing, but the nature of offense was. The home run had never played such an important role in generating runs. Rosters were filled out with players who could hit the occasional home run but couldn't do much else. The reemergence of bases-tealers at the very end of this era offered some hope, however.[36]

2.5 The Pre-Turf Expansion Era (1963–76) and AstroTurf Doubles (1977–84)
Rule Tinkering Triggers Rise in Singles Proportion and Drop in Home-run Proportion (Segment D)

As we saw in Figure 1, the singles proportion experiences only three up cycles after the Deadball Era, and

two of them are quite brief: 1942–46 and 2011–15. The Pre-Turf Expansion Era and subsequent AstroTurf Doubles period, on the other hand, lasted 22 seasons. The period is filled with events that influenced the on-base event proportions and gives us glimpses of our ideal version of the game, so it's very instructive for our purposes and warrants exploration in some depth.

The National and American Leagues each added two new franchises in 1961–62 and two more in 1969. Some observers believe league expansion of this magnitude played an important role in the decline of offense from 1963 to 1984. Normally, the resulting dilution of talent would require teams to diversify their offenses, leading to fewer runs scored. This time, however, any dilution of talent was more than offset by the continued growth in the number of African American players and, to a lesser extent, Latino players throughout this period.[37]

It's more plausible that the decline was initially triggered by Roger Maris breaking Babe Ruth's single-season home run record in 1961. Fearing home runs were becoming too routine, the Baseball Rules Committee decided to expand the strike zone prior to the 1963 season.[38] Unfortunately, they overshot their mark by extending the strike zone both upward from the armpit to the top of the shoulder, and downward from the top of the knee to the bottom of the knee.[39]

The change had a more dramatic effect than the committee likely intended. The singles prop immediately rose to .521 in 1963, a level not seen since the war years. The home-run prop eventually fell as well. From baseball's perspective, the problem was that runs per game collapsed to World War II levels. Pitching dominated because the expansion of the strike zone caused strikeouts to shoot up and walks to drop off dramatically. The quality of batters' contact suffered as well, with hitters being forced to swing at pitches they could previously take for balls. Thus began an era of pitching dominance.

Also helping to suppress runs during this period was the second wave of ballparks that entered the league beginning in 1953 and continuing into the 1960s. Some were new as a result of franchises moving to new locations; others were newly built. Regardless, most were pitcher's parks. On top of that, night baseball was becoming more prevalent during the 1960s. Early lighting technology was primitive by today's standards, so this too favored pitching.[40] Offense eventually crashed to 3.42 runs per game in 1968, a level not seen since 1908, the heart of the Deadball Era. Baseball felt compelled to act again by restoring the smaller strike zone (arm pits to top of knees), lowering the mound, and actually enforcing the standard mound height (several teams with good pitching were believed to have had pitcher's mounds higher than the rules allowed).[41] In addition, league policy finally started requiring that the visual background for the batter (an area located beyond the center-field fence known as the batter's eye) protect the hitter's ability to see an incoming pitch.[42]

These latest changes had their desired effect, jacking offense back up above 4 runs per game in 1969. The singles prop, which had spiked to .537 in 1968, the highest since the war years, now fell back to .507, its largest season-to-season drop to this point in the twentieth century. Predictably, the home-run prop, which had collapsed to .056 in 1968, now jumped back up to 1950s levels.

Strangely, the boost in offense was short-lived. One can only speculate as to why (improved defense?). In any case, the roller-coaster ride of the Expansion Era continued, fueled by baseball's seemingly quixotic search for balance, a balance that stubbornly refused to reveal itself. By 1971, runs per game were back down below 4.0 and the singles prop was back up above .520. The American League, which had been lagging behind the National League in runs per game, brought out the big guns this time by implementing the designated-hitter rule in 1973.[43] This clearly helped run production, at least in the AL. Then, in 1974, a shortage of horsehide prompted the major leagues to start using baseballs covered in cowhide.[44] The singles prop rocketed to a period-high .539 in 1976.

It didn't stay there for long, though. In 1977, MLB's ball supplier changed name from Spalding to Rawlings and it's likely manufacturing changes unintentionally affected the ball.[45] Whether intended or not, the singles prop crashed again every bit as hard as it had in 1969. And with that, the Expansion Era was truly over. Runs per game never fell below 4.0 again. The Rules Committee had come full circle. Runs per game were back up to the levels of the late 1950s, a few years before the decline commenced.

While runs were up, the singles prop and home-run prop continued to oscillate at the same levels through the 1984 season. Both proportions kept fluctuating within intervals signaling greater reliance on the single and less reliance on the home run compared to the preceding postwar period. How was this possible? The singles and homer props aren't telling us the whole story. For the first time since the transition from the Deadball Era to the Live Ball Era, the doubles prop jumped to a new level.

The key driver behind this odd eight-year period was a third wave of ballparks entering the major leagues during the 1970s.[46] The newly constructed parks were sterile and uniform multipurpose sports stadiums. But it was primarily the fast artificial turf playing surfaces in almost all of them that affected the way offenses generated runs. The prototype was Houston's Astrodome, which opened in 1965 and installed AstroTurf in 1966.[47] Six more artificial turf fields were added between 1970 and 1973, and three more in 1977. Except for 1979–81, when there were nine, there would be 10 artificial turf fields in baseball until 1994. Most were in the National League. Groundballs scooted across turf faster than on grass, and line drives and fly balls bounced higher. Speed and quickness now mattered for both batters and fielders more than at any time since the Deadball Era. Balls that weren't hit directly at an infielder could make it to the wall for a double or triple. The overall level of runs, 4.3 per game, was mid-level, historically. But the new playing conditions allowed all aspects of the game to emerge. Teams like the Kansas City Royals and St. Louis Cardinals, who did the best job constructing rosters that would flourish on artificial turf, won many games during the late 1970s and 1980s despite consistently finishing near the bottom of the league in home runs. Singles, doubles, triples, stolen bases, and fielding percentage—these were their marks of honor.

The best thing about these years was that good teams could win in a variety of ways, and good players could possess different skill sets. It was an unintended but welcome respite from the inexorable march of the home run. Baseball had always been more concerned about the balance between offense and pitching. But this was a new type of balance that fans hadn't seen. Attendance increased. But baseball purists struggled with the way the baseball behaved on this new surface. Batted balls that were previously routine outs were now singles, and what had been singles were now doubles or triples. The speed of the game had changed.

2.6 The Single's Last Days (1985–93)
Singles Proportion Collapses Again to Record Low
Before Stabilizing Around All-time Average (Segment E)

The 1985 season saw the beginning of a decline in the singles prop that would eventually take it down to .485 by 1987. Baseball then abolished the high strike, defining the top of the zone as the midpoint between the shoulders and the top of the uniform pants, and the singles prop bounced right back up in 1988 before settling down to average .503 for the period ending in 1993.[48] It wasn't a dramatic change, but it was a distinctly lower level than the singles prop of the Pre-Turf Expansion Era and the AstroTurf period. Predictably, the initial decline in the singles prop brought with it a resurgence in the power-hitting game, with the home-run prop shooting up to a then-record level in 1987. But, unlike in 1950 and 1969, the 1988 contraction of the strike zone had the effect of erasing the home-run prop's gains and then keeping the home-run prop suppressed through the 1993 season. Pitchers were likely working the bottom of the strike zone more intensely once the high strike was abolished.

For the period as a whole, the double and home-run props both bumped up, along with the walks prop, but offense remained around the same 4.3 runs per game achieved during the AstroTurf period of 1977–84. Artificial turf surfaces continued to exert an important influence throughout this period (speed still mattered), but other factors seemed to be coming into play now. We might view this period as an extension of the 1977–84 turf period with a modest increase in the home-run prop and a modest decrease in the singles prop.

The now prevalent use of five-man starting rotations and closers helped support the home-run prop. Adding a starter to the rotation and letting a dominant reliever specialize in preserving narrow leads in the ninth inning likely added to the difficulty of stringing hits together to generate runs, and thus encouraged greater reliance on the home run.[49] Another driver of the home-run prop beginning in the 1990s was players increasingly devoting their offseasons to strength and conditioning programs rather than supplementing their incomes.[50] It was finally acknowledged by everyone in the baseball world that offseason strength training done properly could improve a power hitter's performance. As more and more players participated, and as the programs grew in sophistication, durability and performance improved, and any gains in strength were generally reflected in more extra-base hits for batters and more strikeouts for pitchers. Finally, the explosive growth in the number of Latino players from 1987 to 1999 cannot be ignored, though its effect on the single and home-run props is unclear.[51] Any significant addition to the talent pool would seem to help the home-run prop because it provides teams with the means to implement their preferred strategies: home runs and power pitching. The unanswered question is, What kind of talent was being added?

2.7 The Steroid Era (1994–2010)
The Singles Proportion Topples to New Depths (Segment F)
In the 1990s, the analytics movement was gaining greater acceptance within front offices. It confirmed what many in baseball instinctively knew in earlier eras: Small-ball strategies, featuring speed and contact hitting to advance baserunners, were a relatively inefficient way to score runs. This would become a near-universal mindset as the Steroid Era progressed, and it was reflected in the behavior of the singles and home-run props.[52]

After 1919, the Pre-Turf Expansion Era and its AstroTurf aftermath was the singles prop's lengthiest period above its all-time average of .501 (21 of 22 seasons). Its counterpart below the all-time average was the Steroid Era (17 consecutive seasons). The singles prop set or tied a record low (post-1919) every season from 1994 through 2000, when it bottomed out at .457. For the entire period, it averaged .472, 29 points lower than the next lowest era, the postwar period.

Of course, it wasn't just the singles prop that changed so dramatically. Surpassing their post-1919 record highs (both single-season and era average) were the doubles prop, home-run prop, strikeouts per game, and the hit-by-pitch prop. Run production in the Steroid Era was comparable to that in the Live Ball Era. But it was the outsized role of power hitting in generating runs that characterized this period in the minds of fans and analysts.

As it was all happening, observers naturally credited the ball itself for the power-hitting explosion. Some analysts continue to insist the ball is the only explanation that can plausibly account for such a sudden and large jump. As time passed and further evidence came to light, the more commonly accepted explanation for the power explosion was players' widespread use of performance-enhancing drugs such as steroids.[53] Both the ball and steroids may have been factors, and we'll probably never know to what extent each contributed to this period of sustained power hitting.

The manifest power surge seemed impervious to forces that normally may have hindered it. The majors expanded by two teams in 1993 and two more teams in 1998. On top of that, African American participation was now receding. But any resulting dilution of talent seems to have been more than offset by the continued rapid growth in Latino players until 1999.[54] In 1996, MLB expanded the bottom of the strike zone to the bottom of the knee, but this too had little effect.[55] Other forces driving the home-run prop included a fourth wave of mostly natural grass ballparks (11, to be exact) built during the 1990s. These were generally friendlier toward hitters, and included among them Coors Field (1995), the best hitter's park in the history of baseball. Also, in the early 1990s, baseball implemented a zero-tolerance policy for brushback pitches, automatically expelling a pitcher who threw close to a hitter after a warning. This enabled batters to crowd the plate and drive outside pitches to the opposite field.[56]

These factors, together with steroids, strength-building programs, and a possible lively ball, may have been too much to overcome. In any case, MLB made little effort to do so. With runs per game approaching Live Ball Era levels and fans excited by home-run races, team owners may have viewed the power explosion as a second Ruthian revolution that would increase the popularity of the game. They rode the power wave until the stigma associated with performance-enhancing drugs became too great. Stringent policies against steroid use, with significantly increased penalties, were put in place before the 2005 season, and the length of suspensions for steroid use was increased before 2006.[57] This finally halted the climb in power numbers, but they never returned to pre-Steroid Era levels, and it would be another five seasons before the singles prop and the home-run prop began behaving differently. Drug testing confirmed that some players continued to use steroids.[58] Perhaps more importantly, the power-hitting mindset (wait for your pitch and swing for the fences) had become firmly entrenched, buttressed by strength training, new parks, league policies, and equipment changes (bats and gloves).[59]

The character of the game evolved into something new during the Steroid Era. It produced a limited set of results: doubles, homers, walks, strikeouts, and hit batters. Speed, whether on the bases or in the field, didn't matter as much. Sacrifice hits and advancing baserunners didn't matter as much. Nor did defensive skills in general. Fewer balls were being hit into play, and strategic decision points occurred less frequently. Teams simply sat back and waited for the next power hitter in the lineup to drive in runs. Games were longer and moved along more slowly, so a greater proportion of game time contained no action. But MLB appeared content with the state of the game, so long as offenses were humming and attendance was climbing.

2.8 The Umpire Strikes Back (2011–15)
Conformity to the Rulebook Strike Zone Permits the Singles Proportion One Last Goodbye (Segment G)

In 2011, the singles prop moved toward pre-Steroid Era levels not seen for 18 seasons and remained there for five years. It peaked at .496 in 2014 before retreating again. The 2015 season would be the last with a singles prop above Steroid Era levels.

The doubles and home-run props did not change during this period, but the walks prop plunged to levels not seen since the 1930s, and strikeouts per game set a new record every season. In baseball history, this combination of changes had always been accompanied by a change in the strike zone.

While there was no official change to the strike zone during this period, there is evidence that umpires' enforcement of the strike zone changed after 2009, when MLB began using an improved camera system in all major-league stadiums to, among other things, monitor ball-strike calls by umpires. In addition to the technology change, a new umpire evaluation and training system was implemented following collective bargaining between MLB and the umpires' union in 2009. Umpires began receiving reports of their performance after every game. While this was happening, MLB took unusual disciplinary action by firing three of its seven umpire supervisors because of blown calls made during the 2009 postseason.[60]

A 2014 study by Brian Mills examined, among other things, the impact of changes in monitoring, evaluation, and training on the performance of major-league umpires from 1988 through 2013. Mills found substantial changes in the way umpires enforced the strike zone after 2009. Umpires were now calling balls and strikes in a way that was more consistent with the strike zone defined in the MLB Rulebook. Specifically, they called more strikes near the bottom of the strike zone and fewer strikes off the outside edge of the plate.[61] The net effect, according to Mills, was a large increase in the rate of strikes called by umpires that "likely resulted in a decrease in offense [in 2010–11 runs per game finally started to move down in a significant way from Steroid Era levels] often attributed to the league's crackdown on the use of performance enhancing drugs. …[A]ny claim of success in PED testing should be considered with some skepticism."[62]

Mills' findings provide a sound explanation for the rise in the singles prop during this five-year period. When the strike zone expands, whether the result of a change in the rules or a change in umpire performance, batters are forced to swing at pitches they would otherwise take for balls, and thus make weaker contact. The consequent increase in the singles prop was even more assured in this case because the strike zone, in effect, expanded downward, resulting in more groundballs.[63]

2.9 The Launch Angle Revolution and Reduced Drag (2016–23)
The Single Becomes an Accident (Segment H)

If we use a long-term macro perspective to look back at the singles and home-run props between 1920 and 2015, you could say baseball went through a transformative period during the Live Ball Era that was temporarily interrupted by World War II before settling into relative stability marked by short-term peaks and valleys after 1946. Sometimes offense had the upper hand and other times pitching had the upper hand. Sometimes offense was dominated by the home run and other times the power game was balanced by contact hitters and speed. But neither the singles prop nor the home-run prop strayed very far for very long before turning around and coming back home.

That might have continued indefinitely, but it didn't. Baseball instead headed toward uncharted territory in 2016. Like the Live Ball Era, it was more than a shift in balance; it was a transformation. And if you measure it by the singles prop, it's still happening.

The 2011 to 2015 umpire-driven interlude abruptly ended in 2016, when the singles prop experienced a two-season drop of 30 points to .467, comparable to the singles props of the Steroid Era. The home-run prop rocketed past its Steroid Era levels, rising 22 points over 2015 and 2016 to land at .095. Neither prop stopped there. The singles prop dropped below its all-time low the next season and continued to fall in subsequent years until finally landing at .425 in 2020. Its 71-point fall between 2014 and 2020 was the largest uninterrupted drop in the history of the game. Not to be outdone, the home-run prop experienced a 40-point rise during the five-year period ending in 2019, when it set its all-time high of .113. Baseball was in a different place now.

This time there was hard evidence of the primary causes, thanks to newly available Statcast data and more advanced laboratory testing. An exhaustive report by a group of scientists and mathematicians, commissioned by MLB in 2017 and published in May 2018, pointed to the most notorious catalyst for change throughout baseball history, the baseball.[64] The report found that "changes in the aerodynamic properties of the baseball" resulted in batted balls having greater carry. Balls were traveling farther because of decreased drag.[65] The researchers continued their work through the rest of 2018 and 2019 to try to definitively establish which physical properties changed to reduce air resistance. The report was monumental not only for identifying the primary cause of the latest power explosion, but also for demonstrating that the slightest change in the baseball manufacturing process has the potential to change, intentionally or not, the character of the game. Suddenly, all those who had pointed to the ball to explain previous performance changes throughout history gained a bit more credibility.

In December 2019, another report released by MLB made it apparent the scientists and statisticians were still struggling to identify all the factors affecting the air resistance of the ball.[66] However, by using more sophisticated lab equipment, they were able to determine that differences in seam height accounted for about 35% of the change in drag.[67] According to one of the scientists on the committee, "The change in seam height of a fraction of the thickness of a sheet of paper would give you a measurable effect in the change in the drag." Reduced drag, or increased carry, was again identified as the primary cause of the increase in home runs, accounting for 60%.[68] MLB promised tighter quality control to minimize ball-to-ball variation, but said it would not try to undo the changes that led to the ball's increased carry. After the singles and home-run props went off the charts in 2019 and 2020, MLB did try to deaden the ball for the 2021 season by instructing Rawlings to loosen one of the wool windings.[69] The change had the desired effect for two seasons, but both proportions resumed their journeys into uncharted territory in 2023, and the current version of the game remains vastly different from its historical past—due, at least in part, to the baseball itself.[70]

The 2019 report's conclusion that reduced drag accounted for 60% of the increase in home runs was interesting enough. Just as interesting was the report's conclusion that the other 40% of the increase was attributable to launch conditions. That is, more players were adapting their swing to hit the ball at a higher launch angle (vertical trajectory).[71] Sequential offense was more difficult than ever. Defensive positioning, with its shifting and shading, particularly among infielders, had grown ever more sophisticated.[72] By 2015, exasperated hitters had responded with their own shift—a philosophical one sparked by Marlon Byrd's turnaround season in 2013. This shift has been described as "so dramatic it can safely be called a revolution, with more hitters, armed with better and more extensive data than ever, reaching the conclusion that not only are fly balls, on average, better than grounders but that the latter are to be avoided at all costs."[73] As one proponent, 2015 American League MVP Josh Donaldson, succinctly put it, "Groundballs are outs. If you see me hit a groundball, even if it's a hit, I can tell you: It was an accident."[74]

Teams valued slugging. The stars of the game were paid a lot to slug. That wasn't new. What was new was the recognition by many players that slugging required hitting fly balls, and that they could hit fly balls with greater frequency by training specifically to increase the launch angle at which they hit the ball. Now, thanks to an explosion of newly available launch-angle and other data, they knew the exact launch angles (25 to 35 degrees) and velocities (95 miles per hour or more) needed to hit home runs. Daniel Murphy, another player who turned around his career with higher launch angles, likened it to having some of the answers to the test. The most successful players were able to increase their average launch angle by 10 or 11 degrees from one season to the next. The average launch angle across the majors increased 17% from 2015 to 2023. The result has been a steadily declining league groundball percentage (including a record low 42.3 percent in 2023) and, ultimately, more slugging, including home runs.

NATIONAL BASEBALL HALL OF FAME LIBRARY, COOPERSTOWN, NY

Babe Ruth of the New York Yankees, a hulking figure for the time, seen here with Lloyd Waner, the Pittsburgh Pirates' 150-pound center fielder. Before the 1927 World Series, Ruth said about Lloyd and his brother Paul, "Why, they're just kids. If I was that little, I'd be afraid of getting hurt."[75] Lloyd finished his career with a .700 singles prop, the highest since the end of the Deadball Era. By today's standards, he is considered to have been an excellent contact hitter and center fielder, but probably undeserving of his Hall of Fame election by the Veterans Committee in 1967.

The History of the Singles Proportion: Final Thoughts

Tracing the movement of the singles prop over the last century of National and American League baseball affirms the power of the singles prop to describe how runs are being scored and the game is being played. Time and again, when the singles prop fell, we saw a game moving toward more strikeouts and home runs and less action on the field. In short, the singles prop is a particularly insightful barometer for examining the game at this point in its history, as MLB works toward moving the game back toward its ideal form.

3. THE FUTURE OF THE SINGLE

Will the singles and home-run props ever again approach pre-Steroid Era levels? Will the single ever again be considered something more than the incidental side effect of a failed attempt at a home run?

One opportunity to increase the singles prop might have been the full implementation of an automated ball-strike system (ABS). History has shown that changes to the strike zone or its enforcement can have a powerful influence on how runs are produced. However, MLB now appears intent on implementing ABS with a challenge system rather than on every pitch.[76]

A safer and more reliable way to boost the singles prop may be to simply limit the number of active pitchers to 10.[77] Carrying 10 active pitchers was the norm between World War II and 2000.[78] By codifying what was the normal practice through much of modern baseball history, starting pitchers and at least some relievers would have to get more outs while throwing fewer pitches, lest their pitching staffs run out of arms. Pitchers would pitch to contact more often, batters would put more balls in play and reach base more often, and serial offense would once again be a viable means of scoring runs.[77]

For now, we'll continue to live with more home runs, strikeouts, and hit batters, and fewer singles, triples, sacrifice hits, and balls in play. It all adds up to less action, despite the rule changes that went into effect in 2023 (some of which were suggested by Bill James decades ago). The rule changes were successful in quickening the pace of games and resurrecting base stealing. Perhaps that should give us some hope that contact hitting and defensive athleticism can make a comeback as well. MLB's efforts to move the game in this direction appear sincere, and we now have some powerful tools, the various on-base event proportions, particularly the singles proportion, to help us measure the progress. ■

Appendices

Available on the SABR website: https://sabr.org/journal/article/the-singles-slow-fade-the-diminishing-role-of-the-single-since-the-deadball-era/.
- Appendix A: Summary of Historical Events Impacting the Singles Proportion, 1920–23.
- Appendix B: Career Singles Proportion Leaders (1920–2023).

Notes

1. Anthony Castrovince, "8 Changes Fans Need to Know For the '23 Season," MLB, March 28, 2023, https://www.mlb.com/news/mlb-rules-changes-refresher-2023-season.
2. Harry Enten, "Why is baseball no longer America's Game?" CNN, April 7, 2022, https://www.cnn.com/2022/04/07/sport/mlb-opening-day-baseball-popularity-spt-intl/index.html; Ari Shapiro and Enrique Rivera, "New baseball rule hopes to reverse decades of fan loss," NPR, July 22, 2022, https://www.npr.org/2022/07/22/1113067620/new-baseball-rule-hopes-to-reverse-decades-of-fan-loss.
3. "The State of Baseball: Inside the biggest questions MLB is facing with the future of the sport at stake," ESPN, May 10, 2021, https://www.espn.com/mlb/story/_/id/31394230/the-state-baseball-biggest-questions-mlb-facing-future-sport-stake; Dave Sheinin, "These days in baseball, every batter is trying to find an angle," *Washington Post*, June 1, 2017, https://www.washingtonpost.com/graphics/sports/mlb-launch-angles-story/; Tom Verducci, "There's a Science Behind More High-Velocity Pitches, But There's Also a Cost," *Sports Illustrated*, May 1, 2023, https://www.si.com/mlb/2023/05/01/high-velocity-pitching-what-it-means-for-mlb-pitchers; "Baseball's 'existential crisis': Why pitchers are becoming more unhittable than ever," CBS News, July 8, 2021, https://www.cbsnews.com/news/baseball-pitchers-velocity-increase/.
4. Associated Press, "Average MLB game time dropped to 2:40 with pitch clock," ESPN, October 2, 2023, https://www.espn.com/mlb/story/_/id/38551264/mlb-game-dropped-240-pitch-clock.
5. Jesse Rogers, "Fix baseball? MLB is working on a plan," ESPN, June 24, 2021, https://www.espn.com/mlb/story/_/id/31693901/fix-baseball-mlb-working-plan.
6. Bill James, *The New Bill James Historical Baseball Abstract* (New York: Free Press, 2003), 276–77, 296 .
7. James, *New Historical Baseball Abstract*, 296.
8. James, *New Historical Baseball Abstract*, 120.
9. The singles proportion can be easily calculated by dividing the number of singles by the sum of hits, walks, and hit-by-pitches during a given time period. The proportion for any other on-base event (e.g., home run, walk, double) can be computed in a similar manner, by dividing the number of occurrences of that on-base event by the sum of hits, walks, and hit-by-pitches. "Major League Batting Year-By-Year Batting Averages," Baseball Reference, https://www.baseball-reference.com/leagues/majors/bat.shtml, accessed October 22, 2023.
10. The expression of singles *as a proportion of all on-base events* is critical to the metric's ability to describe *how* runs are being scored. Its power derives from the ratio. Thus, counting stats such as the number of singles or the number of hits are not nearly as informative. Nor are hits per game or batting average. Batting average encompasses all types of hits within the context of opportunities; as such, it's a far better indicator of how many runs were scored than how runs were scored.
11. Jason McDonald, "What Are the Major Eras of Major League Baseball History?" Huffpost, July 4, 2013, updated December 6, 2017, https://www.huffpost.com/entry/what-are-the-major-eras-o_b_3547814.
12. James, *New Historical Baseball Abstract*, 120–22.
13. Joshua Mizels, Brandon Erickson, and Peter Chalmers, "Current State of Data and Analytics Research in Baseball," *Current Reviews in Musculoskeletal Medicine* 15, Issue 4 (2022), 283–90, https://www.ncbi.nlm.nih.gov/pmc/articles/PMC9276858/; Jack Moore,
"Baseball ProGUESTus: The Secret History of Sabermetrics," Baseball Prospectus, July 16, 2013, https://www.baseballprospectus.com/news/article/21234/baseball-proguestus-the-secret-history-of-sabermetrics/.
14. Richard Schell, "SABR, Baseball Statistics, and Computing: The Last Forty Years," *Baseball Research Journal* 40, No. 2 (Fall 2011), https://sabr.org/journal/article/sabr-baseball-statistics-and-computing-the-last-forty-years/, accessed July 25, 2024.
15. Mike Petriello, "Homers are still the key to winning in playoffs," MLB, October 7, 2020, https://www.mlb.com/news/homers-are-still-the-key-to-winning-in-playoffs, accessed July 25, 2024.
16. Sheinin, "These Days in Baseball."
17. Jason Chang and Joshua Zenilman, "A Study of Sabermetrics in Major League Baseball: The Impact of Moneyball on Free Agent Salaries," Olin Blog, April 19, 2013, https://api.semanticscholar.org/CorpusID:37346410; Craig Edwards, "Positional Pricing: Paying for Power and Aces," FanGraphs, March 11, 2015, https://blogs.fangraphs.com/positional-pricing-paying-for-power-and-aces/; Edwards, "Designated Hitter is the Highest Paid MLB Position," FanGraphs, March 18, 2016, https://blogs.fangraphs.com/designated-hitter-is-the-highest-paid-mlb-position/; James, *New Historical Baseball Abstract,* 198, 220–22, 306–10, 316–17; Sheinin, "These Days in Baseball."
18. James, *New Historical Baseball Abstract*, 307; Sheinin, "These Days in Baseball."
19. Dave Sheinin, "Velocity is Strangling Baseball—and Its Grip Keeps Tightening," *Washington Post*, May 21, 2019, https://www.washington-post.com/sports/2019/05/21/velocity-is-strangling-baseball-its-grip-keeps-tightening/; Sheinin, "These Days in Baseball"; Ben Clemens, "How Bigger Bullpens are Constraining Offense," FanGraphs, April 26, 2022, https://blogs.fangraphs.com/how-bigger-bullpens-are-constraining-offense/; Tyler Kepner, "Velocity School: Where Pitchers Pay to Throw Harder," *The New York Times*, September 14, 2017, https://www.nytimes.com/2017/09/14/sports/baseball/mlb-velocity-pitchers.html; Verducci, "There's a Science Behind More High-Velocity Pitches."
20. James, *New Historical Baseball Abstract*, 145, 198, 220–22, 306.
21. "Player Batting Season & Career Stats Finder," Stathead Baseball, https://stathead.com/baseball/.
22. "Major League Batting Year-By-Year Batting Totals," Baseball Reference, https://www.baseball-reference.com/leagues/majors/bat.shtml.
23. Bill James once described the trends toward more homers and more strikeouts as cyclical. (James, *New Historical Baseball Abstract*, 316.) In the short term that may be true, but certainly not in the long term.
24. Singles still produced 27% of all RBIs in 2022, for example. https://www.retrosheet.org/; https://www.kaggle.com/datasets/jraddick/baseball-events-from-retrosheetorg.
25. Koby Close, "Part 1: Investigating Major League Baseball's Home Run Problem," LinkedIn, September 26, 2019, https://www.linkedin.com/pulse/part-1-investigating-major-league-baseballs-home-run-koby-close-eit/.
26. This effort was inspired by Bill James' attempt to identify historical events that divide the history of major-league baseball into distinct eras. He ended up identifying 366 such events falling into 10 broad categories, and concluding that stadium architecture and game equipment were "the two largest dynamics of change in baseball." Bill James, "Dividing Baseball History into Eras," Bill James Online, June 10, 2012, https://web.archive.org/web/20230930165226/https://www.billjamesonline.com/dividing_baseball_history_into_eras/; James, *New Historical Baseball Abstract*, 276.
27. Alan Schwarz, "The History of Rule Changes," ESPN, February 4 (2003), https://www.espn.com/mlb/columns/schwarz_alan/1503763.html; James, *New Historical Baseball Abstract*, 120–22.
28. Tommy Craggs, "Was MLB's Juiced Era Actually a Juiced-Ball Era?" Deadspin, August 29, 2012, https://deadspin.com/was-mlbs-juiced-era-actually-a-juiced-ball-era-5937432; James, *New Historical Baseball Abstract*, 145.

29. James, 250.
30. Jimmy Stamp, "The Invention of the Baseball Mitt," *Smithsonian Magazine*, July 16, 2013, https://www.smithsonianmag.com/arts-culture/the-invention-of-the-baseball-mitt-12799848/; Jim Daniel, "#Goingdeep: The Evolution of Baseball Gloves," National Baseball Hall of Fame, https://baseballhall.org/discover/going-deep/the-evolution-of-baseball-gloves.
31. James, *New Historical Baseball Abstract*, 145.
32. Zachary D. Rymer, "The Evolution of the Baseball From the Dead-Ball Era Through Today," Bleacher Report, June 18, 2013, https://bleacherreport.com/articles/1676509-the-evolution-of-the-baseball-from-the-dead-ball-era-through-today; Craig Calcaterra, "Today in Baseball History: 'Balata Ball' Threatens a New Dead Ball Era," NBC Sports, May 4, 2020, https://www.nbcsports.com/mlb/news/today-in-baseball-history-balata-ball-threatens-a-new-dead-ball-era.
33. Rocco Constantino, "The Top 200 Moments That Shaped MLB's History," Bleacher Report, May 17, 2012, https://bleacherreport.com/articles/1157233-200-events-that-defined-shaped-and-changed-major-league-baseball/.
34. James, *New Historical Baseball Abstract*, 198.
35. Schwarz, "The History of Rule Changes."
36. James, *New Historical Baseball Abstract*, 220, 222, 249.
37. Brian L. Lokker, "History of MLB Expansion Teams and Franchise Moves," How They Play, August 21, 2023, https://howtheyplay.com/team-sports/major-league-baseball-expansion-and-franchise-relocation; Mark Armour, "The Effects of Integration, 1947–1986," *Baseball Research Journal* 35 (2007), https://sabr.org/journal/article/the-effects-of-integration-1947-1986/; Mark Armour and Daniel R. Levitt, "Baseball Demographics, 1947–2012," Society for American Baseball Research, https://sabr.org/research/article/baseball-demographics-1947–2012/; Armour and Levitt, "Baseball Demographics, 1947–2016," Society for American Baseball Research, https://sabr.org/bioproj/topic/baseball-demographics-1947-2016/.
38. Steve Treder, "Re-Imagining the Big Zone Sixties, Part 1: 1963–1965," Hardball Times, November 30, 2004, https://tht.fangraphs.com/re-imagining-the-big-zone-sixties-part-1-1963-1965/.
39. "Strike Zone," MLB, https://www.mlb.com/official-information/umpires/strike-zone; "The Strike Zone: A History of Official Strike Zone Rules," Baseball Almanac, https://www.baseball-almanac.com/articles/strike_zone_rules_history.shtml.
40. James, *New Historical Baseball* Abstract, 250, 276.
41. Schwarz, "The History of Rule Changes"; Constantino, "The Top 200 Moments."
42. James, *New Historical Baseball Abstract*, 276.
43. McDonald, "What Are the Major Eras."
44. Craggs, "Was MLB's Juiced Era Actually a Juiced-Ball Era?"
45. Craggs; Rymer. Numerous analysts speculate about changes in the ball in 1977. Although technically the only change in 1977 was to the name from Spalding to Rawlings, some slight incidental change in the manufacturing process, coinciding with Rawlings beginning to apply its own trademark logo (as well as separate, distinctly colored logos for the National and American Leagues), may have unwittingly caused the singles prop to drop significantly in 1977. (See https://thinkbluela.com/2018/08/rawlings-puts-the-ball-in-baseball-3/ for photos of the two 1977 Rawlings balls.) Many times Rawlings and MLB have insisted that balls are being manufactured to the same specs, only to later acknowledge, based on scientific findings, that different batches of balls can have different properties that impact carry and drag. It's possible that even changing what's stamped on the baseball could alter its properties.
46. James, *New Historical Baseball Abstract*, 277.
47. Constantino, "The Top 200 Moments."
48. "Strike Zone," MLB.
49. Bill James, "The Three-Man Starting Rotation," Bill James Online, November 20, 2015, https://web.archive.org/web/20230930164809/https://www.billjamesonline.com/the_three_man_starting_rotation/.
50. James, *New Historical Baseball Abstract*, 297, 307.
51. Armour and Levitt, "Baseball Demographics, 1947–2012;" Armour and Levitt, "Baseball Demographics, 1947–2016."
52. Taylor Bechtold, "State of Analytics: How the Movement Has Forever Changed Baseball—For Better or Worse," Stats Perform, https://www.statsperform.com/resource/state-of-analytics-how-the-movement-has-forever-changed-baseball-for-better-or-worse/.
53. Craggs, "Was MLB's Juiced Era Actually a Juiced-Ball Era?" Ben Lindbergh, "How Much of a Role Did Steroids Play in the Steroid Era?" The Ringer, September 28, 2018, https://www.theringer.com/mlb/2018/9/28/17913536/mark-mcgwire-sammy-sosa-steroid-era-home-run-chase.
54. Armour and Levitt, "Baseball Demographics, 1947–2012;" Armour and Levitt, "Baseball Demographics, 1947–2016."
55. "The Strike Zone," Baseball Almanac.
56. James, *New Historical Baseball Abstract*, 307–09, 322–23.
57. Zachary D. Rymer, "Full Timeline of MLB's Failed Attempts to Rid the Game of PEDs," Bleacher Report, June 10, 2013, https://bleacherreport.com/articles/1667581-full-timeline-of-mlbs-failed-attempts-to-rid-the-game-of-peds.
58. Lindbergh, "How Much of a Role."
59. Bechtold, "State of Analytics"; Steven Bratkovich, "The Bats…They Keep Changing!" *Baseball Research Journal* 47 (Spring 2018), https://sabr.org/journal/article/the-bats-they-keep-changing/.
60. Brian Mills, "Expert Workers, Performance Standards, and On-the-Job Training: Evaluating Major League Baseball Umpires," SSRN, August 27, 2014, https://ssrn.com/abstract=2478447; Bob Nightengale, "Yer Out! 3 Umps' Bosses Get Thumb Over Bum Calls," *USA Today*, March 8, 2010, 1C.
61. Mills, "Expert Workers."
62. Research by Jon Roegele made similar findings and drew similar conclusions using somewhat different methodologies. Jon Roegele, "The Strike Zone During the PITCHf/x Era," Hardball Times, January 30, 2014, https://tht.fangraphs.com/the-strike-zone-during-the-pitchfx-era/.
63. Joe Lemire, "Why Baseball's Strike Zone Is Changing," Vocativ, May 23, 2016. (Article no longer online.)
64. Jim Albert et al., "Report of the Committee Studying Home Run Rates in Major League Baseball," MLB via Inside SoCal, May 24, 2018, https://www.insidesocal.com/dodgers/files/2021/10/Full-Report-of-the-Committee-Studying-Home-Run-Rates-in-Major-League-Baseball_052418.pdf.
65. Joe Lemire, "MLB Research Determines Reduced Drag Boosted Home Run Surge," Sports Business Journal, May 25, 2018, https://www.sportsbusinessjournal.com/Daily/Issues/2018/05/25/Technology/mlb-baseball-research-home-run-drag-aerodynamics.aspx.
66. Zach Kram, "How the Baseball Became an Unreliable Narrator," The Ringer, December 16, 2019, https://www.theringer.com/year-in-review/2019/12/16/21023481/juiced-dejuiced-ball-home-runs-investigation.
67. Kyle Glaser, "Study Concludes Seam Height Changes Contributed to 2019 Home Run Spike," Baseball America, December 11, 2019, https://www.baseballamerica.com/stories/study-concludes-seam-height-changes-contributed-to-2019-home-run-spike/.
68. Jay Jaffe, "The Home Run Committee's Latest Report Isn't the Final Word on Juiced Baseballs," Fangraphs, December 12, 2019, https://blogs.fangraphs.com/the-home-run-committees-latest-report-isnt-the-final-word-on-juiced-baseballs/.
69. Matt Borelli, "MLB Rumors: Only Baseballs Manufactured After 2021 Production Change Being Used For 2022 Season," Dodger Blue, April 28, 2022, https://dodgerblue.com/mlb-baseballs-manufactured-after-2021-production-change-being-used-for-2022-season/2022/04/28/. Before the 2022 season, MLB made yet another change that impacted the properties of the ball. All 30 MLB teams were required to store their baseballs in a humidor at a specified humidity and temperature prior to games. By doing so, MLB hoped to reduce inconsistencies between balls used in different locales, as both humidity and temperature affect the distance

the ball travels. (David Kagan, "The Physics of Cheating Baseball's Humidors," Hardball Times, June 3, 2019, https://tht.fangraphs.com/the-physics-of-cheating-baseballs-humidors/.) The overall impact of the humidor requirements on league performance is not clear. For one thing, parks that are normally less humid than the standard would be affected differently than parks that are more humid than the standard. Plus, the number of variables involved makes it difficult to isolate cause and effect. (Zach Crizer, "These Nine MLB Ballparks are Using Humidors. What Does It Mean for Baseball's Offensive Downturn?" Yahoo Sports, June 8, 2021, https://sports.yahoo.com/these-9-mlb-ballparks-now-use-humidors-complicating-the-sports-pursuit-of-big-changes-162450868.html.)

70. MLB points to a five-point increase in batting average as evidence that rule changes implemented in 2023 are helping bring more action back into the game. (Tom Stone, "The Impact of the 2023 Rule Changes on MLB Statistics in Historical Context," Now Taking the Field, October 14, 2023, https://nowtakingthefield.substack.com/p/the-impact-of-the-2023-rule-changes.) But at least a part of this increase can be attributed to MLB instructing official scorers to rule batted balls to be hits rather than errors except in the most obvious cases. (Bob Nightengale, "David Cone Recalls Short-Lived Writing Career," *USA Today*, June 5, 2023, 7C.) In any case, the singles proportion is a better measure of action on the field than batting average because it places singles in the context of all on-base events. When the singles proportion rises, the home-run proportion and strikeouts per game fall. Fewer home runs and strikeouts necessarily leads to more action occurring on the field. In 2023, however, the singles proportion fell. The five-point increase in batting average is misleading if interpreted to mean more balls are being put in play.

71. Jaffe, "The Home Run Committee's Latest Report."

72. Taylor Bechtold, "State of Analytics."

73. Sheinin, "These Days in Baseball."

74. Taylor Bechtold, "State of Analytics."

75. Jan Onofrio, *Oklahoma Biographical Dictionary* (St. Clair Shores: Somerset Publishers, 1999), 215–16.

77. Nate Silver, "Relievers Have Broken Baseball. We Have a Plan to Fix It.," FiveThirtyEight, February 25, 2019, https://fivethirtyeight.com/features/relievers-have-broken-baseball-we-have-a-plan-to-fix-it/; Ben Lindbergh, "How Can MLB Fix Its Too-Many-Pitchers Problem?," The Ringer, May 2, 2022, https://www.theringer.com/mlb/2022/5/2/23052714/pitcher-roster-rules-limit; Russell A. Carleton, *The New Ballgame: The Not-So-Hidden Forces Shaping Modern Baseball* (Chicago: Triumph Books, 2023), 138–39.

78. Pete Palmer, "Relief Pitching Strategy: Past, Present, and *Future?*," *Baseball Research Journal* 40, No. 1 (2018), 45–52.

Ghost Stories and Zombie Invasions

Testing the Myths of Extra-Inning Outcomes

Connelly Doan, MA

After several years of testing in Minor League Baseball, Major League Baseball introduced a regular-season extra-inning rule in 2020 by which teams begin each extra inning with a runner on second base. The rule was meant to reduce the length of extra-inning games and save pitching arms while bringing more action to the game.[1] While it was initially enacted to accommodate the 2020 COVID-19 pandemic season, the rule was made permanent by MLB's Joint Competition Committee prior to the 2023 season.[2]

The decision to introduce "ghosts" and "zombies" to MLB was met with polarizing feelings from fans.[3] While there are many debates around the rule, two main topics of argument are: "Does departing from the tradition of the game actually lead to shorter games?" and "Is the strategy of extra-inning games simplified to sacrifice-bunting the automatic runner to third and hitting a sacrifice fly or a single to score, thus making the game even less exciting?"[4]

While these discussions have relied on ample anecdotal evidence, little has been presented in terms of empirical evidence to analyze how extra-inning games used to play out compared to how they've been played since the introduction of the new rules at the big-league level. This paper will present descriptive data from extra-inning games in the 2018–22 regular seasons. These data will be used to test for statistically and practically significant changes in the following game results: average innings per extra-inning game; average extra-inning runs scored per game; frequency of extra-inning bunt attempts and their success; and the game situations when bunt attempts occurred. This analysis will provide concrete evidence about whether and how the automatic-runner rule has impacted games.

DATA OVERVIEW

The raw play-by-play extra-inning game data for this article were scraped from MLB's API game data using Python. Specifically, the raw data comprised extra-inning game data from games in the 2018 regular season through the 2022 regular season. Only games that were originally scheduled to be nine innings were included, as doubleheaders in 2020 and 2021 were scheduled to be seven innings.[5] The line scores of those games were then coded to identify occurrences of interest in extra innings.

Several Python libraries were used for data pulling, cleaning, and analysis. Pybaseball was used to facilitate the ingestion of the raw data.[6] Pandas was used to manipulate the raw data into usable data frames for further analysis. PandaSQL was used to better query the created data frames and shape the variables of interest. Finally, Scipy's Stats was used to run independent T-tests on the variables of interest, treating the 2018–19 and 2020–22 seasons as the independent sample groups.[7]

VARIABLES/DEFINITIONS

Average innings per extra-inning game was defined as named. Average extra-inning runs scored per game by home and away teams only considered the number of runs scored in extra innings.

Variables concerning bunt attempts, successes, and situational context were defined using Statcast's events and descriptions. Statcast events are categories bucketing the outcomes of an at-bat or play (sacrifice bunt, single, etc.). Descriptions further categorize the specific type of action taken within an event (foul bunt, missed bunt, etc.). Additionally, each action within an event is given a full written description. Bunt attempts were defined as any at-bats resulting in a game event of sacrifice bunt or an action described as a foul bunt or missed bunt, as well as any at-bat with an action containing "bunt" in the written description. Successful bunts were defined as a game event of sacrifice bunt or a game event of single with a description containing "bunt" in the written description.

RESULTS

Game and Inning Stats

Table 1 presents both descriptive statistics and relevant T-test results for the variables in this analysis. T-tests determine whether the difference between mean values from two separate populations is statistically significant. The T value measures the size of the difference relative to the variation in the data. In other words, it presents the difference between the population means in standard error units.

The P value resulting from a T-test indicates the likelihood that the two means of comparison came from the same population. The higher the P value, the more similar the means are from the two populations. In other words, the higher the P value, the more likely it is that the means from the two populations could conceivably come from the same population, suggesting that the populations of interest are the same. P values range from 0 to 1, with .05 as the widely accepted maximum P value to indicate statistical significance of a difference.

The sample sizes of extra-inning games were roughly split between the two groups of data, with 425 standard extra-inning games occurring in 2018–19 (Before) and 493 occurring in 2020–22 (After). The average number of innings in Before's games was 11.25, while the average number of innings in After's games was 10.40. The T-test result between these averages was statistically significant, indicating that extra-inning games in Before were longer than in After.

The average number of extra-inning runs scored by the away team in Before's games was 1.14, compared to 1.60 runs in After. Likewise, the average number of extra-inning runs scored by the home team in Before's games was 0.83, compared to 1.25 runs in After. The T-test results between both of these averages were statistically significant, indicating that both home and

away teams scored more runs in extra innings in After's games.

In the Before period, 39.53% of games contained at least one bunt attempt in extra innings by either the home or away teams, while 39.96% of games did in the After period. The T-test result between these percentages was not statistically significant, indicating that games with extra-inning bunt attempts were not different between Before and After. At least one successful bunt was executed in 20.47% Before games and 25.15% of After games. The T-test result between these percentages yielded a P value of 0.09. Based on the previously mentioned 0.05 threshold, the results indicate that games with successful extra-inning bunts were also not different between Before and After.

Before's games saw 0.26 bunt attempts per extra inning, compared to 0.37 in After games. The T-test result between these numbers was statistically significant, indicating that more bunts were attempted per extra inning in After's games than in Before's. Of those attempts, 0.12 bunt attempts per extra inning were successful in Before's games, compared to 0.21 in After's games. This T-test result was also statistically significant, indicating that more bunts were executed per extra inning in After's games over Before's.

Looking more specifically at the metrics by team, 25.65% of the 425 extra-inning games in Before contained at least one bunt attempt in extra innings by the away team, compared to 23.12% of the 493 extra-inning games in After. The T-test result between these percentages was not statistically significant, indicating

Table 1. Comparison Pre- and Post-2020

	Years		T Statistic	P Value
	2018-19	2020-22		
Extra Inning Games	425	493		
Avg. Innings/Game	11.25	10.40	10.23	***
Avg. Away Extra Inning Runs Scored	1.14	1.60	-4.55	***
Avg. Home Extra Inning Runs Scored	0.83	1.25	-5.90	***
Games w/ Bunt Attempt (%)	168 (39.53%)	197 (39.96%)	-0.13	0.89
Avg. Bunt Attempts/Extra Inning	0.26	0.37	-3.68	***
Games w/ Bunt Success (%)	87 (20.47%)	124 (25.15%)	-1.68	0.09
Avg. Bunt Successes/Extra Inning	0.12	0.21	-3.82	***
Games w/ Away Bunt Attempt (%)	109 (25.65%)	114 (23.12%)	0.88	0.37
Avg. Away Bunt Attempts/Extra Inning	0.14	0.19	-2.13	0.03
Games w/ Away Successful Bunt (%)	56 (13.18%)	61 (12.37%)	0.36	0.72
Avg. Away Bunt Successes/Extra Inning	0.07	0.10	1.55	0.12
Games w/ Home Bunt Attempt (%)	91 (21.41%)	119 (24.14%)	-0.98	0.33
Avg. Home Bunt Attempts/Extra Inning	0.11	0.18	-3.14	0.002
Games w/ Home Successful Bunt (%)	40 (9.41%)	75 (15.21%)	-2.65	0.008
Avg. Home Bunt Successes/Extra Inning	0.05	0.11	-3.87	***

P values less than .001 denoted with ***

that games with extra-inning bunt attempts by away teams were not different between Before and After. Similarly, 13.18% of the games in Before contained at least one successful bunt in extra innings by the away team, compared to 12.37% in After. The T-test result between these percentages was not statistically significant, indicating that games with successful extra-inning bunts by away teams were not different between Before and After.

Before's games saw 0.14 away bunt attempts per extra inning, compared to 0.19 in After. The T-test result between these numbers was statistically significant, indicating that more bunts were attempted per extra inning by away teams in After's games over Before's. Of those attempts, 0.07 bunt attempts per extra inning were successful in Before's games, compared to 0.10 in After's games. This T-test result was not statistically significant at 0.12, indicating that there was no difference in executed bunts per extra inning by away teams in After's games over Before's.

In the bottom half of innings, 21.41% of games in Before contained at least one bunt attempt in extra innings by the home team, compared to 24.14% in After. The T-test result between these percentages was not statistically significant, indicating that games with extra-inning bunt attempts by home teams were not different between Before and After. On the other hand, 9.41% of the games in Before contained at least one successful bunt in extra innings by the home team, compared to 15.21% in After. The T-test result between these percentages was statistically significant, indicating that more games in After contained successful extra-inning bunts by the home team than in Before.

Before's games saw 0.11 home bunt attempts per extra inning, compared to 0.18 in After. The T-test result between these numbers was statistically significant, indicating that more bunts were attempted per extra inning by home teams in After's games over Before's. Of those attempts, 0.05 per extra inning were successful in Before's games, compared to 0.11 in After's games. This T-test result was statistically significant, indicating that home teams executed more bunts per extra inning in After's games over Before's.

Bunt Situation Stats

Tables 2 and 3 present the distribution of extra-inning bunt attempts by game situation and team for Before and After. The most frequent extra-inning bunt situations Before came with a runner on first with no outs (38.7%) and with runners on first and second with no outs (18.5%). This pattern held true for both home and away teams, with away teams attempting more bunts. Bases empty with no outs (10.9%) and a runner on second with no outs (10.1%) were the only other situations with a noticeable quantity of attempts.

The most frequent extra-inning bunt situations in After games overwhelmingly came with a runner on second and no outs (69.8%). This pattern held true for both home and away teams, but especially so for

Table 2. Bunt Attempts by Situation and Team (2018–19)

Runner Situation	Outs	Team		Total
		Home	Away	
Bases Empty	0	11	15	26 (10.9%)
Bases Empty	1	6	9	15 (6.3%)
Bases Empty	2	2	4	6 (2.5%)
Runner On First	0	42	50	92 (38.7%)
Runner On First	1	4	8	12 (5.0%)
Runner On First	2	1	2	3 (1.3%)
Runners On First & Second	0	19	25	44 (18.5%)
Runners On First & Second	1	1	2	3 (1.3%)
Runners On First & Second	2	0	1	1 (0.4%)
Runners On First & Third	0	0	1	1 (0.4%)
Runners On First & Third	1	2	4	6 (2.5%)
Runners On First & Third	2	1	0	1 (0.4%)
Runner On Second	0	12	12	24 (10.1%)
Runners On Second & Third	1	0	1	1 (0.4%)
Runner On Third	0	1	1	2 (0.8%)
Bases Loaded	2	0	1	1 (0.4%)
Total		102 (42.9%)	136 (57.1%)	238 (100%)

Table 3. Bunt Attempts by Situation and Team (2020–22)

Runner Situation	Outs	Team		Total
		Home	Away	
Bases Empty	0	0	1	1 (0.4%)
Bases Empty	1	0	1	1 (0.4%)
Bases Empty	2	0	1	1 (0.4%)
Runner On First	0	3	1	4 (1.6%)
Runner On First	1	0	2	2 (0.8%)
Runners On First & Second	0	21	23	44 (17.1%)
Runners On First & Second	1	0	1	1 (0.4%)
Runners On First & Third	0	0	5	5 (1.9%)
Runners On First & Third	1	1	5	6 (2.3%)
Runners On First & Third	2	1	0	1 (0.4%)
Runner On Second	0	99	81	180 (69.8%)
Runner On Second	1	0	1	1 (0.4%)
Runner On Second	2	1	0	1 (0.4%)
Runners On Second & Third	1	0	1	1 (0.4%)
Runners On Second & Third	2	0	1	1 (0.4%)
Runner On Third	1	4	1	5 (1.9%)
Runner On Third	2	0	1	1 (0.4%)
Bases Loaded	0	1	0	1 (0.4%)
Bases Loaded	1	0	1	1 (0.4%)
Total		131 (50.8%)	127 (49.2%)	258 (100%)

home teams. Runners on first and second with no outs (17.1%) was the only other situation with a noticeable number of attempts.

DISCUSSION

Extra-inning game event data from 425 standard extra-inning games occurring 2018–19 (Before) were compared to 493 games occurring 2020–22 (After) to test for statistically different outcomes. Extra-inning games in Before lasted nearly one inning longer than in After, which was statistically significant. This could also be considered a practically significant difference, as the new rule eliminated almost 420 innings (or 46.6 standard games) of gameplay over the 2020–22 seasons. In terms of offensive production in extra innings, both away teams and home teams averaged about half a run more of production in After compared to Before. Given that more extra-inning runs were scored in fewer innings, the empirical evidence seems to support MLB's original goals for implementing the new rule.[8]

In terms of overall gameplay strategy, the percentage of games with extra-inning bunt attempts was nearly identical Before and After, although more bunts were attempted per extra inning in After games. Most Before bunts were attempted with either a runner on first and no outs or with runners on first and second with no outs. Almost all After bunts were attempted with a runner on second and no outs or with runners on first and second and no outs. More After bunt attempts were successful than Before, perhaps due to them occurring without a force on the basepaths. These results align with the narrative that teams will try to take advantage of the automatic runner starting at second base. However, it can be argued that the intent of extra-inning bunts has not changed. Most extra-inning bunts, Before and After, occurred with a runner on base and no outs. While Before teams had to earn a baserunner as opposed to After, the bunt situation distribution suggests that the goal has not changed: Trade a first out to better position a runner to score.

The percentage of games in which the away team attempted a bunt in extra innings decreased slightly between Before and After. The percentage of those games with a successful away-team bunt also slightly decreased. Away teams attempted relatively fewer extra-inning bunts in After. Perhaps away teams are implementing various game theory analyses that suggest that swinging rather than bunting gives them the best chance to score runs in extra innings with the new rules.[9]

As for home teams, the percentage of games with attempted extra-inning bunts increased slightly between Before and After, although not enough to be deemed statistically significant. The number of games with a successful home-team bunt was almost six percentage points higher in After than in Before, which is both statistically and practically different. Additionally, home teams in After attempted and executed more extra-inning bunts than in Before. The difference in extra-inning bunt attempts and success rate between home and away teams in these two periods could suggest a fundamentally different approach to extra innings. It may also be a result of home teams practicing the situation more frequently.

NEXT STEPS

This article provides descriptive data to inform discussions on the impact of the automatic runner rule on extra-inning outcomes. Extra-inning games have been shorter with more extra-inning offense since the implementation of the rule. Extra-inning bunt attempts and successes did increase, although home teams drove these patterns. The vast majority of extra-inning bunt attempts came with no outs and a runner on second; in other words, they occurred at the beginning of half-innings to attempt to advance the automatic runner. While these data provide objective fodder to what up to this point has been a mostly subjective set of discussions, there are additional nuances that can further be explored.

The first could be a more thorough investigation of gameplay sequencing to better understand extra-inning strategy. In this article, extra-inning bunts were only analyzed in terms of frequency and isolated situations. The next level of analysis could extend game event sequences to better understand the impact of bunt attempts on scoring runs and winning games.

Relatedly, this article only considered overall extra-inning offensive production and extra-inning bunt attempts and successes separately; it did not analyze the relationship between successful bunts and eventual runs being scored. Specifically, it did not consider how or if the bunt played a part in runs being scored. Did the automatic runner advance to third on a sacrifice bunt but then score on a double or home run, or did he score on a single or sacrifice fly?

Finally, a third sample group could be introduced beginning in 2023. Several rule changes were introduced before that season, including a pitch timer and limited pickoff attempts.[10] It would be interesting to investigate how these rule constraints affected the approach to extra-inning gameplay with respect to the automatic runner, if at all. ∎

Notes

1. Bill Walker, "New For 2020: MLB Extra Inning Rule," MiLB, August 30, 2020, https://www.milb.com/news/major-league-baseball-extra-inning-rule.

2. Brett Taylor, "Commission Manfred Suggests Extra-Innings Runner-at-Second Rule Could Be Made Permanent," Bleacher Nation, November 2, 2022, https://www.bleachernation.com/cubs/2022/11/02/commission-manfred-suggests-extra-innings-runner-at-second-rule-could-be-made-permanent/; Evan Drellich and Eno Sarris, "MLB Makes Extra-Inning Ghost-Runner Rule Permanent, per Sources: How Has It Changed the Game?" The Athletic, February 13, 2023, https://theathletic.com/4191908/2023/02/13/mlb-extra-innings-position-player-rules/.

3. Joe Rivera, "MLB rule changes for 2022: Why controversial extra-inning ghost runner is sticking around (for now)," *The Sporting News*, March 23, 2022, https://www.sportingnews.com/us/mlb/news/mlb-rule-changes-2022-extra-inning-ghost-runner/pfawy4fmbxzcdlnoolo2bd3p; Associated Press, "MLB, players agree to keep zombie runner for '22," *USA Today*, March 22, 2022, https://www.usatoday.com/story/sports/mlb/2022/03/22/ap-source-mlb-players-agree-to-keep-zombie-runner-for-22/49972101/.

4. Associated Press, "MLB, players agree," Dayn Perry, "MLB's extra-innings rule is back in 2021; here's why baseball should use ties instead," CBS Sports, April 4, 2021, https://www.cbssports.com/mlb/news/mlbs-extra-innings-rule-is-back-in-2021-heres-why-baseball-should-use-ties-instead/; Abbey Mastracco, "Sorry, Purists: MLB's New Extra-Inning Rule Is Great and Should Be Here to Stay," Bleacher Report, April 9, 2021, https://bleacherreport.com/articles/2939660-sorry-purists-mlbs-new-extra-inning-rule-is-great-and-should-be-here-to-stay; Mike Petriello, "To bunt, or not? How to handle new rule in extras," MLB, July 20, 2020, https://www.mlb.com/news/how-teams-should-strategize-extra-innings-rule-in-mlb-in-2020; Craig Calcaterra, "New extra innings rule will not create a sacrifice bunt-fest," NBC Sports, July 9, 2020, https://www.nbcsports.com/mlb/news/new-extra-innings-rule-will-not-create-a-sacrifice-bunt-fest.

5. Thomas Harrigan, "MLB, MLBPA agree to 7-inning twin bills," MLB, July 31, 2020, https://www.mlb.com/news/mlb-mlbpa-agreement-on-seven-inning-doubleheaders#:~:text=In%20the%20interest%20of%20player,1; "MLB, union agree on doubleheaders, extra-inning rules," Reuters, February 8, 2021, https://www.reuters.com/article/us-baseball-mlb-rules-agreement/reports-mlb-union-agree-on-doubleheaders-extra-inning-rules-idUSKBN2A90I3.

6. James LeDoux, "GitHub: jldbc/pybaseball," GitHub, https://github.com/jldbc/pybaseball, accessed November 26, 2023.

7. "scipy.stats.ttest_ind," SciPy, https://docs.scipy.org/doc/scipy/reference/generated/scipy.stats.ttest_ind.html, accessed November 26, 2023.

8. Walker, "MLB Extra Inning Rule."

9. Taylor Bechtold, "Should MLB Teams Be Bunting the Ghost Runner to Third in Extra Innings More Often?" Opta Analyst, March 22, 2023, https://theanalyst.com/na/2023/03/should-mlb-teams-be-bunting-the-ghost-runner-to-third/.

10. Anthony Castrovince, "Pitch timer, shift restrictions among announced rule changes for '23," MLB, February 1, 2023, https://www.mlb.com/news/mlb-2023-rule-changes-pitch-timer-larger-bases-shifts.

Does the Home Team Batting Last Affect Game Outcomes?

Evidence from Relocated Games

Woody Eckard, PhD

Major-league rules have stipulated since 1950 that the home team always bats last. However, as Gary Belleville relates in a recent *Baseball Research Journal* article, an exception has been added to the rulebook:

> Starting in 2007, any team that had to relocate a home game to another city would still bat last. …MLB's revised policy…resulted in the home team batting first in 44 contests between 2007 and 2022.[1]

These relocations were caused by events outside of baseball, completely unrelated to the win-loss records of the involved teams. In other words, they were *random* with respect to the key variable in the present study: club winning averages. As such, these relocations constitute natural experiments that provide an opportunity to estimate the impact on game outcomes of the home team batting first (HTBF) rather than last.

The interesting question, of course, is whether it makes a difference. Do teams win at a lower rate when, instead of batting last at home, they bat first? The common presumption and the basis for the rule change is that batting last provides an advantage that leads to more wins. This article analyzes that question using the above-described natural experiments inadvertently created by the rule change. We find no evidence of a bats-last advantage. To my knowledge, this is the first analysis of this issue for major-league baseball.

The paper proceeds as follows. The first section provides some historical background, including related studies on college baseball. Next is a presentation of our data associated with the 44 HTBF games since 2007 and a discussion of the possible influence of the 28 games from the empty-stadium 2020 COVID-19 season. The third section describes the statistical methodology used to estimate the impact of HTBF. The fourth section presents those estimates in terms of the actual HTBF victories versus a hypothetical expected victory total assuming instead that our sample teams had batted last. The last section summarizes and concludes.

BACKGROUND

Starting in the mid-1880s, major-league home teams were given the choice of batting first or last.[2] During the next several years, they often elected to bat first. But by the mid-1890s, HTBF had declined and, as Belleville put it, "by 1901 teams rarely batted first at home."[3] Finally, after 1914, no home teams batted first through 1949, after which a new rule eliminated the option. In 2007, MLB created the above-noted exception requiring relocated home teams to bat last. In that year, for the first time in over nine decades, teams playing at home batted first rather than last.

As David Nemec notes: "by the early part of the [twentieth] century having your last at bats was viewed as an advantage," and it is still so viewed today.[4] In fact, the relocation exception was apparently created because batting last on the road was presumed to at least partially offset the disadvantage of losing the well-established home-field advantage. But it's not clear why batting last would create an advantage. There is little discussion of the issue today, perhaps because it has been a given for over a century. As Theodore Turocy observes, "Received wisdom…holds that it is a clear and obvious advantage to… have… 'last ups' [and so] no justification is necessary."[5] Be that as it may, before analyzing why the presumed advantage exists, there should first be evidence of its existence. However, there has been little empirical analysis of the issue, likely because of the almost total absence of data.[6] Prior to 2007, there had been no home-team-bats-first major-league games for almost a century. For example, in the above referenced article published in 2008, Turocy notes:

> …because random assignment of teams to the first and last batting roles has [occurred] not at all in 130 years, natural experiments for separating home field advantage from the effects of the order in which teams bat do not exist [for major-league baseball].[7]

As noted above, this circumstance has now changed.

While the absence of data has prevented MLB-focused studies, college baseball has presented some opportunities. In particular, in NCAA national championship tournaments, the batting-last rule often is set aside and batting order is determined by other means, such as a coin flip. This in turn has produced many home-team-batting-first situations, allowing empirical analysis.

There have been two main studies using NCAA tournament data, both finding no support for a bats-last advantage. First, in 2006, Simon and Simonoff examined tournament baseball games to estimate the impact of the batting-last rule on game outcomes. They concluded that "there is little evidence of a 'last licks' effect."[8] Second, in 2007, Bray, Obara, and Kwan similarly examined a different sample of NCAA tournament baseball games for the same purpose. Their results did not support the hypothesis that home teams "would win a greater percentage of the games in which they batted last compared with when they batted first."[9]

It should be noted at the outset that in a closed "league" like major-league baseball, across all clubs the aggregate *league* won-lost record cannot vary from .500, as each game produces both a win and a loss. Thus, for the league as a whole, to the extent that home team batting last impacts home wins, it has an equal but opposite impact on road wins. The issue, therefore, is simply the distribution of all wins between home and road.

DATA

Table 1 displays our sample of 44 relocated games, sorted by year, date, and host team, meaning the team whose stadium the game was played in, as opposed to the "home team," defined in the rules as the team that bats last.[10] The principal source was the above-mentioned Belleville *BRJ* article, supplemented by game logs available from Baseball Reference. We number the games from one to 44 to clearly identify each. The "host teams" in the table constitute our sample because, by playing a game in their own stadium, they ordinarily would have batted last but instead, in effect, were assigned visiting team status. The "relocated home team" is the opponent that was assigned home-team status and batted last. "Host W/L" indicates whether the team playing at home and batting first won or lost the game.

Twenty-eight of our 44 sample games occurred during the COVID-19-shortened 2020 season, 14 occurred prior to 2020, and there was one each in 2021 and 2022. The sample contains 17 different host teams. The Philadelphia Phillies account for five games and the Milwaukee Brewers, San Francisco Giants, and Seattle Mariners each appear four times. Thus, the sample is not dominated by a few teams. On five occasions an entire three-game series was relocated.

The last column of Table 1 gives reasons for the relocations. The most common was concerns over COVID-19 outbreaks in 2020, accounting for 16 relocations from eight cities. Unusual weather, including three hurricanes or tropical storms, caused eight relocations from six cities. Civil unrest forced six relocations from four cities, three in 2020. Smoke from wildfires near Seattle caused five Mariners games to be moved to either San Francisco or San Diego, all in September 2020.

The 28 games in 2020, 70 percent of the sample, raise concerns about the unique circumstance of that season biasing the results. For example, because of the pandemic, all major-league games in 2020 were played in empty stadiums. This eliminated any fan effects often presumed to be important in explaining the home-field advantage. Our host teams had a 14–14 record in 2020, and were 9–7 in the other years. Thus, the winning averages were very similar for the two groups, .500 and .562, respectively.

Also, several formal studies have found that the crowdless 2020 season did not affect home vs. road performance. For example, Daniel and Fullmer examined 8,188 major-league games, comparing the 2020 season to the previous three seasons, and found "no significant effect of crowds on home team performance."[11] Similarly, Chiu and Chang investigated 13,044 regular-season games, comparing 2020 to the previous five seasons. They found that "home advantage in the 2020 season [without fans] was not significantly different from that in 2015–2019 in MLB. …spectators may not be a crucial factor in home advantage."[12] Zimmer, Snyder, and Bukenya also compare the pandemic season to the previous five seasons with the same conclusion: "the lack of fans did not influence game results."[13]

METHODOLOGY

In our 44-game sample, the host team, batting first, won 23 games and lost 21. But what should we compare this to? The ideal is the counterfactual outcomes if the host team had batted last. This, of course, cannot be observed. But we can estimate these hypothetical outcomes using each team's home-road splits based on games involving the home team batting last. The associated home winning averages provide estimates of the probability of home team victory. This in turn can be used to estimate the expected number of counterfactual bats-last victories in our sample games.

For example, assume a given team in a given year has a home winning average of .550. In 20 home games against average teams we would expect $20 \times .550 = 11$ wins. For a single game, the expectation is $1 \times .550 = .550$ wins. In effect, the home winning average is the single game win expectation or probability. We can add this 20 times to get the 20-game expectation of 11. If instead we had 20 games involving clubs of varying

Table 1. Sample of 44 Relocated Home-Team-Bats-First Games, 2007–22

Game	Year	Date	Host Team	Host W/L	Relocated Home Team	Reason for Relocation
1	2007	26-Sep	Mariners	L	Indians	Snowstorm in Cleveland
2	2010	25-Jun	Phillies	W	Blue Jays	Economic Summit in Toronto
3	2010	26-Jun	Phillies	L	Blue Jays	Economic Summit in Toronto
4	2010	27-Jun	Phillies	W	Blue Jays	Economic Summit in Toronto
5	2011	24-Jun	Mariners	W	Marlins	Rock concert in Miami
6	2011	25-Jun	Mariners	L	Marlins	Rock concert in Miami
7	2011	26-Jun	Mariners	W	Marlins	Rock concert in Miami
8	2013	23-Jul	Giants	L	Reds	Rainout in Cincinnati
9	2015	1-May	Rays	W	Orioles	Civil unrest in Baltimore
10	2015	2-May	Rays	L	Orioles	Civil unrest in Baltimore
11	2015	3-May	Rays	L	Orioles	Civil unrest in Baltimore
12	2017	15-Sep	Brewers	W	Marlins	Hurricane in Miami
13	2017	16-Sep	Brewers	L	Marlins	Hurricane in Miami
14	2017	17-Sep	Brewers	W	Marlins	Hurricane in Miami
15	2020	29-Jul	Nationals	W	Blue Jays	Fill-in COVID-19 stadium not ready
16	2020	30-Jul	Nationals	W	Blue Jays	Fill-in COVID-19 stadium not ready
17	2020	5-Aug	Orioles	L	Marlins	COVID-19 concerns
18	2020	5-Aug	Phillies	L	Yankees	Tropical storm in New York
19	2020	6-Aug	Orioles	L	Marlins	COVID-19 concerns
20	2020	17-Aug	Cubs	L	Cardinals	COVID-19 concerns
21	2020	19-Aug	Cubs	L	Cardinals	COVID-19 concerns
22	2020	22-Aug	Nationals	W	Marlins	COVID-19 concerns
23	2020	25-Aug	Mets	L	Marlins	COVID-19 concerns
24	2020	28-Aug	Yankees	L	Mets	COVID-19 concerns
25	2020	30-Aug	Yankees	W	Mets	COVID-19 concerns
26	2020	4-Sep	Pirates	L	Reds	COVID-19 concerns
27	2020	4-Sep	Red Sox	L	Blue Jays	Civil unrest in Buffalo
28	2020	4-Sep	Twins	W	Tigers	Civil unrest in Detroit
29	2020	5-Sep	Angels	W	Astros	Hurricane in Houston
30	2020	5-Sep	Cubs	L	Cardinals	COVID-19 concerns
31	2020	8-Sep	Athletics	W	Astros	COVID-19 concerns
32	2020	16-Sep	Giants	W	Mariners	Wildfire smoke in Seattle
33	2020	17-Sep	Giants	W	Mariners	Wildfire smoke in Seattle
34	2020	17-Sep	Orioles	L	Rays	Civil unrest in Tampa Bay
35	2020	18-Sep	Padres	W	Mariners	Wildfire smoke in Seattle
36	2020	18-Sep	Phillies	W	Blue Jays	COVID-19 concerns
37	2020	18-Sep	Pirates	L	Cardinals	COVID-19 concerns
38	2020	19-Sep	Padres	L	Mariners	Wildfire smoke in Seattle
39	2020	20-Sep	Padres	W	Mariners	Wildfire smoke in Seattle
40	2020	25-Sep	Brewers	W	Cardinals	COVID-19 concerns
41	2020	25-Sep	Giants	W	Padres	COVID-19 concerns
42	2020	26-Sep	Athletics	L	Mariners	COVID-19 concerns
43	2021	10-Aug	Angels	W	Blue Jays	Blue Jay home park rainout
44	2022	10-May	Tigers	W	Athletics	Owners lockout

73

quality, some good and some bad, to get the expected number of wins we would add the appropriate win expectation for each of the 20 games. Algebraically:

$$(1)\ EXPW = SUM\ (EXPW_G),$$

where EXPW is the expected number of wins summed over G games with the appropriate win expectation $EXPW_G$ for each game. If visiting team quality varies, win expectations will also vary. In other words, they would depart from the full-season value that is an average against all visitors and would apply directly only to the typical or average home opponent.

We can estimate the host team win expectation for each game using a formula developed by Bill James.[14]

In particular:

$$(2)\ EXPW_G = (HA - HA*RA_G) / (HA + RA_G - 2*HA*RA_G),$$

where HA is the host team season winning average and RA_G is the relevant relocated home team season winning average. The expected number of host team wins can be calculated, per equation (1), by summing the win expectations for all games involving a relocated home team.

ESTIMATION

To get the expected total wins in our sample, we sum $EXPW_G$ (equation 2) over the 44 games. We are estimating the wins that would have occurred if, for our sample games, the host team had batted last rather than first. Therefore, HA is calculated by removing our sample games from the standard home-road splits because they include *all* home games, regardless of whether the home team batted first or last.[15] This adjustment can be non-trivial during 2020, when the pandemic limited the season to 60 total games and 30 home games for each team. Table 2 shows the calculation of the hypothetical expected total wins assuming that our 44 sample host teams batted last instead of first. The first four columns identify the games and are identical to the first four columns of table 1. Column five of table 2 shows the bats-last-only HA in each game for the appropriate host team and season. The sixth column shows the RA for each game's relocated home team, which equals that team's season winning average. The relocated home teams are shown in the last column. Column seven shows the expected win value $EXPW_G$ for each game, given opponent quality, per equation 2 above.

Summing EXPW over all 44 games gives the total expected wins for our hypothetical bats-last sample. This total is 23.9 wins. We want to compare this to the actual bats-first sample total of 23 wins. The difference of 0.9 is small. But how likely would it be to observe a total of 23 in a sample of 44 games drawn from the *bats-last* distribution? If it's not *un*likely, then our actual bats-first results could well be from the bats-last distribution, i.e., the two distributions are the same. This would support the hypothesis that outcomes are unaffected by batting order.

Recall that our 44 games are a random sample with respect to team winning averages. Of course, in any particular sample of actual games we cannot observe a fractional win total. Thus, all possible samples will yield an actual number of wins different than the expected value of 23.9. And, in general, given sample variability, individual sample means are unlikely to correspond *exactly* with the population mean. The question is how large the difference must be to cause us to reject that they come from the same distribution, i.e., that batting last has an impact.

Using the applicable binomial distribution, we can conduct a formal test of the hypothesis that the actual 44-game home-team-bats-first sample comes from the same win distribution as the counterfactual home-team-bats-last sample.[16] Using a standard 95 percent confidence level (and a two-tailed test), that hypothesis would be rejected if we observed a win total in our 44-game sample less than 18 or greater than 30.[17] Of course, our sample total of 23 is well within that range. In other words, we can be 95 percent confident that our actual sample of 44 home-team-bats-first games is drawn from the same population as the much more common home-team-bats-last games. At the same time, however, there is also a 5 percent probability that we have an unrepresentative sample, i.e., an "outlier" from an HTBF distribution with a significantly different expected number of wins.

SUMMARY AND CONCLUSION

It has long been presumed that, for major-league teams, batting last at home provides an advantage that leads to more victories. However, there has never been any direct evidence of a positive effect because of the almost complete absence of such games since the nineteenth century. However, a new rule in 2007 that requires relocated teams to bat last has changed this, creating 44 games since then in which the team playing in its home park, which we're calling the host team, batted first. These games were determined randomly with regard to the winning averages of the involved teams, and therefore constitute a natural experiment ideal for statistical analysis.

In these 44 games, the host team batting first won

23 and lost 21. We estimate that if the home team had instead batted last in these games the statistically expected number of wins would on average have been 23.9. The difference is small intuitively, and formal tests based on the binomial probability distribution clearly support the hypothesis that there is no difference in expected game outcomes based on team batting order. While 28 of these games occurred dur-

Table 2. Calculation of Hypothetical Expected Wins Assuming Sample Host Teams Batted Last Instead of First

Relocated Game	Year	Date	Host Team	HA	RA	EXPW	Home Team
1	2007	26-Sep	Mariners	0.605	0.593	0.513	Indians
2	2010	25-Jun	Phillies	0.642	0.525	0.619	Blue Jays
3	2010	26-Jun	Phillies	0.642	0.525	0.619	Blue Jays
4	2010	27-Jun	Phillies	0.642	0.525	0.619	Blue Jays
5	2011	24-Jun	Mariners	0.457	0.444	0.512	Marlins
6	2011	25-Jun	Mariners	0.457	0.444	0.512	Marlins
7	2011	26-Jun	Mariners	0.457	0.444	0.512	Marlins
8	2013	23-Jul	Giants	0.519	0.556	0.463	Reds
9	2015	1-May	Rays	0.506	0.500	0.506	Orioles
10	2015	2-May	Rays	0.506	0.500	0.506	Orioles
11	2015	3-May	Rays	0.506	0.500	0.506	Orioles
12	2017	15-Sep	Brewers	0.543	0.475	0.568	Marlins
13	2017	16-Sep	Brewers	0.543	0.475	0.568	Marlins
14	2017	17-Sep	Brewers	0.543	0.475	0.568	Marlins
15	2020	29-Jul	Nationals	0.400	0.533	0.368	Blue Jays
16	2020	30-Jul	Nationals	0.400	0.533	0.368	Blue Jays
17	2020	5-Aug	Orioles	0.433	0.517	0.417	Marlins
18	2020	5-Aug	Phillies	0.600	0.550	0.551	Yankees
19	2020	6-Aug	Orioles	0.433	0.517	0.417	Marlins
20	2020	17-Aug	Cubs	0.633	0.517	0.617	Cardinals
21	2020	19-Aug	Cubs	0.633	0.517	0.617	Cardinals
22	2020	22-Aug	Nationals	0.400	0.517	0.384	Marlins
23	2020	25-Aug	Mets	0.429	0.517	0.412	Marlins
24	2020	28-Aug	Yankees	0.724	0.433	0.774	Mets
25	2020	30-Aug	Yankees	0.724	0.433	0.774	Mets
26	2020	4-Sep	Pirates	0.433	0.517	0.417	Reds
27	2020	4-Sep	Red Sox	0.367	0.533	0.336	Blue Jays
28	2020	4-Sep	Twins	0.767	0.397	0.833	Tigers
29	2020	5-Sep	Angels	0.500	0.483	0.517	Astros
30	2020	5-Sep	Cubs	0.633	0.517	0.617	Cardinals
31	2020	8-Sep	Athletics	0.700	0.483	0.714	Astros
32	2020	16-Sep	Giants	0.533	0.450	0.583	Mariners
33	2020	17-Sep	Giants	0.533	0.450	0.583	Mariners
34	2020	17-Sep	Orioles	0.433	0.667	0.277	Rays
35	2020	18-Sep	Padres	0.655	0.450	0.699	Mariners
36	2020	18-Sep	Phillies	0.600	0.533	0.568	Blue Jays
37	2020	18-Sep	Pirates	0.433	0.517	0.416	Cardinals
38	2020	19-Sep	Padres	0.655	0.450	0.699	Mariners
39	2020	20-Sep	Padres	0.655	0.450	0.699	Mariners
40	2020	25-Sep	Brewers	0.500	0.517	0.483	Cardinals
41	2020	25-Sep	Giants	0.533	0.617	0.415	Padres
42	2020	26-Sep	Athletics	0.700	0.450	0.740	Mariners
43	2021	10-Aug	Angels	0.481	0.562	0.420	Blue Jays
44	2022	10-May	Tigers	0.432	0.370	0.564	Athletics

SUM = 23.87

ing the pandemic season of 2020, there is no evidence of a resulting statistical bias that might affect our findings. These results are consistent with prior studies of the home team batting first in college baseball.

As time passes, additional data no doubt will be added as more game relocations occur, expanding the sample. But that most likely will be a slow process. Our study period included 16 non-pandemic "normal" years, and only 16 of our random relocation events occurred in those years, exactly one per year on average. However, if MLB is interested in further addressing the issue, it could do so with controlled experiments, perhaps in the minor leagues. For example, team batting orders could be randomly switched during the regular season with a game selection process that minimized possible adverse effects on the competition for playoff spots. In the meantime, these 44 data are all we have, and they do not support a bats-last advantage. ■

Notes

1. Gary Belleville, "The Death and Rebirth of the Home Team Batting First," *Baseball Research Journal* 52, No. 1 (Spring 2023), 35.
2. Prior to that, first-last bats were determined by a coin flip, except for a single year, 1877, when the home team was required to bat first. David Nemec, *The Official Rules of Baseball: An Anecdotal Look at the Rules of Baseball and How They Came to Be* (New York: Barnes and Noble Books and Lyons Press, 1999), 62; and Woody Eckard, "The National League's 1877 'Experiment' with the Home Team Batting First," *Nineteenth Century Notes* (SABR), Bob Bailey, ed., (Summer 2024), 5–7. For a succinct history of the home team batting first, see Belleville, "The Death and Rebirth."
3. Belleville, "The Death and Rebirth," 31.
4. Nemec, *The Official Rules of Baseball*, 63.
5. Theodore L. Turocy, "In Search of the 'Last-Ups' Advantage in Baseball: A Game-Theoretic Approach," *Journal of Quantitative Analysis in Sports* (February 2008), 1. https://www.researchgate.net/publication/4985998_In_Search_of_the_Last-Ups_Advantage_in_Baseball_A_Game-Theoretic_Approach.
6. In fact, Belleville does not address the issue, stating that "whether or not there is a benefit in batting last is beyond the scope of this paper." Belleville, "The Death and Rebirth," 30.
7. Turocy, "In Search of the 'Last-Ups,'" 2.
8. Gary A. Simon and Jeffrey S. Simonoff, "'Last Licks': Do They Really Help?," *American Statistician* 60, No. 1 (February 2006), 16.
9. Steven R. Bray, Jeff Obara, and Matt Kwan, "Batting Last as a Home Advantage Factor in Men's NCAA Tournament Baseball," *Journal of Sports Sciences* 23, Issue 7 (February 2007), https://www.tandfonline.com/doi/full/10.1080/026404104000221136?, last accessed January 14, 2024.
10. For example, see Nemec, *The Official Rules of Baseball*, 62.
11. J. Furman Daniel III and Elliott Fullmer, "When the Fans Didn't Go Wild. The 2020 MLB Season as a Natural Experiment on Home Team Performance," *Baseball Research Journal* 50, No. 2 (Fall 2021), 65–73.
12. Yung-Chin Chiu and Chen-Kang Chang, "Major League Baseball During the COVID-19 Pandemic: Does a Lack of Spectators Affect Home Advantage?," *Humanities and Social Sciences Communications* 9, 178 (2022), https://doi.org/10.1057/s41599-022-01193-6, last accessed January 27, 2024.
13. Timothy E. Zimmer, Allison Snyder, and Lawrence Bukenya, "American Baseball Fans Do Not Influence Game Outcomes," *Economics Bulletin* 41, No. 2 (2021), 741–50.
14. See Bill James, "Pythagoras and the Logarithms," *Baseball Abstract*, 1981: 104-110; and Matt Haechrel, "Matchup Probabilities in Major League Baseball," *Baseball Research Journal* 43, No. 2 (2014), 118–23. This calculation is commonly referred to as the "log5 method."
15. The splits are available on Baseball Reference, https://www.baseball-reference.com.
16. The binomial is a discrete probability distribution that applies to a situation with n "trials" (games); two possible outcomes at each trial: "success" (win) or "failure" (loss); and a constant success probability p. In our case, n = 44 and p = .538. The latter is the average of the annual home winning averages based on home-road win splits over 2007–22 available from Baseball Reference. The probabilities for various wins were calculated using Excel's BINOM.DIST function.
17. Recall that sample means from zero to 44 are possible.

The Third Time Is the Charm

The 1939 Pensacola Fliers

Sam Zygner

The white sand beaches and warm waters of the Gulf of Mexico provide a pleasant distraction to the residents and tourists of Pensacola. A sense of optimism swept the Pensacola community in 1939 as the economy took a turn for the better with the ending of the Great Depression. During that summer, another form of amusement provided a diversion to local baseball fans: a case of baseball pennant fever. For the Fliers of the Class B Southeastern League (SEL), it proved to be their most memorable season.

The SEL included teams in Alabama, Mississippi, Florida, and Georgia. During Pensacola's initial years in the circuit, from 1927 to 1930, the club experienced mixed success. The debut season resulted in a respectable record and fourth-place finish in the eight-team league. In 1928, the Fliers (92–54) edged out the Montgomery Lions (91–57) for first place before falling to the Lions in the league championship series, four games to two. However, the Fliers' fortunes crashed in the next two years, landing them in the basement both times before the league folded because of financial reasons.[1]

Pensacola entered the fray again in 1937 in the newly established six-team SEL, led by manager Frank "Pop" Kitchens. The Fliers (83–52) quickly made their mark, finishing five games ahead of the Selma Cloverleafs (78–57), only to lose to the Mobile Shippers in the finals, four games to three.[2] In 1938, ownership of the team transferred to John "Wally" Dashiell, who named himself manager.[3] Dashiell was no stranger to the minor leagues, having toiled in the bush leagues for 15 seasons, including two in Pensacola in 1927 and 1928. In addition, his résumé included one year of piloting the Class C Jacksonville Jax (1934) and three with the Class C Tyler Trojans (1935–37). Dashiell, a sure-handed second baseman, also appeared in one game with the Chicago White Sox in 1924.[4]

Dashiell was a part owner of local radio station WCOA, which broadcast Fliers games, and he possessed a keen business sense.[5] Through clever marketing, the club drew just under 72,000 fans to the corner of G Street and Gregory Street in 1938.[6,7] Among the most popular promotions at Legion Field included Ladies Day (18 games for $3 total) and outlandish events like donkey baseball. Low-priced tickets were available at the famous Pilot Club or Red's News Stand for Tuesday and Friday home games.[8]

Dashiell's leadership experience and discerning eye for evaluating talent proved vital in ensuring a second consecutive first-place finish. The Fliers (95–53), now an affiliate of the Brooklyn Dodgers, easily outdistanced the second-place Selma Cloverleafs by 10½ games. Disappointingly, Pensacola fell to the Mobile Shippers, four games to two, in the first round of the playoffs.[9]

Prospects for 1939 seemed bright. Returning regulars from the 1938 team included first baseman Charley Baron (.280, 69 RBIs), shortstop Bobby Bragan (.298, 69 RBIs), utilityman Rudy Laskowski (.315, 7 HRs, 60 RBIs), second sacker Norris "Gabby" Simms (.322, 86 runs), and outfielder Neal Stepp (.330, 69 RBIs). Furthermore, Kinner Graf (16–13, 3.21 ERA) and Johnny "Big Train" Hutchings (18–6, 2.25) brought experience to the pitching staff.[10] Despite the change of major-league affiliation from the Dodgers to the Philadelphia Phillies, many of the core players remained.

The air was electric with anticipation on Opening Day. Known as "The City of Five Flags," Pensacola, with a population of approximately 37,000, still had a small-town feel.[11] Most people did not lock their doors at night and citizens cared for their neighbors during rough times. The local Jaycees of the Chamber of Commerce announced plans for Opening Day ceremonies. The festivities started with a parade through the streets of downtown to Legion Field. It was led by five local girls, who were followed by vehicles carrying players from the Fliers and their nemeses from the previous two years, the Mobile Shippers. Honors for throwing out the first pitches fell to Pensacola Mayor L.C. Hagler and Mobile Mayor Charles A. Baumhauer.[12]

An estimated crowd of over 6,000 crammed the stands. Southpaw Zack "Dutch" Schuessler, a veteran of four minor-league campaigns, toed the slab for the Fliers. He was coming off his best season, having won 20 games for the Class C Helena (Arkansas) Seaporters of the Cotton State League.[13] Tensions ran high between the teams, with several arguments breaking out during the contest. The Fliers built an early 4–1 lead, with the Shippers cutting the lead to 4–3 in the eighth inning. Schuessler worked out of several jams before the eventual deciding run came in the bottom of the eighth, when Laskowski grounded into an apparent double play, but a bad throw to second allowed Alex Pitko to score. Mobile scored in the ninth but fell short, 5–4.[14] The Shippers would not be a factor for the pennant in 1939. The Fliers and Jackson Senators established themselves as the class of the league, battling for the top spot in the first half of the season. The Sens featured six regulars with batting averages of .294 or better. They savaged SEL pitching, scoring 826 runs to lead the league. Their most proficient batter was minor-league legend Prince Oana, who finished the season slamming 39 home runs and driving in 127; both numbers led the SEL.[15]

On the other hand, Pensacola won with the best pitching in the league and solid fielding. The Fliers' roster was full of talented players. Four regulars—Bobby Bragan, Leslie "Bubber" Floyd, Alex Pitko, and Harry Walker—and pitchers Hutchings and Garth Mann went on to major-league careers.

Scouts considered right-hander Hutchings the most likely to make the majors. At 6-foot-2 and just over 250 pounds, the Big Train's most effective tool was his devastating fastball, which he combined with better-than-average control. As evidence, he finished the season averaging fewer than three walks per nine innings, and his 205 strikeouts led the league.[16] During July's SEL All-Star break, Hutchings represented minor-league stars from around the country and appeared in baseball's centennial game in Cooperstown, New York, pitting the Cartwrights against the Doubledays. Hutchings performed well for the Doubledays, working three scoreless innings while striking out six in a 9–6 victory.[17]

Pensacola and Jackson jockeyed for the top spot until the end of June. The Fliers separated themselves from June 21 through July 1, winning 11 of 12 games. They did not relinquish the league lead.

With two weeks left in the season, Dashiell sent Warren "Red" Bridgens to the mound against the fourth-place Cloverleafs on a typical humid evening in Selma, Alabama. A Jackson loss to Gadsden and a Fliers victory would clinch the pennant. Bridgens was not up to the task, giving up five runs in the third inning, and gave way to Hutchings to finish the game. Pensacola plated a couple of runs in the seventh inning to take a 7–6 lead. Pensacola secured the win in the ninth when Bragan hit a grand slam, ensuring the

11–6 victory. The news soon arrived that Gadsden had upended Jackson, 9–2, and the celebration was on. It was an incredibly satisfying night for the Big Train, who earned his 22nd win of the season.[18]

Table 1. 1939 Southeastern League Standings

Team	W	L	GB
Pensacola Fliers	87	48	–
Jackson Senators	78	60	10.5
Gadsden Pilots	77	66	14
Selma Cloverleafs	68	66	18.5
Anniston Rams	71	70	19
Montgomery Rebels	60	81	30
Mobile Shippers	56	78	30.5
Meridian Scrappers	55	83	33.5

The four-team playoffs used an arrangement called the Shaughnessy format, which pits the top seed against the fourth seed while the second and third seeds play each other, the higher seed getting the home-field advantage. It was devised for the International League in 1933 by Frank Shaughnessy, the general manager of the Montreal Royals. It was quickly adopted by other leagues and is commonly used in many sports today. The strategy was successful in boosting attendance and maintaining fan interest late in the season.[19]

The SEL postseason began with pennant-winning Pensacola facing fourth-place Selma and second-place Jackson opposing third-place Gadsden. The Fliers quickly dispatched the Cloverleafs, sweeping them in four games. Schuessler earned a pair of wins, and Hutchings and Graf hurled shutouts to collect the other victories. That set up the much-anticipated championship, with Jackson (who took their series, 4–1) hoping to play the spoiler.[20]

The Fliers received a scare in the opener at Legion Field, taking a beating by Jackson, 8–4. The visitors pounded out 14 hits against Graf and Hutchings.[21] The Fliers bounced back the next night, winning 7–2. Schuessler scattered eight Senators hits and Stepp accounted for three hits and four RBIs to lead Pensacola before the series switched to Jackson for three games.[22]

The Senators shut out the Fliers, 6–0, in the third game but dropped the next three contests, all in extra innings, by scores of 5–4, 8–7, and 3–2.[23] Schuessler brought the pennant home in style, earning the win in front of nearly 5,000 fans at Legion Field. "Dutch" held Jackson to six hits and struck out Prince Oana three times. A Simms bunt in the bottom of the ninth resulted in the winning run. After two years of frustration, the victory earned the Fliers their first

Southeastern League title.[24] Pandemonium was the day's word as locals partied the night away.

By winning the SEL championship, Pensacola earned the right to play the Augusta Tigers, the South Atlantic League champions (83–56), in the Little Dixie Series, for bragging rights as the top Class B team in the Southeast. The New York Yankees affiliate featured six players who would go on to major-league careers, most famously Billy Johnson, who played the hot corner for the Yankees in 1943 and the postwar years before finishing up with the St. Louis Cardinals.[25]

The best-of-seven series kicked off in Pensacola in front of 5,000 fans. Hutchings started Game One. The Fliers staked themselves to a five-run lead in the first inning. The Tigers offense responded and tied the game in the seventh, 5–5. Dashiell pulled his starter in the eighth inning, but Mann extinguished the fire. The Fliers stayed in the game thanks to some dazzling plays by shortstop Bubber Floyd. Charley Baron scored on a walk-off base on balls in the 10th frame, securing a 6–5 Fliers victory.[26] The Tigers took the next two games, 5–2 and 15–7. Hutchings turned the tide, winning Game Four, 4–2. Graf and Schuessler closed the books on Augusta by winning the final pair, 3–2 and 3–0. It was a perfect end to a magical season, proving the adage that the third time is the charm.

The Fliers had the best pitching staff in the league, led by Hutchings (22–10, 1.97 ERA that led the league), Graf (20–6, 2.65), and Schuessler (20–7, 2.29 ERA). They allowed only 3.35 runs per game.[27] The Gadsden Pilots, their closest competitor, allowed 4.61 runs per game. Although Pensacola ranked fifth in the league in runs scored (651 runs, 4.72 per game), several of their players had productive seasons. Harry Walker (.322) led the team in batting average, followed closely by outfielder Neal Stepp (.316), first baseman Charley Baron and catcher-infielder Rudy Laskowski (both .315), and second baseman Simms (.309), while shortstop-turned-third baseman Bobby Bragan batted .311 and led the team in homers with 12 and RBIs with 95.[28]

The Fliers' regular-season MVP was Hutchings, hands-down, but the postseason honors belonged to Schuessler. The crafty 27-year-old lefty from LaFayette, Alabama, dominated the competition, collecting five wins in the postseason, including a shutout in the finale against Augusta.[29] Dashiell returned for one more season in 1940 and nearly brought home a fourth straight flag. In a taut pennant race, Jackson (89–58) edged out Pensacola (89–60) by one game. The Fliers beat Mobile in the first round of the playoffs, four games to three, but Jackson won the championship series over Pensacola in five games.[30]

"Pop" Kitchens replaced Dashiell in 1941 and finished in fourth place with a 75–67 record. The Fliers were swept in the first round of the playoffs by Mobile. Buster Chatham took over the managerial reins in 1942 and the club finished out of contention before the Southeastern League suspended operations due to World War II.[31]

After the war, Pensacola returned to the reestablished SEL in 1946 and turned in five winning seasons, winning championships in 1949 and 1950, before the league folded. Today, the Pensacola Blue Wahoos are the Double A affiliate of the Miami Marlins in the Southern League. They play home games at Blue Wahoos Stadium at 351 West Cedar Street.[32] The British playwright and actress Shelagh Delaney said it best, and it applies to championships: "You can remember the second and the third and the fourth time, but there's no time like the first. It's always there."[33]

POSTSCRIPT

Charley Baron's real last name was Baronovic, which he changed when becoming a professional baseball player. Writer Phillip Tutor described Baron as playing the game with a brash determination bordering on intimidation. He enjoyed 20 seasons in the minors, from 1931–51, playing in 15 different cities. He served five of those years as a player-manager. The tempestuous batsman rose as high as Triple A in 1946 and 1947 with Rochester of the International League. He had several years in the minors batting over .300 but with little power.[34] After retiring, he worked in maintenance for the St. Louis Public School System. He died on May 1, 1997.[35]

Bobby Bragan was the epitome of a baseball lifer. He made it to the big leagues in 1940 and played three seasons with the Phillies and four with the Dodgers, batting .240 for his career. Bragan, an Alabaman, became infamous for being one of a group of Dodgers who opposed Jackie Robinson being on the team. His attitude later changed, and he developed a friendship with Robinson. After his playing career ended, Bobby had a great deal of success as a manager in the minor and major leagues, including seven years skippering the Pittsburgh Pirates (1956–57), Cleveland Indians (1958), and Milwaukee-Atlanta Braves (1963–66). He also served as the president of the Texas League for seven years, worked in public relations with the Texas Rangers, and served as an assistant to Commissioner Bowie Kuhn. He died on January 21, 2010, at the age of 92.[36]

Leslie "Bubber" Floyd, known later as "Bubba," reached the major leagues in 1944 with the Detroit

Tigers. He appeared in three games, slapping four hits in nine at-bats before his demotion to Buffalo of the International League. After hanging up his spikes, he worked in transportation sales for a car loading company. Floyd lived to be 83, passing away in Dallas on December 15, 2000.[37]

After two dominating seasons in Pensacola, Johnny "Big Train" Hutchings made it to the majors the next season with the Cincinnati Reds. The husky right-hander did well, appearing in 19 games, posting two wins and a 3.50 ERA. He also appeared in the 1940 World Series, giving up one run in one inning of work. His World Series share was a welcome gift, and he earned a championship ring when the Reds defeated the Tigers in seven games. In 1940, Hutchings appeared in 19 games with the Reds and eight more in 1941 before he was traded to the Boston Braves for Lloyd "Little Poison" Waner in June, where he spent four-plus seasons until 1946.[38] He received a modicum of fame when he gave up Mel Ott's 500th home run on August 1, 1945.[39] Hutchings ended his playing career in 1951 with the exception of two games for the Indianapolis Indians of the American Association in 1959. He later managed the Clinton Pirates of the Class D Midwest League (1959) and Indianapolis of the American Association (1960). The "Big Train" died on April 27, 1963, at the age of 47.[40]

Rudy Laskowski was a minor-league nomad. His career stretched from 1932 to 1966. He was first signed by the Class A Knoxville Smokies of the Southern Association. As a player, he clocked in for 17 seasons, reaching as high as Double A in 1934 with Milwaukee, 1935 with Toledo and Louisville, and 1946 with Little Rock of the American Association. He proved a valuable asset, playing at every position except outfielder.[41] In the middle of his career, he missed five seasons serving his country as a TEC 5 in the U.S. Army. He also managed for 11 seasons in eight different cities, including West Palm Beach for three years, Keokuk, Iowa, for two, and Oklahoma City for two. He was not one to rest: He also ran a successful bowling alley in Chicago in 1950.[42] Rudy passed away on June 9, 1993, and was laid to rest in the Florida National Cemetery, Bushnell, Florida.[43]

Garth "Red" Mann played a significant role in the success of the 1940 Pensacola Fliers, winning 20 games. The slender 6-foot Texan pitched professionally for 12 years, rising as high as the Pacific Coast League (1945–47). His best season came in 1942 with Montgomery of the Southeastern League, when he won 18 games and posted a 2.06 ERA.[44] The 1950 Census showed Red working as an assistant warehouseman for an oil company. He died on September 11, 1980, in Waxahachie, Texas.[45]

Zack "Dutch" Schuessler's career looked promising following the championship season. His promotion to Birmingham of the Southern Association brought him closer to his big-league dreams. However, he found facing a higher level of hitters more difficult and struggled to win nine and lose 14 games with a suspect 4.94 ERA. Dutch pitched 10 minor-league seasons, compiling a 93–89 record before hanging up his wool togs[46]. He later became a teacher in West Palm Beach, Florida. He passed away on August 2, 1959.[47]

Norris "Gabby" Simms derived his nickname from being precisely the opposite, a man of few words. The quiet Oklahoman began his baseball career as a batboy for the Oklahoma City Indians. He broke into organized ball with Opelousas of the Class D Evangeline League in 1936. After the 1939 season, Simms moved on to better opportunities financially, working for 65 years for the Oklahoma National Stockyards with the livestock commission. He passed away on May 9, 2007.[48]

Neal Stepp spent three seasons with the Fliers as the starting second baseman (1938–40). In 1941, he enlisted in the Army and served in the 77th Second Field Artillery Battery Battalion. He decided not to return to baseball and worked in a supervisory position with Hickory Industries. He died in Hickory, Georgia, the same town where he was born, on June 26, 2004.[49]

Harry "the Hat" Walker, like Bragan, became a baseball lifer. By 1941, he reached the major leagues with the Cardinals. Walker spent most of his career with the Redbirds and later the Phillies, Chicago Cubs, and Reds. In 1947, he won the National League batting title with a .363 average. In addition, he managed the Cardinals (1955), Pirates (1965–67), and Houston Astros (1968–72). Walker was notorious for bending anyone's ear who would listen about hitting. He died as the result of a stroke on August 8, 1999, in Birmingham, Alabama.[50]

When Wally Dashiell decided to retire from baseball, he put down family roots in Pensacola. He co-owned the Martin-Dashiell Insurance Agency, and his wife, Virginia, remained active in several community organizations. His home in the North Hill area of Pensacola is a registered historic site. Dashiell came up to the plate for the last time on May 20, 1972, leaving a legacy the city of Pensacola holds proud. Wally Dashiell, also known as "Mr. Baseball," continues to be a legendary figure in Pensacola.[51] ∎

Notes

1. "Southeastern League," Baseball Reference, https://www.baseball-reference.com/bullpen/Southeastern_League.
2. "Southeastern League."
3. Frank Pericola, "Sport Slants," *Pensacola News Journal*, January 1, 1938, 2.
4. "Wally Dashiell," Baseball Reference, https://www.baseball-reference.com/register/player.fcgi?id=dashie001joh.
5. Hana Frenette, "If Walls Could Talk—The Wally Dashiell House," *Pensacola Magazine*, March 2017, https://www.ballingerpublishing.com/if-walls-could-talk-the-wally-dashiell-house/, accessed August 14, 2024.
6. "1938 Pensacola Pilots," Baseball Reference, https://www.baseball-reference.com/register/team.cgi?id=05cc7cfa; Matt Colville, "Forgotten Stadiums: Pensacola's Legion Field," Stadium Journey, February 27, 2021, https://www.stadiumjourney.com/stadiums/forgotten-stadiums-pensacolas-legion-field, accessed August 14, 2024. Note: Baseball Reference incorrectly refers to the 1927 and the 1937–42 incarnations of the Pensacola team as the Pilots. It also incorrectly refers to the 1928–30 teams as the Flyers, with a y. From 1927 through 1950, every Pensacola team was known as the Fliers.
7. Colville, "Forgotten Stadiums," Stadium Journey, accessed August 14, 2024.
8. *Pensacola News Journal*, "Baseball Ladies' Night Tickets Now On Sale," April 5, 1939, 5; Pericola, "Local Waste 11 Hits Off Rebel Hurler," *Pensacola News Journal*, June 20, 1939, 2.
9. "1938 Southeastern League," Baseball Reference, https://www.baseball-reference.com/register/league.cgi?id=1104948f, accessed August 14, 2024.
10. "1938 Pensacola Pilots," Baseball Reference. "Gabby," *Shawnee* (Oklahoma) *News-Star*, July 2, 1937. "Big Train," *Pensacola News Journal*, September 5, 1939.
11. "Population of Pensacola, FL,"Population.us, https://population.us/fl/pensacola/, accessed August 14, 2024.
12. "Jaycees Finish Plans For First Baseball Game," *Pensacola News Journal*, April 18, 1939, 10.
13. "Zack Schuessler," Baseball Reference, https://www.baseball-reference.com/register/player.fcgi?id=schues001lew; Pericola, "6,000 Witness Opening Tilt in Local Park," *Pensacola Journal*, April 21, 1939, 10, https://www.newspapers.com/image/352800625/?terms=Pensacola%20Fliers&match=1.
14. Pericola, "6,000 Witness Opening Tilt."
15. "1939 Southeastern League Batting Leaders," Baseball Reference, https://www.baseball-reference.com/register/leader.cgi?type=bat&id=67f2108a.
16. "Johnny Hutchings," Baseball Reference, https://www.baseball-reference.com/register/player.fcgi?id=hutchi001joh.
17. *Pensacola News Journal*, "Big Train of Fliers Fans Six Batsmen," July 10, 1939, 2.
18. *Pensacola News Journal*, "Jackson's Loss to Gadsden Ends Chance for Rag," August 26, 1939, 2.
19. "Shaughnessy Playoffs," Baseball Reference, https://www.baseball-reference.com/bullpen/Shaughnessy_Playoffs.
20. "1939 Southeastern League Batting Leaders."
21. Pericola, "Easy Fly Ball Drops for a Hit to Change Tide," *Pensacola News Journal*, September 12, 1939, 7.
22. Pericola, "Aviators Get 12 Wallops off Four Pitchers," *Pensacola News Journal*, September 13, 1939, 7.
23. "Southeastern Playoff Even," *Huntsville Times*, September 15, 1939, 6; "Defeat Jackson in Fifth Game After 13 Frames," *Pensacola News Journal*, September 16, 1939, 2.
24. Pericola, "Takes 12 Frames to Subdue Wild Senators 3 to 2," *Pensacola News Journal*, September 17, 1939, Section 2, 16.
25. "1939 Augusta Tigers," Baseball Reference, https://www.baseball-reference.com/register/team.cgi?id=693e2f3b. Players who reached the major leagues are Charlie Biggs, Mike Garbark, Ford Garrison, Al Gettel, Billy Johnson, and Art Rebel.
26. Pericola, "Jeffcoat Hurls Great Ball as Relief Chunker," *Pensacola News Journal*, September 19, 1939, 2.
27. "1939 Southeastern League Batting Leaders;" Frenette, "If Walls Could Talk."
28. "1939 Southeastern League Batting Leaders."
29. "Zack Schuessler," Baseball Reference; Pericola, "6,000 Witness Opening Tilt."
30. "Southeastern League," Baseball Reference.
31. "Southeastern League."
32. "Blue Wahoos Stadium," MILB.com, https://www.milb.com/pensacola/team/about.
33. Baseball Reference, https://www.azquotes.com/quote/1344332. Retrieved July 4, 2024.
34. Phillip Tutor, "Baron was the Rams' hittin' manager," The Unforgettable & Irrelevant Anniston Rams, https://annistonrams.com/2022/08/09/combustible-baron-managed-and-hit-rams-to-1948-playoffs/, accessed August 14, 2024.
35. "Charley Baron," Baseball Reference, https://www.baseball-reference.com/register/player.fcgi?id=baron-001cha, accessed August 14, 2024.
36. Maurice Bouchard, David Fleitz, "Bobby Bragan," SABR, https://sabr.org/bioproj/person/bobby-bragan/, accessed August 14, 2024.
37. "Bubba Floyd," Baseball Reference, https://www.baseball-reference.com/register/player.fcgi?id=floyd-001les, accessed August 14, 2024.
38. "Johnny Hutchings," Baseball Reference, https://www.baseball-reference.com/register/player.fcgi?id=hutchi001joh. Retrieved on December 13, 2023; "Casey Plays Hunch And Nabs Hutchings," *The Sporting News*, June 19, 1941, 3.
39. Michael Wilson, "History of the Atlanta Braves," Braves History Blog, https://braveshistoryblog.wordpress.com/2017/08/22/johnny-hutchings-gives-up-500th-career-home-run-to-mel-ott-august-1-1945/. Retrieved on December 13, 2023.
40. "Johnny Hutchings," Baseball Reference.
41. "Rudy Laskowski," Baseball Reference, https://www.baseball-reference.com/register/player.fcgi?id=laskow001rud, accessed August 14, 2024.
42. "Rudolph J. Laskowski in the 1950 United States Federal Census," Ancestry, https://www.ancestry.com/discoveryui-content/view/219495357:62308?tid=&pid=&queryId=93a9460f-44c8-49ab-8749-44a58834b3d7&_phsrc=XPL1&_phstart=successSource, accessed August 14, 2024.
43. "Rudy Laskowski."
44. "Garth Mann," Baseball Reference, https://www.baseball-reference.com/register/player.fcgi?id=mann--001ben, accessed August 14, 2024.
45. "Garth Mann in the 1950 United States Federal Census," Ancestry, https://www.ancestry.com/discoveryui-content/view/187193176:62308, accessed August 14, 2024.
46. "Zack Schuessler," Baseball Reference.
47. "Zack Schuessler," *Roanoke Leader*, August 6, 1959, 6, https://www.newspapers.com/image/554099920/?article=d7436839-6e6a-47a0-aa6c-fcda1b82193d&focus.
48. "Norris Oscar Simms Sr.," Find a Grave, https://www.findagrave.com/memorial/93355198/norris-oscar-simms, accessed August 14, 2024.
49. "Neal Stepp," *Hickory Record*, June 29, 2004, 2. See also Ancestry.com.
50. Warren Corbett, "Harry Walker," SABR, https://sabr.org/bioproj/person/harry-walker/, accessed August 14, 2024.
51. Frenette, "If Walls Could Talk."

Do Baseball Batters Keep Their Eye on the Ball?

Mason Clutter, BS, and Nick Fogt, OD, PhD

One of the best-known pieces of advice in baseball is to keep your eye on the ball. In a recent survey, former college baseball players were asked whether they had been told to keep their eye on the ball when batting.[1] Ninety-eight percent of the players answered yes. Despite the widespread use of this phrase, until about 10 years ago there were only two published eye-tracking studies investigating whether batters can and do keep their eyes on the ball after it is released by the pitcher.[2] While both of these earlier studies continue to be highly influential, the question of whether batters point their eyes at a pitched ball throughout most of its flight remains unanswered.[3]

Recently, several groups have been examining eye- and head-tracking in baseball.[4] Some of these more recent studies made use of wearable video eye trackers that allow for significant freedom of movement. The increase in work in this area has mirrored the remarkable rise in published sports vision studies over the past 15 years.[5] In this paper, we explore aspects of batting, review the results of these papers, and look at future directions. This paper adds to and updates previous reviews on this topic.[6]

THE RELATIONSHIP BETWEEN TIME CONSTRAINTS IN BATTING AND EYE MOVEMENTS

To understand the challenges a batter faces in keeping his eyes on the ball, it is necessary to consider the time constraints involved in batting. A pitch that averages 90 miles per hour and that is released 55 feet from a batter will arrive at the plate in approximately 0.42 seconds, not much longer than a voluntary eye blink.[7] The constraints are even more daunting because the time required to move the bat downward through the hitting zone is about 0.15 to 0.20 seconds.[8]

So in about a quarter of a second, a batter has to decide on the likely trajectory of the ball, whether to swing the bat, and where to move the bat to hit the ball. Once the downward bat swing begins, the batter may be able to "check" the swing. However, if the batter intends to complete the swing it is a matter of

debate as to whether the originally planned swing is modifiable. We will return to this latter point momentarily. In that critical quarter of a second decision-making window after pitch release, the ball travels to within about 22 feet of the batter and the ball's angular velocity is under 30 degrees per second.

Some individuals can smoothly track an object traveling at velocities up to 100 degrees per second using eye movements called smooth pursuits, so maintaining the eyes on the ball during the first 0.25 seconds of the pitch should be relatively easy.[9] As a pitched ball approaches a batter, the ball is effectively accelerating because the angle between the ball and the batter is increasing. However, this acceleration is not particularly dramatic until the ball is within about 10 feet of the batter. In the last 10 feet of ball flight, the ball reaches velocities over 400 degrees per second, easily exceeding the capacity of the eyes to smoothly track the ball.

Eye movements called saccades can rotate the eyes at much greater velocities than smooth pursuit. A saccadic eye movement "jumps" the eyes to a new location, as when reading words on a page or scanning a room for a familiar face. So when the pitched ball's velocity surpasses the limits of smooth pursuit velocity, saccadic eye movements could be used to supplement smooth pursuit or to move the eyes at a similar or even higher velocity than that of the ball. However, vision is blurred during saccades (an effect termed saccadic suppression). This saccade-related blur could, for example, lead to a swinging strike if the batter incorrectly predicts the trajectory of the ball based on visual information prior to a saccade, and then the batter executes a saccade. Saccadic suppression during this saccade would limit the batter's ability to evaluate the actual trajectory of the ball and correct the original trajectory prediction.

Moving both the head and the eyes together can allow batters to track targets at higher velocities than the eyes alone, but head movement introduces additional complexity in that the eyes tend to reflexively move opposite to the head. This reflex, termed the rotational vestibulo-ocular reflex or RVOR, can be canceled or suppressed to varying degrees depending on the velocity of the head, but reducing or eliminating the RVOR requires additional neural computations and may be so imperfect that the reflex pulls the eyes off the ball.[10] The physiological limitations of the eye- and head-tracking systems suggest that a batter will likely struggle to keep his eyes continuously on the ball all the way from the pitcher's hand to the point of contact with the bat.

MODEL-BASED vs. ONLINE MOTOR CONTROL

Of course, if a batter must decide whether to swing the bat and where to swing the bat very early in the pitch when eye and head movements are likely to be small, a reasonable question might be whether there is a point in studying these movements. The answer to this question depends on whether the swing can be altered later in the pitch in response to unfolding visual pitch-trajectory information. In an influential study, Higuchi and colleagues looked at the accuracy and variability of bat-ball contact when college baseball players hit balls pitched from a pitching machine at about 72 or 91 miles per hour.[11] The location on the bat at which it made contact with the ball was assessed using high-speed video cameras. The batter was able to see the entire pitch in some cases, but in other cases the batter's vision was occluded either 0.15 seconds after the pitch was released or 0.15 seconds prior to the pitch arriving at home plate.

There were only nominal differences in the location of bat-ball contact between the various conditions, suggesting that batters only need to see the first 0.15 seconds of the pitch to successfully bat the ball. Higuchi's result seems to support the idea that batting is under model-based motor control, in which the trajectory of the pitch is mostly predicted by the batter very early in the pitch. This prediction is derived by combining information about the game situation (for example, the pitch count), information gained from the pitcher's motion prior to pitch release, and information associated with early ball flight cues, including the launch angle of the ball.

These information sources are used to modify a preexisting motor plan stored in the batter's brain. This motor plan is based on an "internal" model of object trajectory derived from experience with, for example, the motion of projectiles such as pitched baseballs. In a recent paper, Gray challenged the notion that batting is based entirely on model-based control.[12] Gray put forward a number of arguments suggesting that batting movements are altered throughout much of the pitch. In motor control theory, continuously adjusting an ongoing movement based on currently available visual information is termed online control. If baseball batters use online control rather than model-based control, then they may want to track the ball reasonably well for as long as possible.

One particularly compelling result that suggests that batting is under online control is that of Katsumata.[13] In Katsumata's study, college baseball batters hit pitches from a pitching machine. The timing of a number of components of the swing (defined as the entire sequence of batter motions), such as the step, foot landing after the step, and the bat swing, were assessed. Katsumata found that the variability of the earlier components of the swing was larger than that of the later components. This suggests that batters are using online control, in that they are continuously adjusting their swing based on unfolding visual information. Therefore, moving the eyes (and head) with the ball for as long as possible to process current pitch trajectory information may be an important aspect of batting.

EYE MOVEMENTS AND GAZE LOCATION PRIOR TO AND AT THE TIME OF BALL RELEASE

While the focus of this article is on eye and head movements after the pitcher releases the ball, there are interesting studies of batters' eye movements prior to pitch release. For example, one study found that when the pitcher releases the ball, college batters look at the pitcher's elbow while non-expert batters look at the "shoulder-trunk" region.[14] Another study concluded that college batters look at the pitcher's arm and the location of pitch release near the time the pitcher throws the ball, while non-expert batters look at the pitcher's head and face.[15] While these studies suggest that there are differences in where experienced and inexperienced batters look as the pitcher winds up and releases the ball, it is still an open question as to whether there is one fixation strategy that batters should use to maximize performance.[16]

Discussions of batter fixation strategies sometimes include the ideas of "soft focus" and "hard focus." Soft focus is a strategy in which the batter looks in the direction of the pitcher but fixates on nothing in particular. Then, around the time of ball release, the batter shifts attention, or "zooms in," on the ball. In contrast, hard focus is a strategy in which the batter attempts to fixate on something in the same direction as but behind the location where the ball is expected to be released.

Once again, whether either of these strategies is superior to the other is not clear. It could even be the case that a completely different strategy from these techniques, such as shifting gaze from the pitcher's body to the point of release or looking at a reliable visual reference close to but not exactly at the release point, such as the pitcher's elbow (termed the "pivot point strategy" by Gray), might lead to the best batting performance. It is even possible that the best fixation strategy for one batter may not be the same as that for another. A final study that looked at eye movements before the pitcher releases the ball was conducted during batting practice. The investigators reported that professional baseball batters look back and forth between the pitcher and the plate prior to the pitcher's windup and delivery.[17] The frequency of these eye movements was correlated with batting performance, suggesting that these movements may serve to warm up the eyes or the brain in preparation for the pitch. These eye movements may help to focus attention on the potential path of the pitched ball.

EYE AND HEAD MOVEMENTS AFTER BALL RELEASE

Research conducted on eye- and head-tracking after the pitch is released has had a resurgence over the past 10 years. All of the studies on the subject to date are summarized in Table 1.

Hubbard and Seng (1954)

In 1954, Hubbard and Seng published their classic paper on eye and head movements in baseball batting.[18] They observed head movements of college and major-league players in games, and made movies of major leaguers taking batting practice. Hubbard and Seng reported that head movements and eye movements in the direction of the ball were uncommon when batters swung at the ball, but eye movements were more common than head movements. The eye movements that did occur stopped about 8 to 15 feet in front of the plate. Hubbard and Seng suggested that eye movements were either too slow to follow the pitched ball at near distances, or alternatively that there was no reason to look at the ball at very close distances since at that point the swing could not be changed.

Bahill and LaRitz (1984)

In 1984, Bahill and LaRitz published the second classic paper on eye and head movements of baseball batters.[19] The batters included university graduate students who were presumably non-expert baseball batters, college baseball players, and one major-league player. The methods available to measure eye and head movements were much more quantitative than they had been in the 1950s. The batters viewed a ball that was pulled toward them using a pulley system at 60 to 100 mph. Vertical movement of the ball was minimized, so the motion of the ball was not the same as that of a pitched ball in a game. Very little data were gathered (for six pitches eye and head movement data were gathered over the entire pitch and for 15 pitches data were gathered only for a portion of the pitch), but many of the findings from this study are consistent with those from more recent studies.

Bahill and LaRitz found some differences between the major leaguer and the other batters, in that the major leaguer tracked the ball with both eye and head movements while some of the other batters tracked the ball using mostly head movements. Still others used mostly eye movements. The big-leaguer had very fast smooth pursuit eye movements, reaching velocities as high as 120 degrees per second. Combining these exceptionally high-velocity eye movements with head movements allowed him to track the ball until it was about 5.5 feet away. The other participants were only able to track the ball until it was about 9 feet away. One of the batters in the study showed a unique eye movement strategy. Instead of tracking the ball as long as possible, this batter took his eyes off the ball part way through the pitch and rapidly looked at a location ahead of the ball. The rapid eye movement is termed a predictive or anticipatory saccade, because the eyes are placed at or near a location that is expected to be occupied by the ball at some future instant.

As mentioned, saccades can reach velocities far greater than those of smooth pursuit eye movements, but the downside to saccades is that vision is blurred during the brief period of eye movement. Predictive saccades have been reported in many different sports, such as cricket, tennis, and table tennis. The purpose of predictive saccades is not entirely known, but Bahill and LaRitz suggested that predictive saccades could allow batters to see the ball hit the bat, and this would help them to predict the location of pitches in subsequent at-bats.

Fogt and Zimmerman (2014); Fogt and Persson (2017, 2020); Fogt, Kuntzsch, and Zimmerman (2019)

After Bahill and LaRitz published their study, 30 years elapsed before the issue of eye and head movements in baseball batting after pitch release was examined again. In 2014, Fogt and Zimmerman published a study in which 15 college batters tracked tennis balls projected at them by a pneumatic pitching machine.[20] This was the first of several studies from this group in which a wearable eye tracker mounted on a frame and synchronized with one or two head-tracking devices was used.

Table 1. Studies on Eye and Head Movements After Ball Release

Study	Method	Results
Hubbard and Seng (1954)	Head movements of college players and major-league players observed in real games, and major leaguers filmed in batting practice.	Batters' head movements were infrequent when swinging the bat. Eye pursuits stopped at 8–15 feet from the plate.
Bahill and LaRitz (1984)	Graduate students, college players, and one major-league player observing a ball approaching on a fishing line at 60–100 mph. Vertical movement of the ball was minimized. Bat swing was not permitted.	The major leaguer tracked the ball with a combination of eye and head movements while other batters tracked with eye movements only, or mostly head movements. A single predictive saccade was detected for one batter. The major leaguer tracked the ball accurately until about 5.5 feet from the batter.
Fogt and Zimmerman (2014)	15 college players calling out the number and color of the number written on tennis balls. Balls were thrown by a pneumatic pitching machine at 76 mph. Only horizontal eye and head movements were measured. Bat swing was not permitted.	On average, the ball was accurately tracked primarily with batters' head movements, and eye movements were small until late in the pitch. No predictive saccades were found.
Fogt and Persson (2017, 2020)	Two former college players either purposely taking pitches or swinging at pitches thrown by a pneumatic pitching machine at about 75 mph. Both horizontal and vertical eye and head movements were measured.	Batters tracked the ball primarily with head movements, and eye movements were small. The ball was tracked accurately with no predictive saccades until about 5 feet from the batter when swinging, and the head and eyes were moved to the plate ahead of the ball when taking pitches. Batting efficiency was very good for both batters.
Higuchi and colleagues (2018)	Six college players swinging at balls thrown by a pitching machine at about 72 and 91 mph. Horizontal eye and head movements were measured. Movements of the bat were recorded with high-speed video cameras.	Batters tracked the ball with head and eye movements. Head movements were larger than eye movements. Head movements continued for longer periods for some batters than for other batters, but batting efficiency was similar across batters. Predictive saccades were not found.
Nakamoto and Mann (2018)	Two professional players swinging at balls thrown at 75 and 87 mph in virtual reality.	The difference in the ball location and batter's head location at bat-ball contact was the most important determinant of hitting efficiency. Predictive saccades were not mentioned.
Fogt, Kuntzsch, Zimmerman (2019)	Fourteen non-expert batters calling out the number and color of the number written on tennis balls. Balls were thrown by a pneumatic pitching machine at 77 mph. Bat swing was not permitted.	The batters' eyes were kept close to the ball primarily with head movements. Predictive saccades were not reported.
Kishita and colleagues (2020a)	Six professional players (three from top teams, three from farm teams) swinging at pitches thrown by former professional players at speeds between 59 and 80 mph.	Batters kept their eyes close to the ball primarily with head movements combined with eye movements opposite to the head. Predictive saccades occurred on every pitch. The location of the bat at bat-ball contact was correlated with head location for all of the batters, and with head and eye location for two of the farm batters. Batting efficiency was not related to eye and head movements.
Kishita and colleagues (2020b)	Nine college batters swinging at pitches thrown by a pitching machine at speeds from 50 to 87 mph	Batters kept their eyes on the ball early in the pitch primarily with head movements in the direction of the ball. Eye movements early in the flight of the pitch were either very small (faster pitches) or directed opposite to the head (slower pitches). Predictive saccades along with quick head rotations in the direction of the ball occurred on every pitch. The timing of predictive saccades was not based on the pitch speed or the distance of the ball from the batter. Batting efficiency was not related to eye and head movements.

These head-tracking devices included an inertial sensor and magnetic tracking technology. The velocity of the balls was about 76 mph. Batters were not permitted to swing the bat. The tennis balls had either black or red numbers written on them in several locations. The batters' task was to call out the number and the color of the number on each pitched ball. While there was some variability between the batters, they generally followed the ball with their head and moved their eyes relatively little until the ball was very close. Batters tended to keep their eyes on the ball using these head movements, and predictive saccades did not occur. In follow-up studies from the same laboratory, two former college players swung at pitches and deliberately "took" pitches from the same pitching machine used in the original study.[21]

The investigators assessed horizontal eye movements for both the "swing" and "take" conditions in one paper and they looked at vertical eye movements only in the "swing" condition in the other paper.[22] In the "swing" condition, for both the horizontal and vertical directions, the eyes were relatively close to the ball until the ball was about 5 feet from the batters. Once again, head movements were primarily responsible for keeping the eyes near the ball and eye movements were relatively small. There was no clear evidence for predictive saccades. Although there were minor differences between the eye and head movements of the two batters, both batters were very successful in hitting the ball. In the "take" condition, large horizontal head and eye movements occurred that allowed the eyes to be pointed at a location near the ball when the ball arrived at the plate. The behavior in taking a pitch may indicate that looking at the location where the ball is expected to cross the plate can help in predicting the location of future pitches, just as Bahill and LaRitz previously suggested. Finally, in 2019, these same investigators published a paper in which 14 non-expert baseball batters were required to call out numbers and the color of these numbers on tennis balls thrown at 77 mph from the same pitching machine used in previous studies from this group.[23] The batters did not swing at the pitches. Head and eye movements of the non-expert batters were similar to those of college players: Head movements were larger than eye movements. Head movements kept the eyes close to the ball throughout much of the pitch.

Higuchi, Nagami, Nakata, and Kanosue (2018)

In 2018, Higuchi and colleagues published another study on eye and head movements.[24] Six college players hit baseballs thrown from a pitching machine equipped with a mechanical arm at speeds of about 72 and 91 mph. In agreement with the results of several of the studies described above, Higuchi concluded that batters moved the head more than the eyes in tracking the pitch. Some of the batters stopped moving the head when the bat swing began, while others continued to track the ball. One batter tracked the ball all the way to bat-ball contact. Although there were differences in the head-tracking strategies between batters, batting efficiency was similar.

Nakamoto and Mann (2018)

Nakamoto and Mann also published the results of a study in 2018.[25] The study was published as an abstract in the book of abstracts from the 2018 meeting of the North American Society for the Psychology of Sport and Physical Activity. These investigators studied two professional baseball players as they batted balls in a virtual reality setting. The ball speed was either 87 mph (fastballs) or 75 mph (changeups and curveballs). Batting accuracy was correlated with both the difference in locations between the ball and gaze (the location of the eye as determined by both the eye and head) and the difference in location between the ball and the head. The difference in the ball and head location at bat-ball contact was the most important determinant of hitting efficiency.

Kishita, Ueda and Kashino (2020a and 2020b)

Finally, Kishita and colleagues published two studies in 2020. In one, six batters from the Nippon Professional Baseball league in Japan batted baseballs thrown by former professional pitchers at speeds ranging from 59 mph (curveball) to 80 mph (fastball).[26] Three of the batters played for top teams and three played on farm teams.

Overall, batters moved their heads in the direction of the ball throughout much of the pitch, while the eyes at first moved opposite to the head, perhaps because of the rotational vestibulo-ocular reflex. During the early part of the pitch, the head and eye rotations combined to keep the eyes close to the ball. At some point (80–220 milliseconds prior to bat-ball contact), a predictive saccade occurred, directing the eyes near the location of bat-ball contact. Predictive saccades occurred later in the pitch for batters in the top league. Predictive saccades also occurred later for fastballs when the batter knew that the pitch was going to be a fastball, compared to the situation where the batter was not informed whether the pitch was going to be a fastball or curveball. The location of the bat at bat-ball contact was correlated with head location for all of the batters and was correlated with head and eye location for two of the farm batters, but the influence of these correlations on batting efficiency is unclear.

In a second study, Kishita and colleagues studied nine college baseball batters.[27] The players hit baseballs thrown from a pitching machine at speeds from about 50 to 87 mph. The results were similar to the first study, in that head movements in the direction of the ball were common, eye movements early on in the pitch were either very small (faster pitches) or directed opposite to the head and the ball (slower pitches), and predictive saccades along with "quick head rotations" in the direction of the ball occurred at a time after the ball was released. In tracking a moving object with the eyes, saccades can be triggered to get the eyes back on the object when the velocity of the object exceeds the capabilities of the ocular pursuits. However, the batters in the Kishita and colleagues study made predictive saccades before the ball reached velocities exceeding that of the pursuit system, suggesting that these saccades were associated with prediction rather than the speed of the pitched ball. These predictive saccades also occurred before the ball arrived at a distance from the plate at which the batter would be forced to make a saccade in order for the eyes to arrive ahead of the ball's future location.

The idea that the timing of predictive saccades is based on something other than when the ball's speed exceeds some value or when the ball arrives within some distance of the batter is further supported by the fact that the time at which the predictive saccades began was correlated with the time of bat-ball contact and the batter's hip rotation, rather than the speed or distance of the ball from the batter. Finally, batting efficiency was not directly evaluated or related to eye and head movement patterns in this study.

SUMMARY OF EYE AND HEAD MOVEMENT STUDIES

In summary, with the exception of Hubbard and Seng's study, these studies consistently show that head movements in the direction of the ball are common. These head movements, in combination with minimal eye movements, or eye movements opposite to the head, allow batters to keep their eyes on or near the ball at least until a predictive saccade is made. On the other hand, the occurrence of predictive saccades has not been consistent across these studies.

WHY MOVE THE HEAD IN THE DIRECTION OF THE BALL?

There have been attempts to address why batters move the head and eyes as observed in these studies. Moving the head in the direction of an approaching ball is seen

not only in baseball batting but in other sports. For example, Mann and colleagues found that cricket batters make head movements in the direction of the ball.[28] Shinkai and colleagues showed that table tennis players also make such head movements.[29] The fact that these head movements have been found in multiple sports suggests that there is some advantage to this behavior. One potential explanation for this pattern of head movement was proposed by Mann and colleagues.[30]

These investigators suggested that head movement when striking approaching objects allows the ball to be maintained in the same direction relative to the head. Since batting a ball is based on computing the ball's direction relative to the head and body (called the "egocentric" direction), turning the head with the ball and keeping the egocentric direction constant could save valuable time for the batter in determining where the ball will arrive at the plate.

ADVANTAGES OF THE CONTINUOUS TRACKING STRATEGY vs. THE PREDICTIVE SACCADE STRATEGY

Batters keep their eyes on the ball at least through the early portions of ball flight. The advantage of this strategy is that maintaining one's eyes near the ball presumably helps in assessing early ball-flight information. This information includes the pitch's launch angle, the rate of angular expansion of the approaching ball, and the ball's vertical angular velocity, all of which are thought to help the batter to determine when and where the ball will arrive near the plate.[31] After the early portion of the pitch, some studies found predictive saccades while others did not. The following section discusses the potential benefits of differing eye movement strategies.

PREDICTIVE SACCADES vs. CONTINUOUS TRACKING

As mentioned before, predictive saccades may be useful for predicting the trajectory of subsequent pitches.[32] In addition, predictive saccades may shorten the time required by batters to program the bat swing.[33] That is, since eye position can inform the brain about where the bat needs to go in order to hit the ball, placing the eyes at the predicted location of bat-ball contact may facilitate more rapid swing planning. Still another potential benefit of predictive saccades is derived from the finding that the onset of predictive saccades is correlated with the time of bat-ball contact and the batter's hip rotation.[34]

This latter finding suggests that there may be an overall timing sequence involving eye movements, head movements, and body movements. It is possible that disruption of the timing of any of these movements could reduce batting efficiency. While predictive saccades may provide all of these benefits, published results suggest that predictive saccades are often made quite late in the pitch.[35] In those cases, there is likely not enough time to change the bat swing based on eye position information after the saccade. In cases where predictive saccades occur relatively early in the pitch, pitch trajectories tend to be less predictable. This suggests (although it doesn't prove) that predictive saccades are intended primarily to help batters predict pitch trajectories in future at-bats.

It should also be pointed out that predictive saccades may have additional or different benefits (compared to baseball) in sports such as cricket and tennis, where the ball bounces prior to being struck. In those sports, predictive saccades to the predicted location of ball bounce may allow the eyes to track the ball after the bounce even when the ball bounces in an unexpected direction.[36] On the other hand, since batting is likely under online control, if batters want to swing at the ball, then they would want to continuously track the approaching ball in order to adjust the swing as the pitched ball approaches. Support for the continuous tracking strategy when hitting (compared to the predictive saccade strategy) comes from the results of studies demonstrating that estimates of when an approaching object will arrive are better when gaze is maintained on the approaching object compared to when gaze is maintained at the location where the object is expected to arrive.[37] Similarly, estimates of where an approaching object will arrive are also better when the observers follow the object with the eyes.[38]

At this point, in agreement with Bahill and LaRitz, it appears that in baseball, the primary function of predictive saccades is to inform batters about future pitch trajectories. At least from a theoretical point of view, maintaining gaze on the ball is the best strategy when batting the ball, and predictive saccades are perhaps best used in learning new pitch trajectories.

EYE AND HEAD MOVEMENTS AND BATTING PERFORMANCE

While there are proposed advantages of particular eye-tracking and head-tracking strategies in baseball batting, there is only modest evidence thus far to suggest that any particular pattern of eye and head movements leads to better hitting. For example, by showing that eye- and head-tracking patterns were different between a major-league batter and lower-level batters, Bahill and LaRitz provided some indirect evidence that batting could be influenced by these patterns.[39] Similarly, Kishita and colleagues showed that batters at higher levels make later predictive saccades than batters at lower levels, and that head location correlates with bat location for players at higher levels but head and eye location correlate with bat location for some players at lower levels.[40] To date, Nakamoto and Mann have provided the most direct evidence of a relationship between head- and eye-tracking and batting.[41] In their small study, these investigators demonstrated that batting efficiency correlates with alignment of the head and the ball at bat-ball contact. This latter result suggests that moving the head with the ball can directly impact hitting performance, at least in virtual reality.

CORRELATIONS BETWEEN BATTING METRICS AND EYE MOVEMENTS OUTSIDE THE BATTING CONTEXT

There is another aspect of this story that must be mentioned. There are studies that show that saccadic eye movements (measured outside of batting) are faster and more efficient in high-level baseball players.[42] Pursuit eye movements (also measured outside of batting) have also been found to be better in these players.[43] Better eye movements have also been correlated with better batting metrics.[44] How can these studies be reconciled with studies in which batters' pursuit or tracking eye movements are relatively small when hitting? There are several possibilities. It may be that while better eye movements and better batting metrics occur together, faster or more efficient eye movements may not be directly responsible for improved batting. Another possibility is that control of predictive saccadic eye movements may be associated with better batting, and this could partially explain some of the correlations between eye movements and batting.[45] Finally, the neural circuitry in the brain that controls tracking eye movements overlaps substantially with the circuitry that is responsible for combined eye- and head-tracking movements.[46] This may explain why eye movements correlate with batting success even though batters' head movements are usually larger than their eye movements, at least prior to a predictive saccade.

SUMMARY AND FUTURE DIRECTIONS

After the flurry of research activity in this area over the last 10 years, are we any closer to answering the question of whether and how baseball batters keep their eyes on a pitched ball? We believe that we are. In all but one of these studies, the eyes are aimed at the ball at least until a predictive saccade occurs. What is surprising is that when the eyes follow the ball, tracking is primarily accomplished by head movements rather than eye movements.

On the other hand, there are unanswered questions that will need to be addressed in future studies. For example, there are potential sources of variability that have not been fully considered, but that could affect the eye- and head-tracking results. Most of the tracking studies have included relatively few batters, and more studies are needed to determine whether individuals differ in their use of eye and head movements. In addition, for an individual batter, eye and head movements could vary depending on the distance of the ball in front of the plate when bat-ball contact is made, and depending on where the pitch arrives (for example, inside or outside).

Probably the most significant question that has not yet been answered in the area of eye- and head-tracking of pitched balls is whether a particular pattern of eye and head movements directly impacts batting. All of these aforementioned questions will best be answered by testing under game or game-like conditions where the predictability of the pitch is varied.

If it is found that particular patterns of eye and head movements directly impact batting, then it may be possible to train batters to emulate those behaviors that lead to batting success. Clinical trials assessing the efficacy of various forms of vision training for baseball batting have shown some positive effects on batting performance. In a 2021 review paper, Laby and Appelbaum listed seven such clinical trials, two of which included some form of eye movement training (termed oculomotor training).[47] One of these latter trials included one Division I college baseball team.[48] The other included 24 players from two Division I college teams.[49] There is clearly a need for more clinical trials with larger numbers of participants to establish whether and which vision training methods lead to better in-game performance. Further, if it can be established that batting performance is better with a particular pattern of eye and head movements, these clinical trials could incorporate new training methods to teach batters to make use of these patterns.

While more clinical trials are needed to understand whether vision training methods lead to better baseball batting performance, it should be pointed out that these trials are difficult for many reasons. Accessing baseball players to participate in clinical trials, particularly players at the college and professional levels, is difficult.[50] Players often have very limited time, and researchers may be in geographic locations that are not conducive to working with these players. Collaboration between everyone interested in improving baseball batting performance, including but not limited to researchers, sports vision practitioners, coaches, athletic trainers, and baseball teams, can help in facilitating the successful completion of future clinical trials, which may in turn lead to better batting performance in games. ■

Notes

1. Nick Fogt and Jacob Terry, "Survey of visual and predictive aspects of batting and eye care utilization in baseball players," *Journal of Sports and Performance Vision* 5, Issue 1 (2023), e1–e15.
2. Alfred W. Hubbard and Charles N. Seng, "Visual movements of batters," *Research Quarterly. American Association for Health, Physical Education and Recreation* 25, Issue 1 (1954): 42–57.
3. A. Terry Bahill and Tom LaRitz, "Why can't batters keep their eyes on the ball?," *American Scientist* Vol. 72, Issue 3 (1984): 249–53.
4. Andrew J. Toole and Nick Fogt, "Review: Head and eye movements and gaze tracking in baseball batting," *Optometry and Vision Science* 98, Issue 7 (2021): 750–58.
5. Nick Fogt, Lawrence Gregory Appelbaum, Kristine Dalton, Graham Erickson, Rob Gray, "Guest editorial: Visual function and sports performance," *Optometry and Vision Science* 98, Issue 7 (2021), 669–71.
6. Dan Aucoin, "How do batters see the ball? A review of gaze research in batting," *Driveline Baseball*. February 25, 2019. Accessed February 8, 2024: https://www.drivelinebaseball.com/2019/02/batters-see-ball-review-gaze-research-batting/.
7. Kyung-Ah Kwon, Rebecca J. Shipley, Mohan Edirisinghe, Daniel G. Ezra, Geoff Rose, Serena M. Best, and Ruth E. Cameron, "High-speed camera characterization of voluntary eye blinking kinematics," *Journal of the Royal Society Interface* 10, Issue 85 (2013), 20130227.
8. Rob Gray, "A model of motor inhibition for a complex skill: Baseball batting," *Journal of Experimental Psychology: Applied* 15, Issue 2 (2009): 91–105.
9. Craig H. Meyer, Adrian G. Lasker, and David A. Robinson, "The upper limit of human smooth pursuit velocity," *Vision Research* 25, Issue 4 (1985): 561–63.
10. Adam C. Pallus and Edward G. Freedman, "Target position relative to the head is essential for predicting head movement during head-free gaze pursuit," *Experimental Brain Research* 234, Issue 8 (2016), 2107–21.
11. Takatoshi Higuchi, Tomoyuki Nagami, Hiroki Nakata, Masakazu Watanabe, Tadao Isaka, and Kazuyuki Kanosue. "Contribution of visual information about ball trajectory to baseball hitting accuracy," *PLoS One* 11, Issue 2 (2016), e0148498.
12. Rob Gray, "Review: Approaches to visual-motor control in baseball batting," *Optometry and Vision Science* 98, Issue 7 (2021): 738–49.
13. Hiromu Katsumata, "A functional modulation for timing a movement: A coordinative structure in baseball hitting," *Human Movement Science* 26, Issue 1 (2007), 27–47.
14. Takaaki Kato and Tadahiko Fukuda, "Visual search strategies of baseball batters: Eye movements during the preparatory phase of batting," *Perceptual and Motor Skills* 94, Issue 2 (2002): 380–86.
15. Takayuki Takeuchi and Kimihiro Inomata, "Visual search strategies and decision making in baseball batting," *Perceptual and Motor Skills* 108, Issue 3 (2009): 971–80.
16. Rob Gray, "'Soft focus' or visual pivot point: Which should baseball batters use?" *Perception & Action Podcast*, August 9, 2017, https://perceptionaction.com/softfocus/, last accessed July 20, 2024.
17. Melissa Hunfalvay, Claire-Marie Roberts, William Ryan, Nicholas Murray, James Tabano, and Cameron Martin, "An exploration of shifts in visual fixation prior to the execution of baseball batting: Evidence for oculomotor warm up, attentional processes or pre-performance routines?" *International Journal of Sports Science* 7, Issue 6 (2017), 215–22.
18. Hubbard and Seng, "Visual movements of batters."
19. Bahill and LaRitz, "Why can't batters keep their eyes on the ball?"
20. Nicklaus F. Fogt and Aaron B. Zimmerman, "A method to monitor eye and head tracking movements in college baseball players," *Optometry and Vision Science* 91, Issue 2 (2014): 200–11.

21. Nick Fogt and Tyler W. Persson, "A pilot study of horizontal head and eye rotations in baseball batting," *Optometry and Vision* Science 94, Issue 8 (2017): 789–96.

22. Nick Fogt and Tyler W. Persson, "Vertical head and eye movements during baseball batting," *Optometry & Visual Performance* 8, Issue 3 (2020): 129–34.

23. Nick Fogt, Erik Kuntzsch, and Aaron Zimmerman, "Horizontal head and eye rotations of non-expert baseball batters," *Optometry & Visual Performance* 7, Issue 1 (2019): 29–46.

24. Takatoshi Higuchi, Tomoyuki Nagami, Hiroki Nakata, and Kazuyuki Kanosue, "Head-eye movement of collegiate baseball batters during fastball hitting," *PLoS ONE* 13, Issue 7 (2018): e0200443.

25. Hiroki Nakamoto and David Mann, "Keep your "head" on the ball: The relationship between gaze behavior and temporal error in baseball batting in a virtual environment," *Journal of Sport and Exercise Psychology* 40, Supplement (2018): S59-S60

26. Yuki Kishita, Hiroshi Ueda and Makio Kashino, "Eye and head movements of elite baseball players in real batting," *Frontiers in Sports and Active Living* 2, Article 3 (2020).

27. Yuki Kishita, Hiroshi Ueda and Makio Kashino, "Temporally coupled coordination of eye and body movements in baseball batting for a wide range of ball speeds," *Frontiers in Sports and Active* Living 2, Article 64 (2020).

28. David L. Mann, Wayne Spratford, and Bruce Abernethy, "The head tracks and gaze predicts: How the world's best batters hit a ball," *PLoS ONE* 8, Issue 3 (2013): e58289.

29. Ryosuke Shinkai, Shintaro Ando, Yuki Nonaka, Yusei Yoshimura, Tomohiro Kizuka, and Seiji Ono, "Importance of head movements in gaze tracking during table tennis forehand stroke," *Human Movement Science* 90 (2023): 103124.

30. Mann, Spratford, and Abernethy, "The head tracks and gaze predicts."

31. A. Terry Bahill and William J. Karnavas, "The perceptual illusion of baseball's rising fastball and breaking curveball," *Journal of Experimental Psychology: Human Perception and Performance* 19, Issue 1 (1993): 3–14.

32. Bahill and LaRitz, "Why can't batters keep their eyes on the ball?"

33. Kishita, Ueda, and Kashino, "Eye and head movements of elite baseball players in real batting."

34. Kishita, Ueda, and Kashino, "Temporally coupled coordination of eye and body movements in baseball batting for a wide range of ball speeds."

35. Kishita, Ueda, and Kashino, "Eye and head movements of elite baseball players in real batting."

36. Mann, Spratford, and Abernethy, "The head tracks and gaze predicts."

37. Simon J Bennett, Robin Baures, Heiko Hecht, Nicolas Benguigui, "Eye movements influence estimation of time-to-contact in prediction motion," *Experimental Brain Research* 206, Issue 4 (2010): 399–407.

38. Miriam Spering, Alexander C Schütz, Doris I Braun, Karl R Gegenfurtner, "Keep your eyes on the ball: Smooth pursuit eye movements enhance prediction of visual motion," *Journal of Neurophysiology* 105, Issue 4 (2011): 1756–67.

39. Bahill and LaRitz. "Why can't batters keep their eyes on the ball?"

40. Kishita, Ueda, and Kashino, "Eye and head movements of elite baseball players in real batting."

41. Nakamoto and Mann, "Keep your 'head' on the ball."

42. Karla Kubitz, Claire-Marie Roberts, Melissa Hunfalvay, and Nick Murray, "A comparison of cardinal gaze speed between Major League Baseball players, amateur prospects, and non-athletes," *Journal of Sports and Performance Vision* 2, Issue 1 (2020): e17–e28.

43. Yusuke Uchida, Daisuke Kudoh, Takatoshi Higuchi, Masaaki Honda, and Kazuyuki Kanosue, "Dynamic visual acuity in baseball players is due to superior tracking abilities," *Medicine & Science in Sports & Exercise* 45, Issue 2 (2013): 319–25.

44. Sicong Liu, Frederick R. Edmunds, Kyle Burris, and Lawrence Gregory Appelbaum, "Visual and oculomotor abilities predict professional baseball batting performance," *International Journal of Performance Analysis in Sport* 20, Issue 4 (2020), 683–700.

45. Kishita, Ueda, and Kashino, "Eye and head movements of elite baseball players in real batting."

46. R. John Leigh and David S. Zee, *The Neurology of Eye Movements, Fifth Edition* (New York: Oxford University Press, 2015), 289–359.

47. Daniel M Laby, Lawrence Gregory Appelbaum, "Review: Vision and on-field performance: A critical review of visual assessment and training studies with athletes," *Optometry and Vision Science* 98, Issue 7 (2021), 723–31.

48. Joseph F Clark, James K Ellis, Johnny Bench, Jane Khoury, Pat Graman, "High-performance vision training improves batting statistics for University of Cincinnati baseball players," *PLoS One* 7, Issue 1 (2012): e29109.

49. Sicong Liu, Lyndsey M. Ferris, Susan Hilbig, Edem Asamoa, John L. LaRue, Don Lyon, Katie Connolly, Nicholas Port, L. Gregory Appelbaum, "Dynamic vision training transfers positively to batting practice performance among collegiate baseball batters," *Psychology of Sport & Exercise* 51, Issue 3 (2020): 101759.

50. Laby and Appelbaum, "Review: Vision and on-field performance: A critical review of visual assessment and training studies with athletes."

Plummeting Batting Averages Are Due to Far More than Infield Shifting: Part Two

Strikeouts

Charlie Pavitt

In the opener of this two-part series, published in *Baseball Research Journal* 53, Number 1, I described how fielding (infield and outfield shifting) and batting (emphasis on pulling and fly-ball hitting) contributed to the 25-point decrease in batting averages between 2007 and 2022, from .268 to .243. As batting average on balls in play dropped 13 points during that period, it appears that these factors were responsible for about half of the BA slide. It is likely that most of the other half can be attributed to increased strikeout rates. It is helpful to view this issue in long-range historical terms. The following figure, based on data posted at FanGraphs, shows the K trend going back to 1920, when the strategy of swinging hard, exemplified by Babe Ruth, began to take hold (Figure 1).[1]

Strikeout rate has generally been going up since the late 1920s. An exception was a drop during the 1970s, such that K rate did not top those for the 1960s until the 1990s. At least part of the reason for that decrease is instructive as we consider strategies to decrease K rate. In 1950, the size of the "rule book strike zone" (hereafter RBSZ) had been set as between the armpits and the top of the knees.[2] In 1963, probably due to the

perception that offense had become too dominant and therefore that games were too long, the Lords of Baseball increased its size, moving its upper boundary to the top of the shoulders and its lower boundary to the bottom of the knees.[2] Strikeout rates immediately went up, while batting averages and walk and homer rates went down. After remaining about the same for a while, these indices dropped again in 1967 and reached their nadir in 1968, which has come to be known as "the Year of the Pitcher." Run scoring was the lowest since 1908 at 3.42 per team per game, and batting averages were the lowest of the twentieth century at .237. Homers (0.61 per team per game) and walk rate (7.6%) were the lowest in decades. Of 76 pitchers qualifying for the ERA crown (162 or more IP), seven had an ERA below 2.00, led by Bob Gibson at 1.12. Forty-two pitchers had an ERA in the twos, 25 in the threes, and only two were above 4.00.

The Lords of Baseball, seemingly realizing that most fans like offense and that pitcher dominance would decrease their interest, returned the RBSZ to its earlier size for 1969. In addition, the height of the pitching mound was lowered from 15 inches to 10.[3] Run

Figure 1. Strikeouts per 9 Innings, 1920–2023

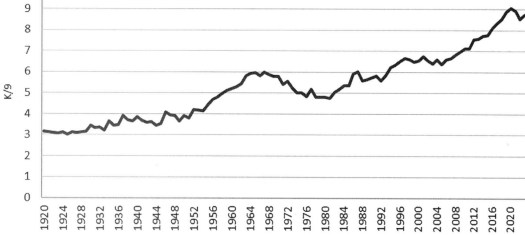

scoring (4.07), batting average (.248), walk (9.1%), and homer (0.8) rates all climbed. With some year-to-year fluctuation, offense drifted upward for the next decade.

Relevant to our interests, the impact on strikeouts took a while to plateau. Strikeout rates per 9 innings, which per Fangraphs were over 5.8 from 1963 to 1969, bottomed out at around 4.8 between 1978 and 1981 before beginning to rise again. Note that after leveling out between 1996 and 2006 at around 6.5 per 9 innings, K rate increased sharply, staying at 8.5 or more in 2018–23 and as high as 8.9 in 2021, the last season with no designated hitter in the National League. In the NL, some of the noticeable drops may have been due to the adoption of the DH, but the AL has seen decreases as well.

The next four sections delve into reasons behind this increase, concentrating on 2007 through 2023 due to the drastic drop in batting average over those years. In short, these include changes in batter behavior, pitch type proportions, pitch velocity and movement, the size and location of the called strike zone, with its implications for pitch location and catcher framing, and foul-ball hitting. Along with summarizing past research, I will be presenting analysis based on Fan-Graphs seasonal data for pitchers accumulating a minimum of 162 innings between 2018 and 2023, excepting the 2020 COVID-19 season, in which no pitchers reached that level of activity. These data include individual pitcher-level information gathered by Statcast across 247 pitcher-seasons for the six most prevalent pitch types compiled by Statcast and listed by FanGraphs, each with annual usage rates of at least 5 percent and as a group comprising more than 95 percent of the total: fastballs (either generic or four-seamed), cutters, sinkers (including those classified separately as two-seamed fastballs in 2018 and 2019), sliders, curves, and changeups. As not all pitchers used each, sample sizes for each pitch type were generally lower that 247, particularly for cutters.[4] Additional pitch location and swinging strike rate data come directly from Statcast via Baseball Savant.[5]

BATTER BEHAVIOR

Changes in batter behavior parallel to those described in part 1 of this series have been contributing to the rise in strikeouts. Using the accepted abbreviations for the included metrics, the following two figures displaying batter plate discipline measures begin our examination (data from Fangraphs; see Slowinski for a description of the metrics).[6] In this and some of the subsequent diagrams, I use ratios as compared with 2007, because, given the large variation in actual percentages among the included indices, changes over time would otherwise become masked (Figures 2 and 3).

O-Swing% and O-Contact% are, respectively, the percentage of pitches outside of the RBSZ that are swung at and the percentage of swings on which contact occurred. By multiplying the first of these (swing per pitch) by the second (contact per swing), I was able to add a line showing contact rate per pitch for non-strike pitches. Z-Swing%, Z-Contact%, and Z-Contact per Pitch% are the counterparts for pitches within the RBSZ. SwStr% and CStr% are the percentage of swinging and called strikes per pitch. Finally, Zone% is the percentage of pitches within the RBSZ.

The picture these data draw is clear. Over the relevant seasons, batters swung more often at pitches both inside (66% in 2007 to 68.8% in 2023) and outside (23.7% in 2007 to 31.9% in 2023) of the RBSZ, and

Figure 2. Swing and Contact Rates Compared to 2007

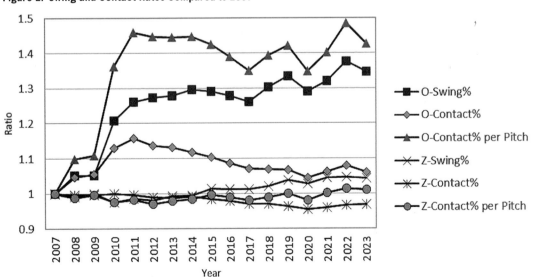

contact rate drifted downward starting in 2011 for those outside (68% down to 62.3% in 2023) and, beginning in 2007, those inside (88.2% down to 85.4% in 2023) the RBSZ. Overall, as making less contact has canceled out the impact of swinging more often, contact rates per pitch stayed within a couple of percentage points from 20 since 2010 for pitches outside and in the mid- and upper-50s during the entire era for pitches inside of the RBSZ (let's call them "real balls" and "real strikes"). As Figure 3 shows, pitches in the strike zone are being called strikes more often.

But pitching strategy changed, as pitchers have been placing more and more pitches outside of the RBSZ (real strikes 51.5% in 2007, 41.9% in 2023). Edwards, using figures for 2002 through 2018, found the percentage of pitches in the RBSZ to correlate very strongly negatively (–0.90) with K rate using the 17 relevant seasons as the data.[7] This method ignores variation in both metrics within seasons, in so doing artificially inflating the correlation, but the implication that more real balls increased strikeouts is certainly valid.

Turning to the 2018–23 pitcher-level data, as contact rate per pitch and per swing were much higher for real

strikes than for real balls, the overall swinging strike rate went up markedly (8.7% in 2007 to 11.2% in 2023). Perhaps due to more real balls, the called strike rate went down, but at a far slower pace than the swing strike rate went up (17.% in 2007 down to 16.4% in 2023). As pitches in the RBSZ have made up a decreasing percentage of total pitches, the outcome has been a lot more swinging strikes, and so a lot more strikeouts. The swinging strike/strikeout relationship, according to Carleton, correlated at 0.71 for 2002 through 2016.[8] Similarly, in the 2018–23 pitcher-level dataset, strikeout rate correlated with O-Contact% at –0.74 and with Z-Contact% at –0.78, and with O-Contact per Pitch% at –0.42 and Z-Contact per Pitch at –0.62.

PITCH TYPE

Batters are, of course, reacting to the pitches they face; let us look next at the progression of average pitch type proportions between 2008 (the first year for which relevant Statcast data are available) and 2023 (Figure 4).[9]

Fastball percentages remain the highest throughout, staying steady until a recent drop. Sinker use has plummeted, with sliders and in particular cutters taking up

Figure 3. Strike Rates Compared to 2007

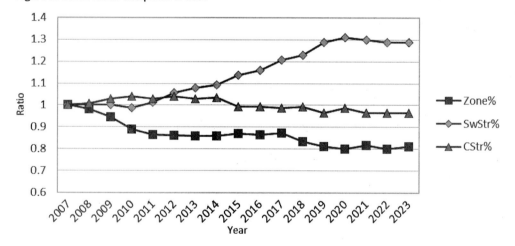

Figure 4. Pitch Type Velocities, 2007–23

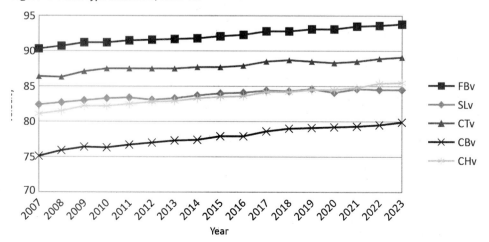

much of the slack. Curves fluctuated a bit over the years before a recent downturn, whereas changeups have gone up a fraction of a percent over the interim.

What is critical here are swinging strike rates for each pitch type. Figure 5 data are directly from Statcast. Swinging strike rate has increased for every pitch type. Comparing across them, the slider, one of the two pitches with increased usage, had the highest SwStr%. With decreased usage, sinkers had the lowest. This is consistent with the just-shown increase in slider use and decrease in sinker use across those years. The other pitch type with markedly increased usage, cutters, also had SwStr% rates well above those for sinkers. Apparently, pitch type repertoire has shifted in favor of pitches more conducive to whiffs.

PITCH VELOCITY AND MOVEMENT

The impact of pitch velocity on strikeout rate appears to be straightforward: faster pitches, more strikeouts.

Figure 6 displays average velocities for five pitch types from 2007 through 2023 (Statcast data posted on FanGraphs). Although the rate of increase might be slowing, every pitch type went up between 2.1 and 4.8 miles per hour over the 17 years included here.

In my analysis of 2018–23 pitcher-level data, higher average pitch velocities were correlated with higher strikeout rates in the following order of relationship strength: fastballs at $+0.59$, sinkers at $+0.54$, cutters at $+0.43$, sliders at $+0.32$, changeups at $+0.28$, and curveballs at $+0.22$. Each pitch type velocity was analogously if negatively correlated with O-Contact%, and all but curves and changeups with Z-Contact%. The impact of pitch velocity is not news; as earlier work uncovered almost perfect relationships between it and SwStr% (Silver at 0.89 for every fastball in 2008) and K rate (Edwards, using the same method as described above, at 0.933).[10] Piling on the evidence: Seidman saw strike percentages rise steadily from 44.6

Figure 5. Pitch Type Swinging Strike Rates, 2008–23

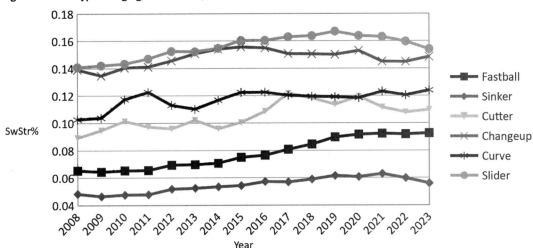

Figure 6. Pitch Type Velocities, 2007–23

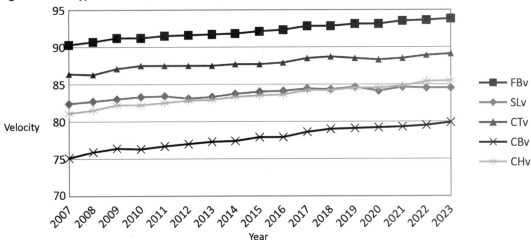

percent to 49.3 percent as fastball velocity rose from 92 to at least 98 mph during 2007; Clemens (2015–19 data) uncovered a median percentage increase of 3.1 in K rate for 23 pitchers who gained at least 1 mph between seasons in four-seamer velocity; and Trueblood observed an average of 0.7 mph difference between pitches resulting in swinging strikes versus batted balls in 2023.[11]

In contrast, the impact of pitch movement on strikeout rate is weak and tied up with pitch velocity. In the 2018–23 pitcher-level dataset, after reversing the sign for the 64 pitcher-seasons thrown by left-handers, the highest correlations with K rate are +0.18 for fastball horizontal movement and +0.25 for fastball vertical movement. Moreover, horizontal and vertical movement were negatively correlated for cutters (–0.50), sliders (–0.40), sinkers (–0.34), and fastballs (–0.13). This tradeoff was observed as far back as 2007, with Seidman noting vertical movement increasing and horizontal movement decreasing as fastball velocity and strikeout rate went up.[12] The quest for higher pitch spin rates may be involved, as Pemstein, with data covering at least 2009 through 2014, discovered that more spin resulted in increased movement but greater decreases in velocity between release point and the plate.[13] Hale, based on 2009 to 2013 data, displayed a diagram showing a three-way association among fastball movement (four- and two-seamers combined), fastball velocity, and swinging strike rate.[14] For fastballs with high velocity (96–100 mph), SwStr% were generally over 50 percent with one to three inches of movement and decreased to about 20 percent with 10 inches of movement. In contrast, swing-and-miss rates increased with higher movement for lower velocity pitches, up to a point where fastballs in the mid-80s

moving 8 to 10 inches had SwStr% close to 40 percent. If Hale's findings are valid, the fastest pitchers want little movement while the slowest pitchers want a lot. Unfortunately, as Hale did not distinguish between vertical and horizontal movement, it is not clear which was more responsible for these data.

Changeups have been a glaring exception. In the Statcast/FanGraphs 2007–23 data, along with increasing in velocity at a greater rate than fastballs (4.4 vs. 3.5 mph), horizontal and vertical movement in changeups both increased; the former from 0.9 inches to 2.8 inches of movement toward left-handed batters and the latter from 3.8 inches above to 2.2 inches above what a pitch with no spin (gyroballs) would move; in other words, more downward motion. Analogously, and unlike most other pitch types, the two directions were positively correlated with one another (+0.30) in the 2018–23 pitcher-level dataset. Pemstein again provided a relevant reason for the difference; SwStr% at intermediate spin rates was highest for changeups but lowest for other pitch types.[15] In addition, Pavlidis, with 2011–12 data, uncovered other clues when examining the relationship between changeups and fastballs.[16] To begin, he calculated a positive (0.28) pitcher-level correlation between fastball velocity and swinging strike rate on changeups. The fastball velocity increase over time implies higher changeup SwSt%. Pavlidis also noted a negative correlation (–0.45) between the usage ratio of fastballs to changeups. As fastball usage decreased and changeup usage remained the same over time, the fastball/changeup ratio became smaller; and as SwStr% is higher in changeups than fastballs, more swinging strikes are again implied. Finally, the difference in vertical movement between changeups and fastballs

Figure 7. Pitch Location Percentages, 2008–23

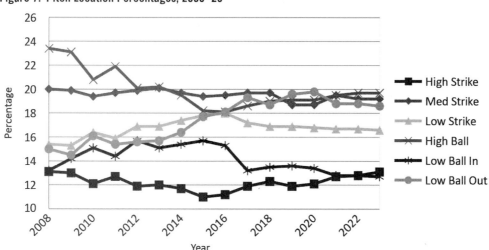

correlated with swinging strike rates at 0.41. As vertical movement for fastballs stayed close to constant, between 8 and 8½ inches, while that for changeups increased, the difference would have gotten larger, once again meaning higher swinging strike rates.

CALLED STRIKE ZONE LOCATIONS AND ITS IMPLICATIONS

We turn next to pitch location. The reason that I have used the specific term "rule book strike zone" (RBSZ) is to distinguish it from the "called strike zone" (CSZ), which is a product of umpire judgment (the terminology comes from Zimmerman, Tang, and Huang).[17] The two are not synonymous. This is speculation, but I wonder if one of the reasons for the delay in RBSZ changes in 1963 and 1969 having their full impact on offense for a few years was that it took some time for umpires to change their CSZ in response to the RBSZ revisions. Pitch location data were not available then, but once they were, researchers began examining the RBSZ/CSZ relationship. Walsh made the first serious measurement of the CSZ using a dataset that was tiny (80,000 pitches) compared to what was available a few years later.[18] Horizontally, the CSZ was on average centered on the RBSZ but two inches wider on both sides for right-handed hitters; for lefties, it was accurate on the inside but 4½ inches too large on the outside. Vertically, the bottom of the CSZ was almost four inches higher and the top more than an inch lower for righty batters and almost 3½ inches lower for lefty batters. As a consequence, the CSZ on average was fatter horizontally, shorter on both vertical ends, and, with those taken together, smaller (475 square inches for right-handed batters, 492 square inches for left-handed batters) than the RBSZ (527 square inches). By 2011, with more than a million pitches at researchers' disposal, it was clear that the CSZ was not only inconsistent with the RBSZ but shaped differently. In two dimensions, the RBSZ is a rectangle whereas Zimmerman et al. (2008–16 data) described the CSZ as a "superellipse," a shape with both elliptical and rectangular features (see https://en.wikipedia.org/wiki/Superellipse for a description).[19] This shape was still present in Porat's examination in 2019.[20]

Over the years, due to the availability of pitch-location data and pressure on umpires from the commissioner's office to call pitches more accurately, the CSZ has steadily become more in line with the RBSZ. Research on pitch-call accuracy has produced ever-increasing figures: 85.6 percent in 2007, 88.14 percent between 2008 and 2016, reaching 90 percent in 2017, and still increasing as I write this—it was 92.8 percent in 2023.[21] A CSZ better reflecting the RBSZ would be larger than earlier, which alone probably increased strikeout rates. Over these years, the CSZ shrunk horizontally, but I want to direct our attention specifically to the vertical dimension. Table 1, below, is a relevant table from Roegele's article, measured in square inches, with the low part of the CSZ defined as less than 21 inches from the ground.[22]

Table 1. Area in Square Inches of Called Strike Zone, 2009–17

Year	Total Area of CSZ	Low Part of CSZ
2009	435	0
2010	436	6
2011	448	11
2012	456	19
2013	460	30
2014	475	47
2015	478	50
2016	474	45
2017	468	42

The low part of the CSZ increased markedly between 2009 and 2014. Strike calls on pitches between 1½ and 2 feet off the ground increased from 29.6 to 43.8 percent from 2009 through 2013.[23] Brian Mills concluded that the bottom part of the strike zone had increased by three inches between 2008 and 2014.[24] As umpires called more low strikes, pitchers responded by throwing more pitches in that location. Between 2007 and 2013, average pitch heights went down steadily from 28.92 inches in 2007 to 27.61 inches in 2013, with the proportion of pitches in that additional three-inch zone increasing from about 22 percent to about 27.5 percent. Batters reacted in turn by raising swing rates on pitches in that zone from about 31 percent to about 34.5 percent, but with the odds of making contact 73.3 percent lower than for pitches above it. Compared to 2008, in 2013 there were 974 more called strikeouts and 685 fewer walks on the final pitch of plate appearances when that pitch was located in the parts of the CSZ that changed during that time period.[25] Mills estimated that the overall improvement in umpire accuracy accounted for between 3.3 and 8.9 percent of the total strikeout rise between 2007 and 2013, with more strike calls on lower pitches responsible for most of this jump.[26]

Returning to Table 1, the increase in the low part of the CSZ slowed down in 2015 and reversed a bit the next two years. At the same time, pitch locations began a partial rebound toward the top. Further, pitchers began responding to where swinging-strike rates were the highest. Figure 6 displays vertical pitch locations for the entire 2008 through 2023 era. Figure 8

Figure 8. SwStr% by Pitch Location, 2008–23

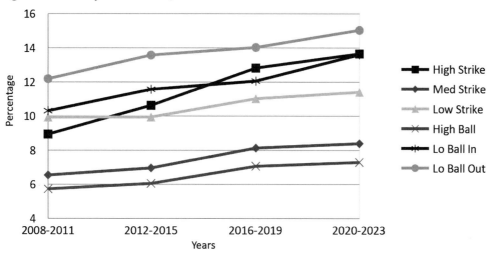

shows swinging strike rates at four-year increments for the same period.

By the end of that time frame, the proportion of high strikes (Zones 1, 2, and 3 in the standard location charts) had rebounded back to its beginning level, but that for high balls (Zones 11 and 12) was still about 3.5 percent lower, low strikes (Zones 7, 8, and 9) about 1.5 percent higher, and low balls outside (Zone 14) about 3.5 percent higher than at the beginning. Now, juxtapose the locations across the two tables. Through 2014, low balls both inside (Zone 13) and outside increased; consistently, these had the highest swinging-strike percentages. Afterward, SwStr% for high strikes rose at a faster pace than the others. In response, its usage proportion went up. In 2017, teams apparently noticed that low balls outside had consistently higher SwStr% than low balls inside; the latter's proportion collapsed by 2.1 percent in one year whereas that of the former went up by 1.9 percent between 2015 and 2019.

Finally, looking back at the metrics displayed in Figure 3, between 2007 and 2023, the percentage of pitches in the RBSZ decreased by a good 10 percent while the drop in called-strike rate went down by only about half of a percentage point. The juxtaposition between the two implies that called strikes outside of the RBSZ probably went up. It is likely that the increased attention to pitch framing by catchers and the teams they played for was involved in this rise. Certainly, at the beginning of this era, the variation in framing skills across catchers was substantial. Kim and King, looking back to 2008 and 2009, calculated that catchers with framing rates one standard deviation better than average received an overall 7 percent increase in the number of called strikes on pitches outside of the RBSZ and a 10 percent decrease in the number of called balls in-side the zone.[27] Not surprisingly, as Carleton pointed out, the better the framing, the more strikeouts.[28]

Again, batters responded. Arthur compared two models predicting swing probability given called strike probabilities for 2014, one including the count and pitch location, and the other adding to those two the identity of the catcher.[29] The second was a better fit for the data, which implies that batters' decisions concerning whether to swing on borderline pitches were influenced by the framing reputation of the catcher. Batters were less willing to swing at borderline pitches if they believed that the catchers were less likely to get a strike call. As the importance of framing skills has become entrenched in our consciousness, front offices are becoming less and less willing to accept a poor framing catcher. Sullivan noted that the standard deviation across teams in pitch framing as estimated by Baseball Prospectus dropped from about 21 in 2011 to about 12 in 2016.[30] This decrease was almost certainly due to the disappearance of poor framers, which means that the tendencies for more called strikes and strikeouts with good framing catchers was becoming more widespread across the major leagues.

FOUL BALLS

Changes over time in foul ball occurrence have had at least some impact on strikeout rates. The foul ball/strikeout relationship is complicated by the fact that fouls hit on zero- and one-strike counts appear to serve a different function than those during two-strike counts, with the former more prevalent for strikeout-prone sluggers and the latter more abundant for strikeout-averse contact hitters. Thus, the foul/strikeout association has been positive for the former and negative for the latter.[31] Most research has suggested that, overall, the prolific foul ball hitter has resembled the slugger more than the contact hitter; for example, Fink, for batters with at least 200 swings in 2021, determined that fouls per swing correlated positively with K rate at 0.17.[32] Although not a large association, a regression equation including both fouls per swing and swinging strike rate increased variance accounted for in strikeout rate to 79 percent from the 69 percent accounted for by SwStr% alone. Chamberlain discovered that, between 2017 and mid-June 2019, K rate was 12 percent for plate appearances with no fouls, 31.3 percent for one foul, and 39.9 and 38.5 percent for two and three fouls; it did dip to 35 percent for 4 or more fouls, perhaps due to greater prevalence of contact hitters achieving this many.[33]

The proportion of contacted balls that went foul has been increasing since at least 1993, from under 47 percent in 2010 up to 51 percent in 2023.[34] As shown in Figure 2 above, contact rate per pitch remained fairly steady over that period while swing rates went up. At the same time, fouls per swing were also stable at close to 40 percent.[35] All of this implies that the foul ball rise was associated with the increased swing rate. In addition, Carleton demonstrated that between 1993 and 2023, foul ball rates increased approximately linearly with higher pitch velocities, from about 47 percent of batted balls in the 88–88.99 mph bin to about 65 percent at 100 mph and faster.[36] Carleton believed that the rise in pitch velocity during those years pictured in Figure 6 was part of the reason for the foul ball increase. In addition, between 2015 and 2021, swing rates increased at about a linear rate with faster pitches, from 41 percent at the 88–88.99 range to 56 percent at 100 + .[37] Putting this all together, as pitch velocity increased and batters swung more, the increase in pitch velocity probably increased the likelihood of batted balls becoming foul, and the additional strikes resulted in a few more strikeouts. As Andrews recently noted, "A foul ball has never been closer to a whiff than it is today."[38]

CONCLUSION

To summarize both parts of this study: The 25-point decrease in mean batting average between 2007 and 2022 was a result of several factors; changes in strategies for fielding (infield and outfield shifting), batting (increased swinging, more fly balls, more pulling, with the byproduct of more popups, and more foul balls), and pitching (higher pitch velocities, more pitches to locations with higher swinging-strike rates, particularly outside of the RBSZ, with fewer sinkers, more sliders and cutters, and more effective changeups). More accurate umpiring and better catcher framing conspired to increase swing rate on pitches outside of the RBSZ and harder-to-hit pitches within it.[39]

The banning of the full infield shift had some impact on batting averages in 2023, but if the Lords of Baseball want to get BAs back to their pre-2007 levels, it will not be sufficient. They might consider other options. Most of the other relevant factors are not subject to legislation, with restrictions on outfield shifting the only possibility. As described earlier, when faced with less offense than desired in 1969, the Lords of Baseball lowered the mound and shrunk the strike zone. These moves certainly had a positive impact on offense, but part of that effect was an increase in home-run rate, and I would venture to guess that this would not be desirable at present. One proposal that was tried was moving the pitching mound back one foot partway through the 2021 Atlantic League season. Before the experiment, and based on Alan Nathan's Trajectory Calculator, Arthur made the following predictions for a two-foot shift, as shown in Table 2.[40]

Given the loss of velocity and the greater distance to cover, meaning the calculated increase in pitch flight time to home, Schoenfield and Passan estimated the visual equivalent of a loss of three mph, with the predicted resulting increase of 26 BA, 31 OBA, and 68 SLG points, which would change the face of the game.[41] However, the Atlantic League experiment backfired, with the strikeout, fly ball, and popup rates increasing and line-drive rate decreasing, resulting in an eight-point BA drop after the move.[42] Speculation was that added pitch movement canceled out any lower pitch velocity. The experiment was not repeated in 2022. ∎

Table 2. Predicted Impact on Pitches if Pitching Mound Moved Two Feet Back

Pitch Type	Velocity at Home Plate	Time to Home	Horizontal Break	Vertical Drop
95 mph fastball	-0.3 mph	~.015 seconds more	~1 inch more	~1 inch more
78 mph curveball	-0.2 mph	~.02 seconds more	~1 inch more	~4 inches more
85 mph slider	-0.3 mph	~0.18 seconds more	~1.5 inches more	~3 inches more

Acknowledgments

Thanks to Dick Cramer for writing suggestions, Pete Palmer for always reading what I write, the two anonymous reviewers for their work, and most of all Cliff Blau, fact checker.

Notes

1. "Major League Leaders, Pitching, League Stats, 2007–23," FanGraphs, https://www.fangraphs.com/leaders/major-league?pos=all&stats= pit&lg=all&qual=0&type=1&month=0&ind=0&rost=0&age=0&fil- ter=&players=0&startdate=&enddate=&team=0%2Css&season1= 2007&season=2023&sortcol=0&sortdir=default&pagenum=1.

2. Steve Treder, "Re-Imagining the Big Zone 1960s, Part 1: 1963-1965," FanGraphs, November 30, 2004, https://tht.fangraphs.com/ re-imagining-the-big-zone-sixties-part-1-1963-1965/.

3. Baseball Almanac, "Baseball Rule Changes," https://www.baseball- almanac.com/rulechng.shtml, accessed August 16, 2024.

4. These were 240 for fastball, 228 for changeup, 204 for sinker, 200 for slider, 180 for curve, and 110 for cutter.

5. https://baseballsavant.mlb.com/statcast_search.

6. Piper Slowinski, "Plate Discipline (O-Swing%, Z-Swing%, etc.)," FanGraphs, February 18, 2010, https://library.fangraphs.com/offense/ plate-discipline/.

7. Craig Edwards, "Don't Blame Hitters for All the Strikeouts" FanGraphs, June 6, 2018, https://blogs.fangraphs.com/dont-blame-hitters-for-all- the-strikeouts/.

8. Russell A. Carleton, "Fire Up the Time Machine," Baseball Prospectus, June 6, 2017, https://www.baseballprospectus.com/news/article/ 31995/baseball-therapy-fire-up-the-time-machine/.

9. Pre-Statcast pitch-type proportions reported by FanGraphs for 2007 are so markedly different from afterward that different classification criteria must have been in use.

10. Mike Silver, "Breaking Down a Pitcher's Stuff: Fastball Velocity," Statistically Speaking Archive, September 29, 2009, https://statspeakmvn.wordpress.com/2009/09/29/breaking-down- a-pitchers-stuff-fastball-velocity/; Edwards, "Don't Blame Hitters."

11. Eric Seidman, "Breaking Down the Heater," Statistically Speaking Archive, June 19, 2008, https://statspeakmvn.wordpress.com/ 2008/06/19/breaking-down-the-heater/; Ben Clemens, "What Happens a Year After a Velocity Spike?" FanGraphs, December 21, 2020, https://blogs.fangraphs.com/what-happens-the-year-after-a-velocity- spike/; Matthew Trueblood, "Does it Matter How Fast the Fastballs You Hit (and Miss) Are?" Baseball Prospectus, January 8, 2024, https://www.baseballprospectus.com/news/article/87555/flyover- country-fastball-speeds/.

12. Seidman, "Does Movement Influence BABIP?" Statistically Speaking Archive, June 26, 2008, https://statspeakmvn.wordpress.com/2008/ 06/26/does-movement-influence-babip/.

13. Jonah Pemstein, "On Rotation, Part 1: The Effects of Spin Rate on the Flight of a Pitch," FanGraphs, June 1, 2015, https://blogs.fangraphs.com/ the-effects-of-spin-on-the-flight-of-a-pitch/.

14. Jonathan Hale, "Is Speed Enough?: A PITCHf/x Look at the Effect of Fastball Velocity and Movement," Baseball Prospectus, October 30, 2013, https://www.baseballprospectus.com/news/article/22139/baseball- proguestus-is-speed-enough-a-pitchfx-look-at-the-effect-of-fastball- velocity-and-movement/.

15. Pemstein, "On Rotation, Part 2: The Effects of Spin on Pitch Outcomes," FanGraphs, June 3, 2015, https://blogs.fangraphs.com/on-rotation- part-2-the-effects-of-spin-on-pitch-outcomes/.

16. Harry Pavlidis, "What Makes a Good Changeup: An Investigation, Part 1," Baseball Prospectus, May 10, 2013, https://www.baseballprospectus.com/ news/article/20539/what-makes-a-good-changeup-an-investigation- part-1/.

17. Dale L. Zimmerman, Jun Tang, and Rui Huang, "Outline Analyses of the Called Strike Zone in Major League Baseball," *Annals of Applied Statistics* 13, no. 4 (2019), 2416–51.

18. John Walsh, "The Eye of the Umpire," July 25, 2007, FanGraphs, https://tht.fangraphs.com/the-eye-of-the-umpire/.

19. Zimmerman, Tang, and Huang, "Outline Analyses"

20. Eli Ben-Porat, "Rethinking the Strike Zone: It's Not a Square," FanGraphs, February 19, 2019, https://tht.fangraphs.com/rethinking-the-strike- zone-its-not-a-square/.

21. Tobias J. Moskowitz and L. Jon Wertheim. *Scorecasting: The Hidden Influences Behind How Sports Are Played and Games Are Won* (New York: Crown Archetype, 2011); James Zhan, John Polimeni, and Luke Gerstner, "Measuring the Impact of Robotic Umpires," MIT Sloan Sports Analytics Conference, March 6–7, 2020, https://www.sloansportsconference.com/ research-papers/measuring-the-impact-of-robotic-umpires; Davy Andrews, "Pitch Framing is Evolving Along with the Strike Zone." FanGraphs, February 27, 2023, https://blogs.fangraphs.com/pitch- framing-is-evolving-along-with-the-strike-zone/; Andrews, "Strike three?! Let's check in on umpire accuracy," FanGraphs, February 1, 2024, https://blogs.fangraphs.com/strike-three-lets-check-in-on-umpire- accuracy/.

22. Jon Roegele, "The 2017 Strike Zone," FanGraphs, March 28, 2018, https://tht.fangraphs.com/the-2017-strike-zone/.

23. Roegele, "The Living Strike Zone," Baseball Prospectus, July 24, 2013, https://www.baseballprospectus.com/news/article/21262/baseball- proguestus-the-living-strike-zone/.

24. Brian Mills, "Expert Workers, Performance Standards, and On-the-Job Training: Evaluating Major League Baseball Umpires," Social Science Research Network, August 27, 2014, https://ssrn.com/abstract=2478447 or http://dx.doi.org/10.2139/ssrn.2478447; see also Brian M. Mills, "Policy Changes in Major League Baseball: Improved Agent Behavior and Ancillary Productivity Outcomes," *Economic Inquiry* 55, no. 2 (2017), 1104–18.

25. Roegele, "The Strike Zone During the PITCHf/x Era," in *The Hardball Times Baseball Annual 2014*, ed. Dave Studenmund, Paul Swydan (FanGraphs, 2014), 233–44.

26. Mills, "Policy Changes in Major League Baseball."

27. Jerry W. Kim and Brayden G. King, "Seeing Stars: Matthew Effects and Status Bias in Major League Baseball Umpiring," *Management Science* 60, no. 11 (2014), 2619–44.

28. Carleton, "The Dark Side of Pitch Framing?" Baseball Prospectus, February 2, 2016, https://www.baseballprospectus.com/news/ article/28350/baseball-therapy-the-dark-side-of-pitch-framing/.

29. Robert Arthur, "How Jonathan Lucroy Makes Batters Swing at Bad Pitches," Baseball Prospectus, February 11, 2015, https://www.baseball- prospectus.com/news/article/25564/moonshot-how-jonathan-lucroy- makes-batters-swing-at-bad-pitches/.

30. Jeff Sullivan, "Pitch Framing Data Is Going Insane," November 8, 2017, FanGraphs, https://blogs.fangraphs.com/pitch-framing-data-is- going-insane/.

31. Pizza Cutter (Russell A. Carleton), "The Foul Ball, Part 1: What Does it Tell Us About a Batter?" Statistically Speaking Archives, https://statspeakmvn.wordpress.com/2008/04/15/the-foul-ball- part-one-what-does-it-tell-us-about-a-batter/.

32. Devan Fink, "Unpacking the Impact of Foul Balls on Strikeouts," FanGraphs, May 21, 2021, https://blogs.fangraphs.com/unpacking-the-impact-of- foul-balls-on-strikeouts/.

33. Alex Chamberlain, "Are Foul Balls Good or Bad?" FanGraphs, June 22, 2019, https://fantasy.fangraphs.com/are-foul-balls-good-or-bad/.

34. Carleton, "When It All Went Foul." Baseball Prospectus, May 1, 2024, https://www.baseballprospectus.com/news/article/90085/baseball- therapy-when-it-all-went-foul-foul-balls/; Andrews, "What Is a Foul Ball Anyway?" FanGraphs, February 16, 2024, https://blogs.fangraphs.com/ what-is-a-foul-ball-anyway/.

35. Andrews, "What Is a Foul Ball Anyway?"

36. Carleton, "When It All Went Foul."

37. Carleton, "Slow Down on the Slowing Down to Speed Up," June 15, 2022, https://www.baseballprospectus.com/news/article/75296/baseball- therapy-slow-down-on-the-slowing-down-to-speed-up/.

38. Andrews, "What Is a Foul Ball Anyway?"

39. Improved pitch framing increased the number of called strikes both outside and inside the rule book strike zone. Whereas the former would decrease umpire accuracy, the latter would counterbalance it, and with the greater attention paid to it, overall umpire accuracy steadily improved.

40. Alan M. Nathan, "Trajectory Calculator," The Physics of Baseball, http://baseball.physics.illinois.edu/trajectory-calculator.html; Robert Arthur. "Moving the Mound will Change Everything," Baseball Prospectus, March 15, 2019, https://www.baseballprospectus.com/news/article/47832/moonshot-moving-the-mound-will-change-everything/.

41. David Schoenfield and Jeff Passan, "How soon could robot umps and 62-foot, 6-inch mound come to MLB?" ESPN, March 8, 2019, https://www.espn.com/mlb/story/_/id/26191979/how-soon-robot-umps-62-foot-6-inch-mound-come-mlb.

42. Robert Arthur, "Moving the Atlantic League Mound Back Has Had Mixed Effects," Baseball Prospectus, August 24, 2021, https://www.baseball-prospectus.com/news/article/69212/moonshot-moving-the-mound-back-has-had-mixed-effects/; Ben Lindbergh and Rob Arthur, "MLB Just Tried a Bunch of Experimental Rules in the Minors. How Well Did They Work?" The Ringer, October 21, 2021, https://www.theringer.com/mlb/2021/10/21/22736400/experimental-rules-atlantic-league-robo-umps.

Scanning the World of Baseball Streaks: Part Two

Ed Denta

In "Going Beyond the Baseball Adage 'One Game at a Time': A Geek's Peek at Streaks," published in the Spring 2024 *Baseball Research Journal*, I developed a set of mathematical expressions to predict the frequency and length of baseball's winning and losing streaks. In this paper, I will highlight the historical content I uncovered during my research, diving into notable accomplishments such as the longest winning and losing streaks in each season and for each franchise, and crowning the streakiest teams of all time. If you are fascinated by baseball history and crave new insights into the triumphs and tribulations of some of the best and worst teams of all-time, this paper is for you.

STREAKS DEFINED

Of the 206,711 games in my data set played from 1901 to 2023, 777 had no determined winner. Ties and suspended games were quite common in the first half of the twentieth century, mainly due to fields not having lights. Suspended games were not always completed at a later date, and 89.6% of all games with no determined winner occurred by 1960. The last tie game occurred on September 29, 2016, when rain halted the Cubs and Pirates in the top of the sixth inning with the score tied, 1–1. The game was called rather than suspended because it was late in the season and the result would have had no effect on the standings. Table 1 shows the number of winnerless games by decade.

For purposes of this paper, games with no winner are considered a neutral result. They neither terminate nor extend a streak. For example, the nine-game sequence WWWTWWTWW is considered a seven-game win streak. This paper addresses only streaks that occur within a single season and does not differentiate between home and away games. Home and road streaks are thought-provoking topics for another report.

LONGEST STREAKS BY SEASON

Table 2 (page 104), shows the longest winning and losing streaks in each season from 1901 through 2023. All current franchises (including the defunct Baltimore Orioles) have led (or tied) for the longest seasonal win streak at least once, except for the Marlins. The Yankees have done so most often, posting the longest win streak 16 times. Only the Padres have never had the longest losing streak, while Red Sox own the dubious distinction of running the longest losing streak in 18 different seasons. In 1971, the Royals, Phillies, and Senators tied for the longest losing streak in baseball with eight consecutive losses. That was the only season where the leader in either wins or losses had fewer than nine. In 1918, the Cubs and Giants led baseball with nine-game win streaks, while the Reds, Phillies, and Brooklyn Robins led with nine-game losing streaks, making it the only season when no team reached double digits in either category.

Table 1. Winnerless Games by Decade

Decade	Ties	Cumulative Ties	Cumulative Tie %
1901–1910	215	215	27.7%
1911–1920	167	382	49.2%
1921–1930	62	444	57.1%
1931–1940	98	542	69.8%
1941–1950	99	641	82.5%
1951–1960	55	696	89.6%
1961–1970	36	732	94.2%
1971–1980	14	746	96.0%
1981–1990	18	764	98.3%
1991–2000	8	772	99.4%
2001–2010	4	776	99.9%
2011–2023	1	777	100.0%
Total	**777**		

Table 2. Longest Streaks by Season (1901 – 2023)

Season	Longest Winning Streak		Longest Losing Streak	
1901	Baltimore Orioles (Defunct)	11	Cleveland Blues	11
1902	Pittsburgh Pirates / Philadelphia Athletics	10 / 10	New York Giants	13
1903	Pittsburgh Pirates	15	St. Louis Browns / St. Louis Cardinals	11 / 11
1904	New York Giants	18	Washington Senators(1)	13
1905	New York Giants	13	St. Louis Cardinals	14
1906	Chicago White Sox	19	Boston Americans	20
1907	New York Giants	17	Boston Americans / Boston Doves	16 / 16
1908	Chicago White Sox	13	New York Highlanders	12
1909	Pittsburgh Pirates	16	Boston Doves / St. Louis Cardinals	15 / 15
1910	Philadelphia Athletics	13	St. Louis Cardinals	13
1911	Pittsburgh Pirates	13	Boston Red Sox	16
1912	Washington Nationals(1)	17	Boston Braves	10
1913	Philadelphia Athletics	15	New York Yankees	13
1914	Philadelphia Athletics	12	Cincinnati Reds	19
1915	Chicago White Sox	11	Philadelphia Athletics	11
1916	**New York Giants**	**26**	Philadelphia Athletics	20
1917	Boston Red Sox / Cleveland Indians / Chicago Cubs	10 / 10 / 10	Washington Nationals(1)	10
1918	Chicago Cubs / New York Giants	9 / 9	Cincinnati Reds / Philadelphia Phillies / Brooklyn Robins	9 / 9 / 9
1919	Cincinnati Reds / Chicago White Sox / Cleveland Indians	10 / 10 / 10	Philadelphia Phillies	13
1920	New York Yankees / Brooklyn Robins / St. Louis Browns	10 / 10 / 10	Philadelphia Athletics	18
1921	Washington Nationals(1) / Brooklyn Robins	11 / 11	Chicago White Sox	11
1922	Pittsburgh Pirates	13	Philadelphia Phillies	12
1923	New York Giants	11	Philadelphia Athletics / Boston Braves	12 / 12
1924	Brooklyn Robins	15	Chicago White Sox	13
1925	Detroit Tigers	10	Philadelphia Athletics / Brooklyn Robins	12 / 12
1926	New York Yankees	16	Boston Red Sox	17
1927	Detroit Tigers	13	Boston Red Sox / Boston Braves	15 / 15
1928	Chicago Cubs	13	Philadelphia Phillies	12
1929	Philadelphia Athletics	11	St. Louis Cardinals / Boston Braves	11 / 11
1930	Brooklyn Robins	11	Boston Red Sox	14
1931	Philadelphia Athletics	17	Cleveland Indians	12
1932	Chicago Cubs	14	St. Louis Browns / Boston Red Sox	11 / 11
1933	Washington Nationals(1)	13	Cincinnati Reds	10
1934	Detroit Tigers	14	Chicago White Sox	10
1935	Chicago Cubs	21	Boston Braves	15
1936	New York Giants / Chicago Cubs	15 / 15	Philadelphia Phillies	14
1937	Boston Red Sox	12	Philadelphia Athletics	15
1938	Pittsburgh Pirates	13	Chicago White Sox / St. Louis Browns	10 / 10
1939	New York Yankees / Cincinnati Reds / Boston Red Sox	12 / 12 / 12	Pittsburgh Pirates	12
1940	Cincinnati Reds	11	St. Louis Browns	11
1941	New York Yankees	14	Washington Nationals(1)	12
1942	Cleveland Indians	13	Philadelphia Phillies	13
1943	St. Louis Cardinals	12	Philadelphia Athletics	20

Season	Longest Winning Streak		Longest Losing Streak	
1944	Chicago Cubs	11	Brooklyn Dodgers	16
1945	Chicago Cubs / Brooklyn Dodgers	11 / 11	Philadelphia Athletics	14
1946	Boston Red Sox	19	Philadelphia Athletics	11
1947	New York Yankees	19	Washington Nationals(1)	11
1948	Boston Red Sox	13	Washington Nationals(1)	18
1949	Boston Red Sox	11	Washington Nationals(1) / St. Louis Browns	11 / 11
1950	Boston Red Sox	11	Cincinnati Reds / Philadelphia Athletics	10 / 10
1951	New York Giants	16	New York Giants / Washington Nationals(1)	11 / 11
1952	St. Louis Cardinals	10	Boston Braves / Pittsburgh Pirates	10 / 10
1953	New York Yankees	18	St. Louis Browns	14
1954	New York Yankees	13	Baltimore Orioles	14
1955	Brooklyn Dodgers / Philadelphia Phillies	11 / 11	Philadelphia Phillies	13
1956	New York Yankees / Milwaukee Braves	11 / 11	Chicago White Sox / Washington Nationals(1)	11 / 11
1957	Cincinnati Redlegs	12	Kansas City Athletics	11
1958	New York Yankees	11	Washington Senators(1)	13
1959	Kansas City Athletics	11	Washington Senators(1)	18
1960	New York Yankees	15	Detroit Tigers / Boston Red Sox / Kansas City Athletics	10 / 10 / 10
1961	New York Yankees	13	**Philadelphia Phillies**	**23**
1962	Los Angeles Dodgers	13	New York Mets	17
1963	St. Louis Cardinals / Minnesota Twins	10 / 10	New York Mets	15
1964	New York Yankees / Los Angeles Angels	11 / 11	Philadelphia Phillies	10
1965	San Francisco Giants	14	New York Mets	11
1966	San Francisco Giants	12	Cincinnati Reds	11
1967	Boston Red Sox / Chicago White Sox	10 / 10	Houston Astros	10
1968	Detroit Tigers	11	Pittsburgh Pirates / Chicago White Sox	10 / 10
1969	New York Mets / Baltimore Orioles	11 / 11	Montreal Expos	20
1970	Chicago Cubs / Atlanta Braves	11 / 11	Washington Senators(2)	14
1971	Baltimore Orioles / Pittsburgh Pirates	11 / 11	Kansas City Royals / Washington Senators(2) / Philadelphia Phillies	8 / 8 / 8
1972	New York Mets	14	Texas Rangers	15
1973	Baltimore Orioles	14	Chicago Cubs	11
1974	Baltimore Orioles	10	California Angels	11
1975	Cincinnati Reds / Boston Red Sox	10 / 10	Detroit Tigers	19
1976	Los Angeles Dodgers	16	Atlanta Braves	13
1977	Kansas City Royals	16	Atlanta Braves	17
1978	Baltimore Orioles	13	Oakland Athletics / St. Louis Cardinals	11 / 11
1979	Montreal Expos / Milwaukee Brewers / California Angels / Cleveland Indians	10 / 10 / 10 / 10	Seattle Mariners	11
1980	Minnesota Twins	12	New York Mets	13
1981	Oakland Athletics	11	Chicago Cubs / Toronto Blue Jays	12 / 12
1982	Atlanta Braves	13	New York Mets	15
1983	Philadelphia Phillies	11	Milwaukee Brewers	10
1984	Philadelphia Phillies	10	Milwaukee Brewers	10
1985	New York Yankees	11	Chicago Cubs	13

Season	Longest Winning Streak		Longest Losing Streak	
1986	New York Mets	11	Kansas City Royals	11
1987	Milwaukee Brewers	13	Milwaukee Brewers[A]	12
1988	Oakland Athletics	14	Baltimore Orioles	21
1989	Houston Astros	10	Detroit Tigers / Seattle Mariners	12 / 12
1990	New York Mets	11	Minnesota Twins / Kansas City Royals	9 / 9
1991	Minnesota Twins	15	New York Mets / Montreal Expos	11 / 11
1992	Atlanta Braves	13	Seattle Mariners	14
1993	Los Angeles Dodgers	11	Colorado Rockies	13
1994	Kansas City Royals	14	Milwaukee Brewers	14
1995	Boston Red Sox	12	Houston Astros	11
1996	Pittsburgh Pirates	11	Detroit Tigers	12
1997	Anaheim Angels / Montreal Expos	10 / 10	Chicago Cubs	14
1998	San Diego Padres / San Francisco Giants / Toronto Blue Jays	11 / 11 / 11	Cincinnati Reds / Tampa Bay Devil Rays / Florida Marlins	11 / 11 / 11
1999	San Diego Padres	14	Philadelphia Phillies / Anaheim Angels	11 / 11
2000	Atlanta Braves	15	Colorado Rockies	11
2001	Seattle Mariners	15	Milwaukee Brewers	11
2002	Oakland Athletics	20	Tampa Bay Devil Rays	15
2003	Arizona Diamondbacks	12	Detroit Tigers	11
2004	Houston Astros / Tampa Bay Devil Rays	12 / 12	Arizona Diamondbacks	14
2005	New York Yankees / Washington Nationals	10 / 10	Kansas City Royals	19
2006	Boston Red Sox	12	Pittsburgh Pirates / Kansas City Royals	13 / 13
2007	Colorado Rockies	11	Tampa Bay Devil Rays	11
2008	New York Mets / Minnesota Twins / Toronto Blue Jays	10 / 10 / 10	Kansas City Royals / Washington Nationals / Seattle Mariners	12 / 12 / 12
2009	Boston Red Sox / Colorado Rockies	11 / 11	Baltimore Orioles	13
2010	Philadelphia Phillies / Texas Rangers / Chicago White Sox	11 / 11 / 11	Pittsburgh Pirates	12
2011	Texas Rangers / Detroit Tigers	12 / 12	Seattle Mariners	17
2012	Cincinnati Reds / New York Yankees	10 / 10	Houston Astros / Kansas City Royals / Chicago Cubs	12 / 12 / 12
2013	Atlanta Braves	14	Houston Astros	15
2014	Los Angeles Angels / Washington Nationals / Kansas City Royals	10 / 10 / 10	Tampa Bay Rays / Boston Red Sox	10 / 10
2015	Toronto Blue Jays / New York Mets	11 / 11	Cincinnati Reds	13
2016	Cleveland Indians	14	Minnesota Twins	13
2017	Cleveland Indians	22	Los Angeles Dodgers	11
2018	Houston Astros	12	San Francisco Giants / Detroit Tigers	11 / 11
2019	Oakland Athletics	11	Detroit Tigers / Kansas City Royals / Baltimore Orioles	10 / 10 / 10
2020	New York Yankees	10	Detroit Tigers / Boston Red Sox	9 / 9
2021	St. Louis Cardinals	17	Baltimore Orioles	19
2022	Atlanta Braves / Seattle Mariners	14 / 14	Los Angeles Angels	14
2023	Tampa Bay Rays	13	Oakland Athletics	11

LONGEST STREAKS BY FRANCHISE

Table 3, opposite, shows the Longest Winning Streak (LWS) and Longest Losing Streak (LLS) for each current franchise. The Miami Marlins are the only franchise without a double-digit win streak.

LONGEST STREAKS BY WINNING AVERAGE

Table 4, opposite, buckets teams based on their winning average, then shows the longest winning and losing streaks for each bucket. For example, of the 23 teams with a winning average below .300, the 1909 Boston Doves, 1945 Phillies, and 2019 Tigers were the only squads that put together a five-game winning streak. The 1939 Yankees stand alone as the only team to run a six-game losing streak despite achieving a winning average above .700.

In 1953, the Yankees posted a 99–52 record, good for a .656 winning average, and cruised to the American League pennant by 8½ games. A week after reeling off 18 consecutive wins from May 27 through June 14, they proceeded to lose nine games in a row. These two streaks represent the longest winning and losing streaks for a team that finished the season with a winning average above .650.

LONGEST ALL-TIME STREAKS

Table 5 (page 106), lists the longest winning and losing streaks of all-time. The 1916 New York Giants had two winning streaks that made the list: a 17-game streak in May and a 26-game streak (interrupted by a tie) in September. Amazingly, the May streak occurred entirely on the road while the September streak took place exclusively at home. Sadly, the Giants finished in fourth place at 86–66–3, seven games behind the pennant-winning Brooklyn Robins.

Table 3. Longest Streaks by Franchise

Current Franchise	Longest In-Season Streaks by Franchise				
	LWS	Seasons		LLS	Seasons
Atlanta Braves	15	2000		19	1906
Arizona Diamondbacks	13	2017		17	2021
Baltimore Orioles (defunct)	11	1901		11	1902
Baltimore Orioles	14	1916, 1973		21	1988
Boston Red Sox	15	1946		20	1906
Chicago Cubs	21	1935		14	1997
Chicago White Sox	19	1906		13	1924
Cincinnati Reds	12	1939, 1957, 2023		19	1914
Cleveland Guardians	22	2017		12	1931
Colorado Rockies	11	2007, 2009		13	1993
Detroit Tigers	14	1909, 1934		19	1975
Houston Astros	12	1999, 2004, 2018		15	2013
Kansas City Royals	16	1977		19	2005
Los Angeles Angels	11	1964		14	2022
Los Angeles Dodgers	15	1924		16	1944
Miami Marlins	9	1996, 2004, 2006, 2008		11	1998, 2011
Milwaukee Brewers	13	1987		14	1994
Minnesota Twins	17	1912		18	1948, 1959
New York Mets	11	1969, 1972, 1986, 1990, 2015		17	1962
New York Yankees	19	1947		13	1913
Oakland Athletics	20	2002		20	1943
Philadelphia Phillies	13	1991		23	1961
Pittsburgh Pirates	16	1909		13	2006
San Diego Padres	14	1999		13	1994
Seattle Mariners	15	2001		17	2011
San Francisco Giants	26	1916		13	1902, 1944
St. Louis Cardinals	17	2021		15	1909
Tampa Bay Rays	13	2023		15	2002
Texas Rangers	14	1991		15	1972
Toronto Blue Jays	11	1987, 1998, 2013, 2015		12	1981
Washington Nationals	10	1979, 1980, 1997, 2005, 2014		20	1969

Table 4. Longest Streaks by Winning Average

Winning Average Range		Team-Seasons in Range	Longest Winning Streak	Team(s) with the Longest Winning Streak	Longest Losing Streak	Team(s) with the Longest Losing Streak
Greater Than	Less Than or Equal To					
.000	.300	23	5	1909 Boston Doves 1945 Philadelphia Phillies 2019 Detroit Tigers	20	1916 Philadelphia Athletics
.300	.350	89	9	1907 St. Louis Cardinals 1949 Washington Senators	23	1961 Philadelphia Phillies
.350	.400	195	10	1976 Chicago White Sox	19	1914 Cincinnati Reds 1975 Detroit Tigers
.400	.450	411	12	2004 Tampa Bay Devil Rays	18	1959 Washington Senators
.450	.500	596	14	1999 San Diego Padres	14	1994 Milwaukee Brewers 2022 Los Angeles Angels
.500	.550	578	17	1907 New York Giants	12	1931 Cleveland Indians 1970 Chicago Cubs
.550	.600	476	26	1916 New York Giants	12	1925 Philadelphia Athletics 1927 Washington Senators 1987 Milwaukee Brewers
.600	.650	217	22	2017 Cleveland Indians	11	1951 New York Giants 2017 Los Angeles Dodgers
.650	.700	50	18	1904 New York Giants 1953 New York Yankees	9	1953 New York Yankees
.700	1.000	11	17	1931 Philadelphia Athletics	6	1939 New York Yankees
Total Team-Seasons		2646				

Table 5. Longest All-Time Streaks

	Current Franchise	Team	Longest Winning Streaks		Season Summary
			Games	Season	
1	San Francisco Giants	New York Giants	26**	1916	86–66–3, 4th of 8
2	Cleveland Guardians	Cleveland Indians	22	2017	102–60, won AL Central, lost ALDS
3	Chicago Cubs	Chicago Cubs	21	1935	100–54, won NL pennant, lost WS
4	Oakland Athletics	Oakland Athletics	20	2002	103–59, won AL West, lost ALDS
5	New York Yankees	New York Yankees	19	1947	97–57, won AL pennant, won WS
5	Chicago White Sox	Chicago White Sox	19**	1906	93–58–3, won AL pennant, won WS
7	New York Yankees	New York Yankees	18	1953	99–52, won AL pennant, won WS
7	San Francisco Giants	New York Giants	18	1904	106–47–5, won NL pennant, no WS played
9	St. Louis Cardinals	St. Louis Cardinals	17	2021	90–72, 2nd of 5, lost WC game
9	Oakland Athletics	Philadelphia Athletics	17	1931	107–45–1, won AL pennant, lost WS
9	San Francisco Giants	New York Giants	17*	1916	86–66–3, 4th of 8
9	Minnesota Twins	Washington Nationals(1)	17	1912	91–61–2, 2nd of 8
9	San Francisco Giants	New York Giants	17	1907	82–71–2, 4th of 8
14	Kansas City Royals	Kansas City Royals	16	1977	102–60, won AL West, lost ALCS
14	San Francisco Giants	New York Giants	16	1951	98–59, won play–off game to win NL pennant, lost WS
14	New York Yankees	New York Yankees	16	1926	91–63–1, won AL pennant, lost WS
14	San Francisco Giants	New York Giants	16	1912	103–48–3, won NL pennant, lost WS
14	Pittsburgh Pirates	Pittsburgh Pirates	16	1909	110–42–2, won NL pennant, won WS

	Current Franchise	Team	Longest Losing Streaks		Season Summary
			Games	Season	
1	Philadelphia Phillies	Philadelphia Phillies	23	1961	47–107, 8th of 8
2	Baltimore Orioles	Baltimore Orioles	21	1988	54–107, 7th of 7
3	Washington Nationals	Montreal Expos	20	1969	52–110, 6th of 6
3	Oakland Athletics	Philadelphia Athletics	20	1943	49–105–1, 8th of 8
3	Oakland Athletics	Philadelphia Athletics	20	1916	36–117–1, 8th of 8
3	Boston Red Sox	Boston Americans	20	1906	49–105–1, 8th of 8
7	Baltimore Orioles	Baltimore Orioles	19	2021	52–110, 5th of 5
7	Kansas City Royals	Kansas City Royals	19	2005	56–106, 5th of 5
7	Detroit Tigers	Detroit Tigers	19	1975	57–102, 6th of 6
7	Cincinnati Reds	Cincinnati Reds	19	1914	60–94–3, 8th of 8
7	Atlanta Braves	Boston Nationals	19	1906	49–102–1, 8th of 8
12	Minnesota Twins	Washington Senators(1)	18	1959	63–91, 8th of 8
12	Minnesota Twins	Washington Nationals(1)	18	1948	56–97–1, 7th of 8
12	Oakland Athletics	Philadelphia Athletics	18	1920	48–106–2, 8th of 8
15	Arizona Diamondbacks	Arizona Diamondbacks	17	2021	52–110, 5th of 5
15	Seattle Mariners	Seattle Mariners	17	2011	67–95, 4th of 4
15	Atlanta Braves	Atlanta Braves	17	1977	61–101, 6th of 6
15	New York Mets	New York Mets	17	1962	40–120–1, 10 of 10
15	Boston Red Sox	Boston Red Sox	17	1926	46–107–1, 8th of 8

* Second long streak by 1916 New York Giants
** Interrupted by a single tie game

SHORTEST LOSING STREAKS

Great teams are resilient after a loss, finding ways to avoid long losing streaks. Table 6, opposite, lists all the teams that lost no more than three consecutive games in a season. That is, their longest seasonal losing streak (LLS) was no more than three games. Entries are sorted by LLS and then by winning average.

Only two teams have ever gone through an entire season without losing more than two games in a row: the 1902 Pirates and the 2020 Dodgers. The Pirates lost consecutive games eight times during 1902. On July 7, they avoided a three-game losing streak by scoring three runs in the bottom of the eighth inning to pull out a 5–3 victory over the Phillies. These juggernaut Pirates, led by future Hall of Famers Honus Wagner, Fred Clarke, and Jack Chesbro, outscored their opponents 775 to 440, finished with a 103–36–3 record, and cruised to the pennant with a 27½ game cushion over the second place Brooklyn Superbas. Only two other National League teams finished above .500 that season.

During the abbreviated 2020 season, the Dodgers lost consecutive games four times. They came closest to losing three in a row on September 8 against the Diamondbacks. Trailing 6–2 after six innings, they scored four runs in the top of the seventh to tie the game. In the 10th inning, they scored four runs to Arizona's three, scraping by with a 10–9 victory.

There have been 41 other occasions when a team did not lose more than three games in a row. Of those clubs, only the 1906 Chicago Cubs were able to limit their three-game losing streak to a single occurrence. At .763, they also posted the highest winning average on the list. On the other hand, the 1972 New York Mets lost three consecutive games on 12 occasions and their .532 winning average was the lowest of the group. In 1954, despite posting a .669 winning average and losing three games in a row just twice, the Yankees missed the playoffs. Despite running four different losing streaks of at least three games, including two in the first nine games of the season, the Cleveland Indians—not included in the table due to a four-game losing streak—ran away with the pennant with a record of 111–43–2, for a winning average of .721.

SHORTEST WINNING STREAKS

Bad teams find it difficult to break out of downward spirals. Any combination of factors can inform their struggles: inferior talent, leadership, or ownership, a poor clubhouse atmosphere, injuries, or maybe even just bad karma. Table 7 (page 108), lists all teams that

Table 6. Teams Without a Four-Game Losing Streak

#	Current Franchise	Team	Season	Smallest Longest Losing Streaks (LLS) within a Season								Season Summary
				LLS	No. of Times	W	L	T	AVG	LWS	Finish	
1	Pittsburgh Pirates	Pittsburgh Pirates	1902	2	8	103	36	3	.741	10	1st of 8	Won NL pennant, lost World Series
2	Los Angeles Dodgers	Los Angeles Dodgers	2020*	2	4	43	17		.717	7	1st of 5	Won NL pennant, won World Series
1	Chicago Cubs	Chicago Cubs	1906	3	1	116	36	3	.763	14	1st of 8	Won NL pennant, lost World Series
2	New York Yankees	New York Yankees	1932	3	3	108	47	1	.697	10	1st of 8	Won AL pennant, won World Series
3	New York Yankees	New York Yankees	1954	3	2	103	51	1	.669	13	2nd of 8	**Missed playoffs**
4	Boston Red Sox	Boston RedSox	2018	3	4	108	54		.667	10	1st of 5	Won AL pennant, won World Series
5	Baltimore Orioles	Baltimore Orioles	1970	3	2	108	54		.667	11	1st of 6	Won AL pennant, won World Series
6	New York Yankees	New York Yankees	1936	3	3	102	51	2	.667	7	1st of 8	Won AL pennant, won World Series
7	Boston Red Sox	Boston Americans	1903	3	3	91	47	3	.659	11	1st of 8	Won AL pennant, won World Series
8	New York Yankees	New York Yankees	1928	3	2	101	53		.656	8	1st of 8	Won AL pennant, won World Series
9	Cincinnati Reds	Cincinnati Reds	1940	3	4	100	53	2	.654	11	1st of 8	Won NL pennant, won World Series
10	New York Yankees	New York Yankees	1923	3	4	98	54		.645	9	1st of 8	Won AL pennant, won World Series
11	New York Yankees	New York Yankees	1957	3	4	98	56		.636	10	1st of 8	Won AL pennant, lost World Series
12	San Francisco Giants	New York Giants	1917	3	3	98	56	4	.636	6	1st of 8	Won NL pennant, lost World Series
13	New York Yankees	New York Yankees	1980	3	3	103	59		.636	9	1st of 7	Won AL East, lost ALCS
14	New York Yankees	New York Yankees	1947	3	4	97	57	1	.630	19	1st of 8	Won AL pennant, won World Series
15	Atlanta Braves	Atlanta Braves	2022	3	4	101	61		.623	14	1st of 5	Won NL East, lost NLDS
16	New York Mets	New York Mets	2022	3	5	101	61		.623	7	2nd of 5	Lost NL Wild Card game
17	Atlanta Braves	Atlanta Braves	2003	3	5	101	61		.623	8	1st of 5	Won NL East, lost NLDS
18	Oakland Athletics	Philadelphia Athletics	1905	3	3	92	56	4	.622	7	1st of 8	Won AL pennant, lost World Series
19	St. Louis Cardinals	St. Louis Cardinals	2005	3	3	100	62		.617	6	1st of 6	Won NL Central, won NLDS, lost NLCS
20	Atlanta Braves	Milwaukee Braves	1957	3	8	95	59	1	.617	10	1st of 8	Won NL pennant, won World Series
21	Pittsburgh Pirates	Pittsburgh Pirates	1927	3	5	94	60	2	.610	11	1st of 8	Won NL pennant, lost World Series
22	Baltimore Orioles	St. Louis Browns	1922	3	5	93	61		.604	5	2nd of 8	Missed playoffs
23	Oakland Athletics	Oakland Athletics	2020*	3	2	36	24		.600	9	1st of 5	Won AL West, won WC series, lost ALDS
24	Boston Red Sox	Boston RedSox	2013	3	5	97	65		.599	7	1st of 5	Won AL pennant, won World Series
25	Los Angeles Dodgers	Brooklyn Robins	1924	3	7	92	62		.597	15	2nd of 8	Missed playoffs
26	Philadelphia Phillies	Philadelphia Phillies	1901	3	7	83	57		.593	10	2nd of 8	No playoffs played
27	Atlanta Braves	Atlanta Braves	2004	3	6	96	66		.593	6	1st of 5	Won NL East, lost NLDS
28	Cincinnati Reds	Cincinnati Reds	1999	3	8	96	67		.589	10	2nd of 6	Missed playoffs
29	Minnesota Twins	Washington Nationals(1)	1913	3	2	90	64	1	.584	6	2nd of 8	Missed playoffs
30	Cleveland Guardians	Cleveland Indians	2016	3	7	94	67		.584	14	1st of 5	Won AL pennant, lost World Series
31	Los Angeles Dodgers	Los Angeles Dodgers	1988	3	10	94	67	1	.584	7	1st of 6	Won NL pennant, won World Series
32	Los Angeles Dodgers	Los Angeles Dodgers	2014	3	3	94	68		.580	6	1st of 5	Won NL West, lost NLDS
33	Baltimore Orioles	Baltimore Orioles	1965	3	6	94	68		.580	9	3rd of 10	Missed playoffs
34	Cleveland Guardians	Cleveland Indians	1918***	3	2	73	54	2	.575	7	2nd of 8	Missed playoffs
35	San Francisco Giants	San Francisco Giants	1989	3	6	92	70		.568	7	1st of 6	Won NL pennant, lost World Series
36	Detroit Tigers	Detroit Tigers	1971	3	6	91	71		.562	7	2nd of 6	Missed playoffs
37	Atlanta Braves	Boston Braves	1947	3	5	86	68		.558	5	3rd of 8	Missed playoffs
38	Kansas City Royals	Kansas City Royals	1994**	3	6	64	51		.557	14	3rd of 5	No playoffs played
39	San Francisco Giants	San Francisco Giants	1968	3	6	88	74	1	.543	5	2nd of 10	Missed playoffs
40	Detroit Tigers	Detroit Tigers	1923	3	6	83	71	1	.539	5	2nd of 8	Missed playoffs
41	New York Mets	New York Mets	1972	3	12	83	73		.532	11	3rd of 6	Missed playoffs

* COVID-19 season
** Strike season
*** World War I season

won no more than three consecutive games in a season. That is, their longest seasonal winning streak (LWS) was no more than three games. Entries are sorted by LWS and then by winning average.

Four teams have failed to win more than two consecutive games during an entire season: the Philadelphia Athletics of 1916 and 1919, the 1939 St. Louis Browns, and the 1952 Pirates. Each of these abysmal squads did win consecutive games at least six times. From 1909 through 1914, the Athletics were the top team in baseball, winning four pennants and three World Series, and never finishing worse than third in the American League. The roster was decimated for 1915, when frugal owner (and manager) Connie Mack sold Eddie Collins to the White Sox, had Home Run Baker sit out the season due to a contract dispute, and allowed Eddie Plank and Chief Bender to jump to the new Federal League by failing to offer comparable salaries. The basement of the AL became Mack's home for the next seven seasons.

In the eight seasons from 1950 to 1957, the Pirates finished in last place in the National League five times and second-to-last three times. Despite reaching their nadir in 1939, the Browns hadn't won more than four straight games in any of the three previous seasons.

There have been 47 other occasions when a team failed to win more than three games in a row, including 10 teams that only managed one single three-game winning streak. The 1936 Brooklyn Dodgers had 12 three-game win streaks and finished with a .435 winning average, the best of the group. Between 1915 and 1950, Philadelphia was home to 13 teams that failed to win more than three in a row. In the 1940 season, neither the Phillies nor the Athletics did so. The Phillies finally brought some elation to the long-suffering fans of Philadelphia by capturing the National League pennant in 1950. Unfortunately, joy turned to disappointment when the Yankees swept the World Series, holding the Phillies to just five runs in four games.

MEASURING STREAKINESS

"A Geek's Peek at Streaks" established a method for quantifying a team's streakiness. Win Streak Quotient (WSQ) and Loss Streak Quotient (LSQ) represent the ratio of wins or losses, respectively, that occur during winning or losing streaks of at least five games. Total Streak Quotient (TSQ) combines those two numbers, showing the ratio of all decisions (wins and losses, but not ties) that occur during either a winning or losing streak. Table 8 (page 109), displays the teams with the

Table 7. Teams Winning No More Than Three Consecutive Games in a Season

	Current Franchise	Team	Smallest Longest Winning Streaks (LWS) within a Season								
			Season	LWS	No. of Times	W	L	T	AVG	LLS	Finish
1	Oakland Athletics	**Philadelphia Athletics**	1916	2	6	36	117	1	.235	20	8th of 8
2	Oakland Athletics	**Philadelphia Athletics**	1919	2	10	36	104		.257	9	8th of 8
3	Pittsburgh Pirates	**Pittsburgh Pirates**	1952	2	9	42	112	1	.273	10	8th of 8
4	Baltimore Orioles	**St. Louis Browns**	1939	2	9	43	111	2	.279	11	8th of 8
1	New York Mets	New York Mets	1962	3	2	40	120	1	.250	17	10th of 10
2	Minnesota Twins	Washington Senators(1)	1904	3	1	38	113	6	.252	**13**	8th of 8
3	Minnesota Twins	Washington Nationals(1)	1909	3	2	42	110	4	.276	11	8th of 8
4	Philadelphia Phillies	**Philadelphia Phillies**	1942	3	1	42	109		.278	**13**	8th of 8
5	Philadelphia Phillies	**Philadelphia Phillies**	1941	3	2	43	111	1	.279	9	8th of 8
6	Boston Red Sox	Boston Red Sox	1932	3	2	43	111		.279	11	8th of 8
7	Oakland Athletics	**Philadelphia Athletics**	1915	3	1	43	109	2	.283	11	8th of 8
8	Atlanta Braves	Boston Rustlers	1911	3	2	44	107	5	.291	16	8th of 8
9	Baltimore Orioles	St. Louis Browns	1937	3	3	46	108	2	.299	12	8th of 8
10	Philadelphia Phillies	**Philadelphia Phillies**	1938	3	3	45	105	1	.300	9	8th of 8
11	Baltimore Orioles	St. Louis Browns	1910	3	1	47	107	4	.305	**12**	8th of 8
12	Boston Red Sox	Boston Red Sox	1925	3	2	47	105		.309	9	8th of 8
13	Oakland Athletics	**Philadelphia Athletics**	1920	3	6	48	106	2	.312	18	8th of 8
14	Arizona Diamondbacks	Arizona Diamondbacks	2004	3	3	51	111		.315	14	5th of 5
15	Pittsburgh Pirates	Pittsburgh Pirates	2020*	3	2	19	41		.317	8	5th of 5
16	Baltimore Orioles	Baltimore Orioles	2021	3	4	52	110		.321	19	5th of 5
17	Philadelphia Phillies	**Philadelphia Phillies**	1923	3	2	50	104	1	.325	7	8th of 8
18	Philadelphia Phillies	**Philadelphia Phillies**	**1940**	3	2	50	103		.327	9	8th of 8
19	New York Yankees	New York Highlanders	1908	3	5	51	103	1	.331	12	8th of 8
20	Toronto Blue Jays	Toronto Blue Jays	1977	3	4	54	107		.335	11	7th of 8
21	Chicago White Sox	Chicago White Sox	1948	3	5	51	101	2	.336	9	8th of 8
22	Atlanta Braves	Atlanta Braves	1988	3	5	54	106		.338	10	6th of 6
23	Oakland Athletics	Kansas City Athletics	1956	3	4	52	102		.338	6	8th of 8
24	Baltimore Orioles	St. Louis Browns	1951	3	1	52	102		.338	**9**	8th of 8
25	Oakland Athletics	**Philadelphia Athletics**	1950	3	1	52	102		.338	**10**	8th of 8
26	Philadelphia Phillies	**Philadelphia Phillies**	1930	3	5	52	102	2	.338	11	8th of 8
27	Washington Nationals	Washington Nationals(2)	2022	3	5	55	107		.340	9	5th of 5
28	Atlanta Braves	Boston Braves	1912	3	1	52	101	2	.340	**10**	8th of 8
29	Oakland Athletics	**Philadelphia Athletics**	**1940**	3	1	54	100		.351	9	8th of 8
30	Pittsburgh Pirates	Pittsburgh Pirates	1985	3	1	57	104		.354	**9**	6th of 6
31	Kansas City Royals	Kansas City Royals	2004	3	3	58	104		.358	8	5th of 5
32	Baltimore Orioles	St. Louis Browns	1933	3	3	55	96	2	.364	7	8th of 8
33	Baltimore Orioles	St. Louis Browns	1917	3	6	57	97	1	.370	8	7th of 8
34	Baltimore Orioles	St. Louis Browns	1913	3	1	57	96	2	.373	9	8th of 8
35	Pittsburgh Pirates	Pittsburgh Pirates	2021	3	6	61	101		.377	10	5th of 5
36	Arizona Diamondbacks	Arizona Diamondbacks	2014	3	5	64	98		.395	7	5th of 5
37	Chicago Cubs	Chicago Cubs	1949	3	5	61	93		.396	8	8th of 8
38	Boston Red Sox	Boston RedSox	2020*	3	2	24	36		.400	9	5th of 5
39	Chicago Cubs	Chicago Cubs	1951	3	5	62	92	1	.403	8	8th of 8
40	Kansas City Royals	Kansas City Royals	2010	3	6	67	95		.414	7	5th of 5
41	Minnesota Twins	Washington Nationals(1)	1944	3	7	64	90		.416	11	8th of 8
42	Kansas City Royals	Kansas City Royals	1997	3	5	67	94		.416	12	5th of 5
43	Philadelphia Phillies	**Philadelphia Phillies**	1935	3	7	64	89	3	.418	9	7th of 8
44	San Diego Padres	San Diego Padres	2016	3	6	68	94		.420	5	5th of 5
45	Milwaukee Brewers	Milwaukee Brewers	1971	3	6	69	92		.429	8	6th of 6
46	New York Mets	New York Mets	2020*	3	2	26	34		.433	5	4th of 5
47	Los Angeles Dodgers	Brooklyn Dodgers	1936	3	12	67	87	2	**.435**	9	7th of 8

* COVID-19 season

largest WSQs and LSQs. The streak lengths are listed in the order that they occurred during the season.

Table 9 displays the teams with the 10 largest seasonal Total Streak Quotients (TSQ). All streaks of five or more games are listed.

Most of the teams in the top 10 were streaky in one particular direction: four only had losing streaks and one only had winning streaks. Despite finishing in last place in the NL, the most balanced team in the top 10 (not counting 2020) is the 1914 Cincinnati Reds, who ranked eighth with a TSQ of .487. Those Reds had five

winning streaks and five losing streaks of at least five games, totaling 29 streak wins and 46 streak losses.

BACK-TO-BACK-TO-BACK-TO-BACK STREAKS

Back-to-back streaks of at least five games each (a winning streak followed immediately by a losing streak, or vice versa) occur with reasonable regularity. Back-to-back-to-back streaks are not that uncommon. However, stringing together four streaks in a row is a rarity. It has happened just four times and only once since 1920. Table 10 shows these extremely rare streak sequences.

Table 8. Teams with the Largest Seasonal Win and Loss Streak Quotients (WSQ, LSQ)

	Current Franchise	Team	Season *COVID-19 year	Total Wins	Streak Wins	WSQ	Win Streak Lengths	W													Win Streaks =>5
1	**New York Yankees**	**New York Yankees**	**2020***	**33**	**23**	**.697**	7	6	10												3
2	New York Yankees	New York Yankees	1939	106	71	.670	12	6	5	5	8	5	5	10	8	7					10
3	Chicago Cubs	Chicago Cubs	1906	116	75	.647	10	5	6	7	5	11	14	12	5						9
4	Chicago Cubs	Chicago Cubs	1910	104	66	.635	6	11	5	6	5	5	8	5	10	5					10
5	San Francisco Giants	New York Giants	1912	103	65	.631	9	9	9	6	16	5	6	5							8
6	Boston Red Sox	Boston Red Sox	1915	101	62	.614	5	8	7	7	7	7	7	7	7						9
7	Pittsburgh Pirates	Pittsburgh Pirates	1977	96	58	.604	5	11	6	5	8	6	5	7	5						9
8	New York Yankees	New York Yankees	1994	70	42	.600	6	10	8	5	5	8									6
9	St. Louis Cardinals	St. Louis Cardinals	1930	92	54	.587	9	8	5	6	9	7	5	5							8
10	Cleveland Guardians	Cleveland Indians	1954	111	65	.586	6	11	9	8	6	9	5	11							8

	Current Franchise	Team	Season	Total Losses	Streak Losses	LSQ	Loss Streak Lengths	L													Loss Streaks =>5
1	**Oakland Athletics**	**Philadelphia Athletics**	**1919**	**104**	**75**	**.721**	5	6	5	6	6	6	8	6	9	5	8	5			12
2	Detroit Tigers	Detroit Tigers	2003	119	85	.714	9	8	6	7	8	9	6	5	11	6	10				11
3	Oakland Athletics	Oakland Athletics	1979	108	73	.676	5	8	5	7	8	8	5	5	5	5	6	6			12
4	Minnesota Twins	Washington Nationals(1)	1909	110	73	.664	5	5	5	6	5	5	6	7	6	11	6	6			12
5	New York Mets	New York Mets	1962	120	79	.658	9	17	5	11	5	13	5	7							9
6	Baltimore Orioles	St. Louis Browns	1949	101	66	.653	7	10	11	5	5	8	6	7	7						9
7	Atlanta Braves	Boston Doves	1909	108	69	.639	13	6	11	5	5	15	5	9							8
8	Baltimore Orioles	St. Louis Browns	1950	96	61	.635	5	7	9	6	5	7	5	5	7	5					10
9	Detroit Tigers	Detroit Tigers	1996	109	69	.633	8	6	12	7	5	5	8	12	6						9
10	New York Yankees	New York Highlanders	1908	103	65	.631	5	7	8	8	7	12	7	5	5	5					10

Table 9. Teams with the Largest Seasonal Total Streak Quotients (TSQ)

	Current Franchise	Team	Season *COVID-19 year	W	L	T	Streak Wins	Streak Losses	Non-Tie Games	TSQ	Streak Lengths	W	L									Streaks =>5
1	**New York Yankees**	**New York Yankees**	**2020***	**33**	**27**		**23**	**12**	**60**	**0.583**	7	6	7	5	10							5
2	Oakland Athletics	Philadelphia Athletics	1919	36	104		0	75	140	0.536	5	6	5	6	6	6	8	6	9	5	8	5	12
3	Detroit Tigers	Detroit Tigers	2003	43	119		0	85	162	0.525	9	8	6	7	8	9	6	5	11	6	10		11
4	New York Yankees	New York Yankees	1939	106	45	1	71	6	151	0.510	12	6	5	5	6	8	5	5	10	8	7		11
5	Baltimore Orioles	St. Louis Browns	1949	53	101	1	11	66	154	0.500	7	10	11	5	5	5	6	8	6	7	7		11
6	New York Mets	New York Mets	1962	40	120	1	0	79	160	0.494	9	17	7	5	11	5	13	5	7				9
7	Chicago Cubs	Chicago Cubs	1906	116	36	3	75	0	152	0.493	10	5	6	7	5	11	14	12	5				9
8	Cincinnati Reds	Cincinnati Reds	1914	60	94	3	**29**	**46**	**154**	**0.487**	5	6	7	7	5	8	6	19	5				10
9	Atlanta Braves	Boston Doves	1909	45	108	2	5	69	153	0.484	13	6	11	5	5	15	5	5	9				9
10	Minnesota Twins	Washington Nationals(1)	1909	42	110	4	0	73	152	0.480	5	5	5	6	5	5	6	7	6	11	6	6	12

Table 10. Back-to-Back-to-Back-to-Back Streaks

			Streak Type and Length						
Current Franchise	Team	Season	First	Second	Third	Fourth	Total Games	Season Summary	Notes
Baltimore Orioles	St. Louis Browns	1903	W8	L7	W5	L11	31	65–74, 6th of 8	No other streaks >5 games
Pittsburgh Pirates	Pittsburgh Pirates	1914	W8	L6	W8	L10	32	69–85–4, 7th of 8	One tie in each loss streak
Chicago Cubs	Chicago Cubs	1920	W9	L10	W6	L5	30	75–79, 5th of 8	
Oakland Athletics	Philadelphia Athletics	1948	L5	W5	L8	W5	23	84–70, 4th of 8	

STREAKS OF 10 OR MORE GAMES BY FRANCHISE

Table 11 lists the total number of winning and losing streaks of 10 or more games for each current franchise. The Yankees boast the most winning streaks and the fewest losing streaks. They are also one of just nine franchises with more winning streaks than losing streaks.

In order to provide a better comparative assessment, Figure 1 normalizes the data in Table 11 based on the number of seasons each franchise has played.

Table 11. Streaks of 10 or More Games by Franchise

Current Franchise	First Season	No of Seasons	W	L	PCT
Atlanta Braves	1901	123	16	27	.372
Arizona Diamondbacks	1998	26	2	5	.286
Baltimore Orioles	1901	123	15	34	.306
Boston Red Sox	1901	123	25	13	.658
Chicago Cubs	1901	123	23	18	.561
Chicago White Sox	1901	123	12	13	.480
Cincinnati Reds	1901	123	12	20	.375
Cleveland Guardians	1901	123	23	11	.676
Colorado Rockies	1993	31	3	4	.429
Detroit Tigers	1901	123	14	22	.389
Houston Astros	1962	62	14	8	.636
Kansas City Royals	1969	55	5	12	.294
Los Angeles Angels	1961	63	5	9	.357
Los Angeles Dodgers	1901	123	27	14	.659
Miami Marlins	**1993**	**31**	**0**	**4**	**.000**
Milwaukee Brewers	1969	55	7	8	.467
Minnesota Twins	1901	123	17	30	.362
New York Mets	1962	62	9	13	.409
New York Yankees	**1903**	**121**	**32**	**2**	**.941**
Oakland Athletics	1901	123	22	34	.393
Philadelphia Phillies	1901	123	8	32	.200
Pittsburgh Pirates	1901	123	28	16	.636
San Diego Padres	1969	55	5	8	.385
Seattle Mariners	1977	47	4	9	.308
San Francisco Giants	1901	123	26	8	.765
St. Louis Cardinals	1901	123	12	12	.500
Tampa Bay Rays	1998	26	3	9	.250
Texas Rangers	1961	63	4	11	.267
Toronto Blue Jays	1977	47	6	3	.667
Washington Nationals	1969	55	5	6	.455

Figure 1. Streaks of 10 or More Games per Season With Winning Average

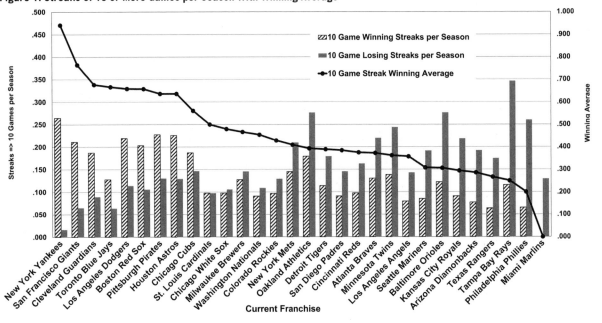

The Yankees and the Marlins represent opposite ends of the streak spectrum.

In their 121-year history, the Yankees have gone on more than twice as many winning streaks of five or more games per season than the Miami Marlins (4.19 to 1.77). They have also gone on fewer than half as many losing streaks (1.57 to 3.26). This disparity is even more pronounced when considering streaks of 10 games or more. The Yankees have had 32 winning streaks, while the Marlins have had zero in their 31 years of existence. On the losing side, the Marlins have had four losing streaks of 10 or more games, while the Yankees have had half as many in nearly four times as many seasons. Perhaps more impressive, neither of the Yankees' losing streaks of ten-plus games have come in the last 110 years.

The only long losing streaks in Yankees history were 12 games in 1908 (when they were sometimes also called the Highlanders) and 13 games in 1913. The 1908 season represents the nadir of the franchise. They finished in last place in the American League, 39½ games out, with a record of 51–103–1. On June 9, they had a winning record of 23–20. They then proceeded to lose 52 of their next 62 games, including 19 losses in 20 games starting on July 23. By August 18, they had fallen to 33–72. In 1912, the team went 50–102–1, with a season-long losing streak of nine games. On June 6, 1913, following a 13-game losing streak, the Yankees found themselves with a record of 9–34–2. They then rallied to compile a 48–60 record over the final 108 games, escaping the American League cellar and finishing at 57–94–2. Never again would they finish a season with a winning average below .414 (Figure 2).

Table 12. Total Streak Details for Yankees and Marlins

		New York Yankees		Miami Marlins	
	First Season >	1903		1993	
	No. of Seasons >	121		31	
		Total	Per Season	Total	Per Season
Streaks from 5 - 9	W	475	3.93	55	1.77
	L	188	1.55	97	3.13
	AVG	.716		.362	
Streaks =>10	W	32	0.26	0	0.00
	L	2	0.02	4	0.13
	AVG	.941		.000	
All Streaks => 5	W	507	4.19	55	1.77
	L	190	1.57	101	3.26
	AVG	.727		.353	

Figure 2. New York Yankees Winning Averages

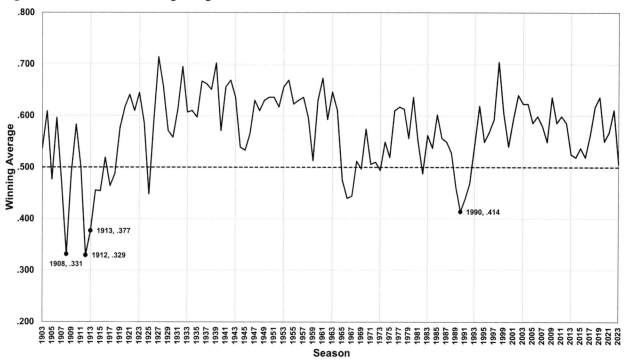

SEASONAL YIN AND YANG

Table 13 shows the 23 teams with both a winning streak and a losing streak of at least 10 games in the same season. The 1982 Atlanta Braves and the 1987 Milwaukee Brewers ran off 13-game winning streaks to start their seasons, then later had losing streaks of 11 and 12 games, respectively. The Tampa Bay Rays started 2023 with a 13-game win streak, but never lost more than seven games in a row that season. Table 14 summarizes the highs and low of various entries.

FINAL REMARKS

Winning and losing streaks are an under-researched corner of baseball history, making the news only when some particularly great or terrible team approaches a record. In writing this paper, I uncovered many new insights that helped me foster a keener awareness of baseball's rich history:

- The Marlins are the only team that has never run the longest winning streak, while only the Padres have never run the longest losing streak. The Yankees have led baseball with the longest seasonal winning streak 16 times, but only twice with the longest losing streak.

- The 1982 Braves, 1987 Brewers, and 2023 Rays are the only teams ever to begin a season with

Table 13. Teams with Both 10-Game Winning and Losing Streaks in the Same Season

	Current Franchise	Team	Season	W	L	T	AVG	LWS	LLS	Streak Total	Sequence	Start Game	Gap	End Game
1	Minnesota Twins	Washington Nationals(1)	1921	80	73	1	.523	11	10	21	WL	97	16	133
2	Minnesota Twins	Washington Nationals(1)	1927	85	69	3	.552	10	12	22	WL	61	43	126*
3	Cleveland Guardians	Cleveland Indians	1931	78	76	1	.506	10	12	22	LW	19	3	43
4	Pittsburgh Pirates	Pittsburgh Pirates	1932	86	68	0	.558	11	10	21	LW	98	17	135
5	Los Angeles Dodgers	Brooklyn Dodgers	1943	81	72	0	.529	10	10	20	LW	94	16	129
6	Chicago Cubs	Chicago Cubs	1944	75	79	3	.487	11	13	24	LW	2	71	96
7	San Francisco Giants	New York Giants	1951	98	59	0	.624	16	11	27	LW	4	96	126
8	Philadelphia Phillies	Philadelphia Phillies	1955	77	77	0	.500	11	13	24	LW	16	57	96
9	Cincinnati Reds	Cincinnati Redlegs	1957	80	74	0	.519	12	10	22	WL	12	87	120
10	Oakland Athletics	Kansas City Athletics	1959	66	88	0	.429	11	13	24	WL	89	26	138
11	Chicago Cubs	Chicago Cubs	1970	84	78	0	.519	11	12	23	WL	5	45	72
12	Chicago White Sox	Chicago White Sox	1976	64	97	0	.398	10	10	20	WL	26	14	59
13	Cleveland Guardians	Cleveland Indians	1979	81	80	0	.503	10	10	20	LW	63	23	105
14	Atlanta Braves	Atlanta Braves	1982	89	73	0	.549	13	11	24	WL	1	90	114
15	Minnesota Twins	Minnesota Twins	1985	77	85	0	.475	10	10	20	WL	12	16	47
16	Milwaukee Brewers	Milwaukee Brewers	1987	91	71	0	.562	13	12	25	WL	1	10	35
17	Baltimore Orioles	Baltimore Orioles	1987	67	95	0	.414	11	10	21	LW	52	26	98
18	New York Mets	New York Mets	1991	77	84	0	.478	10	11	21	WL	74	24	118
19	Cincinnati Reds	Cincinnati Reds	1998	77	85	0	.475	10	11	21	LW	69	6	95
20	Baltimore Orioles	Baltimore Orioles	1999	78	84	0	.481	13	10	23	LW	70	58	150
21	Tampa Bay Rays	Tampa Bay Devil Rays	2004	70	91	0	.435	12	12	24	WL	56	60	139
22	Cleveland Guardians	Cleveland Indians	2008	81	81	0	.500	10	10	20	LW	81	32	132
23	Los Angeles Dodgers	Los Angeles Dodgers	2017	104	58	0	.642	11**	11	22	WL	85	38	144

* The 1927 Washington Nationals had a tie game within their 12-game losing streak

** In addition to the 11-game winning streak, the 2017 LA Dodgers had a 10-game winning streak

Table 14. Parametric Highs and Lows of Table 13

Item of Interest	Team	Season	Value	
Lowest winning average	Chicago White Sox	1976	.398	
Highest winning average	Los Angeles Dodgers	2017	.642	
Highest combined streak lengths	New York Giants	1951	27 (LWS 16, LLS 11)	
Most Wins	Los Angeles Dodgers	2017	104	
Fewest Wins	Chicago White Sox	1976	64	
Most Losses	Chicago White Sox	1976	97	
Fewest Losses	Los Angeles Dodgers	2017	58	
Only year with two teams		1987	Milwaukee Brewers and Baltimore Orioles	
Earliest start of first streak	Atlanta Braves	1982	Game Number	1
Earliest start of first streak	Milwaukee BrewersA	1987		1
Latest start of first streak	Pittsburgh Pirates	1932		98
Smallest gap between streaks	Cleveland Indians	1931		3
Largest gap between streaks	New York Giants	1951		96
Earliest finish of second streak	Milwaukee Brewers	1987		35
Latest finish of second streak	Baltimore Orioles	1999		150
More than two => 10 game streaks	Los Angeles Dodgers	2017	Winning Streaks 10 and 11 Losing Streak 11	

13 straight wins. Both the Braves and the Brewers ran a losing streak of at least 11 games later during the same season.

- The 1916 New York Giants lost 13 of their first 15 games, then came back to post winnings streaks of 26 games (all at home, with one tie) and 17 games (all on the road). They finished in fourth place in the eight-team National League.

- In 1940, neither Philadelphia team won more than three games in a row.

- Only four teams have strung together four alternate decision streaks of at least five games in a row: 1903 St. Louis Browns, 1914 Pirates, 1920 Cubs, and 1948 Philadelphia Athletics.

- Only once have two teams in the same season had both winning and losing streaks of at least 10 games: the 1987 Milwaukee Brewers and Baltimore Orioles.

- Starting on May 7, 1931, the Cleveland Indians lost 12 games in a row, won one, lost two, then proceeded to reel off 10 straight wins.

- If you count the short 2020 season, then the 2020 Yankees were the streakiest team of all time, with 58.3% of their decisions coming during a streak. If you discount 2020, the crown belongs to the 1919 Philadelphia Athletics, who went 36-104 and notched 12 different losing streaks of at least five games for a TSQ of 53.6%.

The research for this paper and its predecessor has been challenging, time-consuming, and extremely gratifying. Baseball's history is laden with countless hidden treasures still to be discovered. The SABR archives and research tools, along with many other online resources, allow an inspired fan to explore just about any aspect of baseball history that stimulates their curiosity. My next goal is to convert the interactive database I developed for this project into a hands-on tool that allows fans to visualize and explore the world of baseball streaks. ∎

Acknowledgments
During the SABR52 convention in Minneapolis this past summer (my very first), I met many ardent baseball fans who share my passion for research and history. The panel discussions with Hall of Famers, other players, and team executives were priceless. I encourage all serious baseball fans to seek out a local SABR chapter to join and collaborate with people who share your enthusiasm for our national pastime.

Jews and Baseball: Part Two

Anti-Semitism, Superstars, Rebels, Owners, Managers, and Executives

Peter Dreier

Part One of this article, "Jews and Baseball," can be found in the last issue of BRJ *(Vol 53 No 1).*

ANTI-SEMITISM

As millions of immigrants arrived in the late nineteenth and early twentieth centuries, America became a cauldron of nativist and anti-Semitic vitriol. Jews were the subject of vicious stereotypes in films, books, plays, and other forms of popular culture. They faced discrimination in jobs and housing. Colleges imposed quotas on Jewish students. Many hotels, resorts, and clubs barred Jews.[1] Anti-Jewish stereotypes were common and widely promulgated. For example, during World War I, a US Army manual published for recruits stated, "The foreign born, and especially Jews, are more apt to malinger than the native-born."[2] Jews in general, and Jewish ballplayers, faced constant verbal and physical abuse.

Anti-Semitism was exacerbated by the 1919 Black Sox Scandal, when the Chicago White Sox threw the World Series to the Cincinnati Reds. Gamblers Arnold Rothstein and former featherweight boxing champion Abe Attell, both Jews, were implicated in the fix. Auto magnate Henry Ford blamed Jews for the entire scandal. His anti-Semitic newspaper, the *Dearborn Independent*, published articles with titles such as "Jewish Gamblers Corrupt American Baseball" and "The Jewish Degradation of American Baseball." In one article, Ford wrote, "If fans wish to know the trouble with American baseball, they have it in three words—too much Jew."[3]

The Sporting News, the influential weekly baseball newspaper, blamed "outsiders" for threatening the sanctity of baseball. The anti-Jewish stereotypes were unmistakable. The paper claimed that "a lot of dirty, long-nosed, thick-lipped, and strong-smelling gamblers butted into the World Series—an American event, by the way."[4]

Like other Jewish players, Andy Cohen, who played for the New York Giants from 1926 to 1929, had to endure being called epithets like "kike" and "Hebe." After a spectator called him "Christ Killer" during a minor-league game, Cohen, bat in hand, found the offending fan and shouted, "Yeah, come down here and I'll kill you, too."[5]

Prior to the 1930s, many Jewish ballplayers changed their names, hoping to avoid anti-Semitism. At least five players named Cohen played in the big leagues during that period, but only one, Andy Cohen, used his birth name. The others called themselves Cooney, Bohne, Corey, and Ewing. Joseph Rosenblum played one game in the major leagues in 1923 as Joe Bennett. (The losing pitcher for the Philadelphia Phillies that day was Lefty Weinert. It marked the first time that two Jewish teammates appeared in the same major-league game).

While a member of the minor-league Los Angeles Angels in the 1920s, Jimmie Reese, who would play for the New York Yankees and St. Louis Cardinals in 1930–32, played in an exhibition game against Hollywood celebrities and retired major leaguers. The celeb team's battery consisted of two Jews—pitcher Harry Ruby, the composer of many hit songs, including "I Wanna Be Loved By You," "Three Little Words," and "Who's Sorry Now?" and minor-league catcher Ike Danning. Rather than use conventional hand signals, Danning called the game in Yiddish, certain that no Angels players would understand. Reese had four hits. After the game a surprised Ruby remarked, "I didn't know you were that good a hitter, Jimmie." Reese said, "You also didn't know that my name was Hymie Solomon."[6]

Sportswriters of that era routinely mentioned players' religion when known. Barney Pelty—an outstanding pitcher for the St. Louis Browns from 1903 to 1912—was called the "Yiddisher curver."[7] While pitching for the Brooklyn Dodgers' minor league franchise in Allentown, Pennsylvania, in 1936, Sam Nahem used an alias, "Sam Nichols," but his secret wasn't very well-hidden. The *Allentown Call* noted that "The Allentown Brooks this season may have one of the rarities of organized baseball, an all-Jewish battery," explaining that the catcher, Jim Smilgoff, was "of Hebraic extraction" while Sam Nichols was "also of Jewish parentage."[8]

A 1938 poll found that about 60 percent of Americans held a low opinion of Jews, labeling them "greedy," "dishonest," and "pushy." In 1939, a Roper

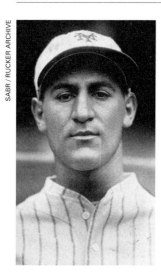

Andy Cohen played shortstop and second base in three seasons with the New York Giants.

poll found that only 39 percent of Americans felt that Jews should be treated like other people. Fifty-three percent believed that "Jews are different and should be restricted" and 10 percent believed Jews should be deported. A 1945 survey found that 23 percent of Americans would vote for a congressional candidate who declared "himself as being against the Jews."[9]

As Jews gained more acceptance and self-confidence in America, fewer Jewish ballplayers changed their names, but anti-Semitism didn't disappear.

During spring training in 1934, the Giants were staying in a hotel in Florida with a "no Jews" policy. The hotel refused to allow two Jewish players—Phil Weintraub and Harry Danning, Ike's more famous younger brother—to register. Manager Bill Terry threatened to take the entire team to another hotel. The hotel manager backed down.[10]

Hank Greenberg, the first Jewish superstar, who played from 1930 to 1947, faced persistent anti-Semitism. Although he wasn't religious, Greenberg was proud of his Jewish identity and knew he was a role model for Jews and a symbol of his people to non-Jews. On September 18, 1934, when he was leading the American League in RBIs and his Detroit Tigers were in first place, he attended Yom Kippur services rather than play in that day's game. When he arrived at the synagogue, the congregation gave him a standing ovation.

Detroit was among the country's most anti-Semitic cities—home of not only Ford but also radio priest Charles Coughlin. When the US government agreed to accept some Jewish refugees from Germany in the mid-1930s, Coughlin said, "Send the Jews back where they came from in leaky boats."[11]

According to fellow Tiger Birdie Tebbetts, "There was nobody in the history of the game who took more abuse than Greenberg, unless it was Jackie Robinson."[12]

During his playing career, the 6-foot-4 Greenberg occasionally challenged bigots to fight him one-on-one. He often said that he felt every home run he hit was a home run against Hitler. "How the hell could you get up to home plate every day and have some son-of-a-bitch call you a Jew bastard and a kike and a sheenie and get on your ass without feeling the pressure?" he said. "If the ballplayers weren't doing it, the fans were. I used to get frustrated as hell. Sometimes I wanted to go into the stands and beat the shit out of them."[13]

During the 1935 World Series, umpire George Moriarty warned Chicago Cubs players to stop screaming anti-Semitic insults at Greenberg and Jewish umpire Dolly Stark (whom Cubs players called a "Christ killer"). By the time the game was over, Moriarty had cleared much of the Cubs dugout. Commissioner Kenesaw Mountain Landis fined Moriarty $250 for his actions but did not discipline the bigoted players.[14]

In 1938, when Greenberg hit 58 home runs, two short of Babe Ruth's 1927 record, he faced regular anti-Semitic insults from fans who hated the idea that a Jew might overtake the beloved Babe's milestone. There is evidence that as Greenberg closed in on the record late in the season, pitchers pitched around him to make sure he didn't break it.[15] Tebbetts recalled that one pitcher shouted to Greenberg, "You're not going to get any home runs off me, you Jewish son of a bitch." Greenberg hit two home runs against him.[16]

But Greenberg had his allies. St. Louis Browns first baseman George McQuinn "deliberately dropped a foul ball to give me another chance," Greenberg remembered.[17]

According to Greenberg, "Being Jewish and being the object of a lot of derogatory remarks kept me on my toes all the time. I could never relax and be one of the boys, so to speak. So I think it helped me in my career because it always made me aware of the fact that I had a little extra burden to bear and it made me a better ballplayer."[18]

After Greenberg, the next Jewish superstar was Al Rosen. During his playing career, from 1947–56, all with the Cleveland Indians, Rosen banged 192 homers, drove in 717 runs, and batted .285. He played in every All-Star Game from 1952–55 and won the American League MVP Award in 1953, leading the league in homers (43) and RBIs (145) while batting .336.

Rosen grew up Miami—in the only Jewish family in a Cuban neighborhood. He got into many fights when others called him anti-Semitic names, which led him to become an excellent boxer in college and in the military during World War II. He dropped out of the

University of Florida to play in the minors, where he constantly faced anti-Semitic taunts, especially in Southern towns. The anti-Semitism didn't stop when he reached the majors. After a White Sox player called him a "Jew bastard," Rosen walked over to the dugout and asked whoever called him that name to step forward. No one did. "When I was in the majors," Rosen said, "I always knew how I wanted it to be about me....Here comes one Jewish kid that every Jew in the world can be proud of."[19]

Dodgers pitcher Don Newcombe recalled that behind Sandy Koufax's back, his own teammates called him "this kike," "this Jew bastard," and "Jew sonofabitch....They hated Jews as much as they hated Blacks."[20] After a spring-training night game in Miami during the mid-1950s, some Dodgers complained about having to ride a non-air-conditioned bus. Coach Billy Herman, sitting across from Koufax, yelled loudly, "You can give this damn town back to the Jews." After a few moments of silence, Koufax tried to defuse the situation: "Now, Billy, you know we've already got it."[21]

Ken Holtzman, the only Jew on the Chicago Cubs' roster from 1966 to 1971, faced anti-Semitic bigotry from manager Leo Durocher. The poorly-educated Durocher resented Holtzman's college education, his cerebral manner (he would read books in airport terminals while waiting for a flight), his ability to beat Durocher at gin rummy, and his strong pro-union attitude. Durocher (who also referred to Marvin Miller, the head of the players' union, as "that goddam Jew bastard") constantly berated Holtzman and called him a "kike" and "gutless Jew" in front of his teammates. In 1970, Durocher removed Holtzman from a game he was winning 6-4 with two outs in the fifth inning. Had he stayed in and gotten one more out, Holtzman would have been the winning pitcher. According to one analysis, "Holtzman's background—specifically his upbringing as an observant Jew who refused to pitch on Jewish holidays and who adhered to Jewish dietary laws—contributed to Durocher's increasingly antagonistic behavior toward Holtzman." Durocher demeaned other players as well; he referred to Ron Santo as a "wop," called the college-educated Don Kessinger a "dumb hillbilly," and degraded the Cubs' Black players. The players rebelled and by the 1972 All-Star game, Durocher was fired.[22]

MISTAKEN IDENTITY

Some players with Jewish-sounding names have been mistaken for Jews by fans, sportswriters, and players. The Jewish Baseball News website even has a "Not a Jew" section identifying non-Jewish players with Jewish-sounding names like Blum, Eckstein, Lowenstein, Rosenberg, Rosenthal, and Weiss.[23] For example, Charley "Buck" Herzog, joined the New York Giants in 1908. Sportswriters wrongly assumed he was Jewish because of his name and facial features and claimed that he attracted fans among fellow Jews. "The long-nosed rooters are crazy whenever young Herzog does anything noteworthy," one sportswriter wrote, adding that "there would be no let-up even if a million ham sandwiches suddenly fell among these believers in percentages and bargains."[24]

Avowedly Christian ballplayers with Jewish ancestry are not considered Jews by Jewish Baseball News (nor by themselves), but that did not stop them from facing anti-Semitism. Charles Solomon (Buddy) Myer Jr. played for 17 years (1925–41) with the Washington Nationals and Boston Red Sox, won a batting title, was a two-time All-Star (although he played his first seven years before the first All-Star Game), and had a lifetime .303 batting average. Jewish sportswriters such as the *Washington Post*'s Shirley Povich, who covered the Nationals every day, routinely referred to him as a Jew. After he led the AL in batting in 1935 with a .349 average, *The Sporting News*, baseball's paper of record, reported that the Yankees were trying to purchase Myer's contract from the Senators. The headline on its story: "Yanks Hope to Dress in Myer a Tailor-Made Jewish Star." The story said that the Yankees hoped that New York's "big army of Jewish fans...would be lured into the park by a Jewish star." Sportswriter Fred Lieb ranked Myer as the second-greatest Jewish player of all time, after Greenberg.[25] (This was before Rosen and Koufax.)

Myer faced anti-Semitic abuse. Opposing players called him a kike. Pitchers threw at his head. In 1933, Yankees outfielder Ben Chapman (a notorious bigot who later taunted Jackie Robinson with racist slurs) intentionally spiked Myer when he slid into second base. The two players got into a fistfight that led to a benches-clearing brawl requiring police intervention. The next day, Povich wrote that Chapman "cut a swastika with his spikes on Myer's thigh."[26] After AL President William Harridge fined and suspended both players, Myer protested. "Chapman had it coming to him and I gave it to him," he said, recalling that he'd spiked him in the past. "I had to retaliate to stop him before he ended my baseball career."[27] Many newspapers reported the incident, but few mentioned its cause.

Myer is included in Peter S. and Joachim Horvitz's *The Big Book of Jewish Baseball*, Burton A. and Benita W. Boxerman's multi-volume *Jews and Baseball*, and Erwin Lynn's *The Jewish Baseball Hall of*

SABR / RUCKER ARCHIVE

Barney Pelty pitched for the St. Louis Browns 1903–12.

Fame.[28] In 1992, he was inducted into the International Jewish Sports Hall of Fame. These errors are understandable. His birth name was Charles Solomon Myer. And his father owned a clothing store.

But Myer wasn't Jewish.

Myer was born in Ellisville, Mississippi, in 1904, the fourth of five children of Charles Solomon Myer and the former Maud Stevens. The family were originally German Jews but had converted to Christianity at least two generations before Buddy was born. When he died in 1974, his obituary listed him as a member of the First Baptist Church in Baton Rouge, Louisiana.[29] "He was raised Baptist," his son Dick said. "He didn't think it was right when they inducted him into the Jewish Hall of Fame, but he didn't correct them because he was afraid it would be taken the wrong way."

Such misidentification was not left behind in the twenty-first century. On May 28, 2006, as part of the Florida Marlins' Jewish Heritage Day promotion, the team gave away Mike Jacobs jersey T-shirts to young fans in attendance. The Marlins mentioned their third baseman in the promotion material for the event. But Jacobs isn't Jewish.

Some lists of Jewish players incorrectly include Hall of Famer Lou Boudreau, but although he had a Jewish mother, he was raised as a Catholic and did not identify as a Jew. Some include Johnny Kling and Rod Carew, who both married Jewish women but did not convert to Judaism. Some writers have mentioned longtime player, pitching coach, and manager Larry Rothschild and former player and current San Francisco Giants manager Bob Melvin as Jews.[31] Rothschild had a Jewish father and Melvin had a Jewish mother, but both were raised as and identify as Christians.

HALL OF FAMERS, ALL-STARS, AND RECORD BREAKERS

There are five Jews in the National Baseball Hall of Fame in Cooperstown, not to mention the two who have served as president, **Jeff Idelson** (2008–19) and **Josh Rawitch** (2021–present). Two are players: **Greenberg** and **Koufax**. **Marvin Miller** was the first executive director of the Major League Baseball Players Association. **Barney Dreyfuss** of the Pittsburgh Pirates and **Bud Selig** of the Milwaukee Brewers were owners (although Selig was inducted as a commissioner).

Twenty-two Jews have been selected to major-league All-Star teams, as shown in Table 1. (All tables can be found in the Appendix in the digital version of this article on the SABR website.) Ryan Braun and Koufax each made the team six times, Greenberg (who missed all of three seasons and parts of two others for service during World War II) was selected five times, and Harry Danning, Al Rosen, and Ian Kinsler made it four times.[32]

Some additional facts of note about Jews and baseball's record books:

- Three Jewish players have made the same All-Star game three times: 1939 (Greenberg, Morrie Arnovich, and Danning); 1999 (Brad Ausmus, Shawn Green, and Mike Lieberthal); and 2008 (Kevin Youkilis, Braun, and Kinsler).

- Four Jews have won the MVP Award: Greenberg (1935 and 1940) and Rosen (1953) in the AL; Koufax (1963) and Braun (2011) in the National League.[33]

- Seven Jews have won Gold Glove Awards: Green (1999); Lieberthal (1999); Ausmus (2001, 2002, 2006); Youkilis (2007); Kinsler (2016, 2018), Max Fried (2020–22); and Harrison Bader (2021).[34]

- One Jew has won the Rookie of the Year Award: Braun in the NL in 2007.[35]

- Lipman Pike led his league (the National Association 1871–73 and the National League in 1877 in home runs four times. Greenberg led the AL in homers four times (1935, 1938, 1940, 1946 in the AL). Rosen did it twice (1950, 1953 in the AL) and Braun once (2012 in the NL).

- League RBI leaders have been Pike in the National Association (1872) Greenberg (1935, 1937, 1940, 1946) and Rosen (1952–53) in the AL.

- Two Jews have won the Cy Young Award: Koufax (1963, 1965, 1966) in the NL and Steve Stone (1980) in the AL.[36]

- Koufax led the NL in wins in 1963, 1965, and 1966. Stone earned that honor in the AL in 1980.

- In 1951, Saul Rogovin had the lowest ERA of any pitcher in the AL.

- Koufax is the only NL pitcher to lead the league in ERA for five years in a row (1962–66). He was the major-league strikeout leader in 1961, 1963, 1965, and 1966.

Some major league records owned by Jewish players:

- Green set the record for most total bases in one game (19) on May 23, 2002. He went 6-for-6, with four home runs (tying the record), a double, and a single (his five extra-base hits tied the record), scored six runs, and had seven RBIs. Green's four home runs tied the record (with 17 others) for most homers in one game.

- On August 22, 1917, Jake Pitler had 15 putouts at second base in a 22-inning game.

- On August 12, 1966, Art Shamsky became the first (and still only) player to hit three home runs in a game he didn't start.
- Youkilis had 2,002 consecutive chances at first base without an error and 238 consecutive games at first base without an error. Those streaks ended on June 7, 2008.

- On April 6, 1973, Ron Blomberg of the Yankees became major-league baseball's first designated hitter. Boston Red Sox pitcher Luis Tiant walked him on five pitches with the bases loaded.

- On August 1, 1918, Erskine Mayer participated in one of the greatest pitching duels in history. Starting for the Pirates against the Braves at Boston, he and Braves starter Art Nehf pitched scoreless baseball for 15 innings. Wilbur Cooper finally relieved Mayer with one out in the 16th inning and got the win when the Pirates pushed across two runs against Nehf in the 21st.[37]

On April 30, 1944, the New York Giants scored 26 runs in a game at the Polo Grounds against the Brooklyn Dodgers. The Giants' Jewish first baseman, Phil Weintraub, knocked in 11 of those runs, one short of the record set by Jim Bottomley in 1924. He went 4-for-5, with two doubles, a triple, and a home run, as well as two walks. Mark Whiten of the St. Louis Cardinals tied Bottomley's record in 1993. So Weintraub's 11 RBIs in one game remains the third most in major league history, tied with Tony Lazzeri.[38]

The "wandering Jew" award goes to pitcher Craig Breslow, who played for 7 different teams during his 12-year career (2005–17). Breslow graduated from Yale, but Moe Berg, a graduate of both Princeton and Columbia University Law School, had two Ivy League degrees. Berg (1923–39) worked as a spy for the predecessor to the CIA and allegedly spoke 12 languages—"but," a teammate once said, "he can't hit in any of them."

NOT QUITE A MINYAN

No major-league team has ever had a minyan—the quorum of 10 Jews required for a worship service. But there have been occasions when an unusual number of Jews were on the same team or on the field at the same time.

At Sid Gordon's first major-league game, on September 11, 1941, the Giants had four Jewish players on the roster: Gordon, Morrie Arnovich, Harry Feldman, and Harry Danning. All four of them played in the same game on September 21. That number has never been surpassed. The 1946 Giants had five Jewish players—Arnovich, Gordon, Feldman, Goody Rosen, and Mike Schemer, the most Jews on one team in one season—but they were never all on the field at the same time.

On August 8, 2005, the Red Sox set an AL record when three Jewish players (Youkilis, Adam Stern, and Gabe Kapler) took the field at the same time. The following year, Breslow joined the Red Sox, setting an AL record of four Jews on the same roster during a season, but Stern had left the team by the time Breslow arrived. Breslow, Youkilis, and Kapler tied the record by playing at the same time in several games.[39]

There have been at least nine all-Jewish batteries, when a Jewish pitcher and Jewish catcher played on the same team and in at least one game together. These include Feldman and Danning (1941–42 Giants); brothers Larry and Norm Sherry, as well as Norm catching Koufax (1959–62 Los Angeles Dodgers); Rogovin and Joe Ginsberg (1950–51 Tigers); Jason Hirsh and Ausmus (2006 Houston Astros); Breslow and Ryan Lavarnway (2012 Red Sox); Eli Morgan and Lavarnway (2021 Indians); Bubby Rossman and Garrett Stubbs (2022 Phillies); and Max Lazar and Stubbs (2024 Phillies).[40]

There have been a handful of trifectas. On May 2, 1951, Rogovin was pitching for the Tigers, Ginsberg was catching, and Lou Limmer came to bat for the Philadelphia Athletics.[41] Twice since then, a Jewish battery faced a Jewish hitter. On August 15, 2013, Breslow, pitching for the Red Sox, struck out Toronto Blue Jay Kevin Pillar with Lavarnway behind the plate. On June 22, 2021, with Lavarnway catching for the Indians, Morgan pitched to Cubs outfielder Joc Pederson three times. On August 10, 2024, in his major league debut, Max Lazar, pitching for the Phillies to catcher Garrett Stubbs, struck out the Diamondbacks' Pederson.[42]

In the bottom of the second inning of Game Six of the 2021 World Series, Alex Bregman of the Astros flied out to right field against Braves pitcher Fried. The ball was caught by Pederson.

On September 18, 1996, near the Jewish High Holidays, the Brewers hosted the Blue Jays at County Stadium. When Shawn Green game to bat, he greeted Jesse Levis, the Milwaukee catcher, with a friendly "L'shana tova," Hebrew for happy new year. Then, to Green and Levis' surprise, home-plate umpire Al Clark offered his own "L'shana tova." Clark had grown up as an Orthodox Jew.[43]

In 1966, Koufax and Ken Holtzman of the Cubs told their managers that they wouldn't pitch on Yom Kippur. Instead they pitched the following day, September 25, at Wrigley Field. Koufax lost a 2–1 game to Holtzman. Both pitched complete games. Holtzman had a no-hitter going until the ninth inning, when he gave up two hits. Koufax gave up four hits on the day. Since then, Jewish starting pitchers have faced off four times: On June 20, 1971, Steve Stone of the Giants started against the Padres' Dave Roberts. As a Yankee, Holtzman started a game against Roberts, then with the Tigers, on September 24, 1976, and again on June 22, 1977. Fried, with the Braves, battled Dean Kremer of the Baltimore Orioles on May 5, 2023.

With a few exceptions (including Greenberg, Koufax, Holtzman, Green, and Youkilis) most Jewish players have chosen to play on Yom Kippur. Some have wondered whether there was a "Koufax curse" for Jews who played on the holiest of Jewish holidays. One study identified 36 Jewish players—18 non-pitchers and 18 pitchers—whose teams have been in the World Series since 1966, the year of the Koufax-Holtzman match-up. In 120 games, teams are 53–67 (a .442 winning average) when a Jewish player plays on Yom Kippur. Teams won six of 23 games in which a pitcher is Jewish, a terrible .261 winning average. Although their teams performed poorly, the individual Jewish players performed relatively well. As a group,

the hitters' performance on Yom Kippur matched their career batting average and OPS. Pitchers' performances have been mixed, with several good starts and relief appearances balanced against some poor games.[44]

JEWISH MANAGERS AND COACHES

At least nine Jews have managed big-league teams and at least six Jews have been major-league coaches, as shown in Table 2 in the Appendix online.

Lipman Pike—the first Jewish professional ballplayer and the first home-run slugger—was a player/manager for the Cincinnati Reds (1877).

For most of **Jacob (Jake) Morse**'s career, he was an influential sportswriter in Boston, but in 1884 he managed the Boston Unions during the second half of the season. Born in 1860 in New Hampshire to Jewish immigrants from Bavaria, he was one of 10 children who grew up in Boston, where his extended family, including his uncles, operated a clothing store, worked as lawyers, and were active in politics. Morse attended Harvard and then Boston University's law school. While in law school he wrote articles for several Boston newspapers. He graduated in 1884, the same year St. Louis millionaire Henry Lucas organized the Union Association to compete with the National League and American Association in protest of the owners of the two leagues adopting a reserve clause in players' contracts.

Morse edited the *Union Association Guide* and became friends with Boston's first baseman, Tim Murnane, who was also the field manager. Morse not only wrote articles about the Union Association and the Boston Unions for local papers but helped Murnane manage the team during the latter part of the season, although it is unclear what his responsibilities were. After the Union Association folded at the end of the season, Morse became the full-time sports editor for the *Boston Herald*, a position he held for 20 years. He also wrote a book, *Sphere and Ash: History of Baseball*, published in 1888. By 1892, he and Murnane—who by then was sports editor of the *Boston Globe*—became the administrative staff for the New England League, a minor league. In 1895, he became president of the New England Association, another minor league with teams in Massachusetts. In 1908, Morse founded *Baseball Magazine*, the first monthly periodical devoted to baseball.[45]

Louis (Louie) Heilbroner was an even more unlikely figure to become a major-league manager. He was the St. Louis Cardinals' business manager and manager of concessions in 1900. He had no knowledge of baseball and, at 4-foot-9, had never played the game. But on August 19, 1900, Cardinals manager Patsy Tebeau quit. The team's president and owner, Frank Robison, was desperate to find someone to replace him. He first offered the job to third baseman John McGraw, who turned it down. So Robison handed the job to Heilbroner, with the understanding that McGraw would actually manage the team from third base. (McGraw went on to become one of baseball's great managers, briefly for the Orioles and then for the Giants). Heilbroner managed the Cardinals' last 50 games and had a record of 23 wins, 25 losses, and 2 ties. When the season ended, the Cardinals hired Patsy Donovan to manage and Heilbroner returned to his job as business manager, which he held until 1902. In 1909, he founded Heilbroner's Baseball Bureau Service, the first commercial firm to focus on baseball statistics.[46]

When a long minor-league career and a brief one in the majors with the Giants (1926–29), **Andy Cohen** managed in the minor leagues between 1939 and 1958. In 1960, he was a coach for the Phillies. After manager Eddie Sawyer stepped down after losing the first game of the 1960 season, the Phillies hired Gene Mauch as his replacement, and Cohen managed one game before Mauch could join the team. As a result, Cohen had a perfect 1–0 record as a big-league manager.

In 1963, he became the head coach at the University of Texas at El Paso, remaining in that position until 1978. Cohen Stadium in El Paso is named after Andy and his brother Syd, who pitched in the major leagues from 1934–37. The brothers grew up in El Paso and attended El Paso High School, where Andy was a star in basketball and football and Syd was a star in baseball and was captain of the basketball teams that went to the state finals in his junior and senior years.

Alon Leichman, assistant pitching coach for the Cincinnati Reds, was born in and grew up on a kibbutz in Israel. He played for Cypress (California) College and the University of California at San Diego. Leichman coached Team Israel at the 2017 World Baseball Classic in South Korea and Japan, then pitched for Israel at the 2019 European Baseball Championship, the Africa/Europe 2020 Olympic Qualification tournament, and the 2020 Summer Olympics, held in Tokyo in 2021.[47]

JEWISH UMPIRES

A 2017 article in *USA Today* claimed that John and Mark Hirschbeck and Tim and Bill Welke are the only sets of brothers to be major-league umpires.[48] But brothers **Israel** and **Lipman Pike** both held that job during baseball's early days. Israel was likely the first Jewish professional umpire, working in the National Association in 1875. Lipman also umpired after his playing days were over, in 1887 and 1889 in Double A and in 1890 in the NL.

Since 1900, at least four Jews have worked as major-league umpires, and each of them faced tragedy and/or scandal.

Dolly Stark was born on November 4, 1897, to a poor Jewish family on Manhattan's Lower East Side. After his father died and his mother became blind, Stark was briefly homeless until a policeman arranged for him to live in an orphanage. Turning to baseball, the 115-pounder played second base in an industrial league and then in the minors from 1917–21 and tried out unsuccessfully for the Yankees and Nationals. A friend asked him to umpire a college game in Vermont, which led to more work in college and Eastern League games. After three weeks, his impressive performance led to his promotion to the NL, where he umpired from 1928–40, except during the 1936 season, when he and Bill Dyer formed the Phillies' first radio announcing team on WCAU. He was the first big-league umpire to move around to be in position to make the right call. From 1923–36, during much of his umpiring career, he also coached the Dartmouth College basketball team.[49]

A trick knee forced Stark to retire from umpiring at the age of 44. No team would hire him as a manager, coach, or scout. He designed women's clothes and briefly had a successful line of apparel called the Dolly Stark Dress. But he couldn't make ends meet. He supported his blind mother and his sister, who was in poor health and eventually committed suicide. Baseball had no pension system and his Social Security check was insufficient. He died of a heart attack in 1968 at the age of 71.

Stan Landes pitched in the low minors in 1946 and 1947, posting a 2–2 record. When it was clear his playing days were numbered, he switched to umpiring. After a few years in the minor leagues, he made it to the majors in 1955, working until 1972. During his 18-year big-league career he umpired 2,874 regular season games, working three World Series and three All-Star Games. He was also an NBA referee. In 1964, he was elected president of the Umpires Association and for years was publicly critical of the NL's treatment of umpires. In 1968, he complained about the players and umpires being forced to play a World Series game during a rainstorm. In 1970, he joined other umpires in picketing outside the NL playoffs in Pittsburgh. In November 1972, the day after Landes was outspoken about umpires' low pay and working conditions at an Umpires Association meeting, he received a letter from NL President Charles Feeney firing him without providing an explanation. "He won't answer my calls and he won't answer my letters," said Landes. Umpires, he noted, "are usually treated as the lowest form of labor."[50] A year later, he was working in a hardware store in Milwaukee. He died in 1994, aged 70.[51]

Al Forman umpired his first game in 1953, during the Korean War, while he was serving in the military in Virginia. After leaving the military the next year, he attended Fairleigh Dickinson University for two years and then completed the Al Somers Umpire School in 1956. He umpired in the minor leagues before being promoted to the majors in 1961, filling that role for the NL through 1965, when he was let go for unspecified reasons other than "we thought someone else could do a better job."[52] He continued to umpire at the college level for many years, and was hired by the AL as a "replacement"— which his colleagues called a strikebreaker—for four games when umpires went on strike in 1978 and 1979. He couldn't make ends meet from the $30 a game he received as a college umpire so he also worked as a sales representative for a liquor company in New Jersey.[53]

Al Clark's father, sports editor of the *Trenton Times*, raised his son as an Orthodox Jew. Al began umpiring while he was still in high school. After college, he attended umpire school and apprenticed in the minors before being promoted to the major leagues, umpiring from 1976 to 2001. He was the first umpire to wear glasses on a regular basis and one of the first AL umps to abandon using the old-style outside chest protector. In his 26-year career, he umpired 3,392 major-league games and worked two All-Star Games and two World Series. In 2001, MLB fired Clark for downgrading his first-class airline tickets to economy class and pocketing the difference. In 2004, Clark was indicted on federal mail fraud charges for participating in a scam in which baseballs were falsely authenticated as having been used in noteworthy games, inflating their value when sold to collectors. He pled guilty and was sentenced to four months in prison, followed by four months under house arrest. His memoir, *Called Out but Safe: A Baseball Umpire's Journey*, was published in 2014.[54]

BASEBALL REBELS

Jewish players, as well as Jewish sportswriters and others, have played significant roles in challenging racial, sex, and other barriers in the sport.[55]

When **Morrie Arnovich** was inducted into the Army in 1942, he was assigned to Fort Lewis, Washington, and was named manager of the base's team. He assembled one of the first integrated baseball teams

Morrie Arnovich played for the Phillies, Reds, and Giants in his major-league career. In 1942, he was put in charge of the Fort Lewis (Washington) baseball team, and assembled a racially integrated team.

to play on US soil since the sport was segregated in the late 1800s.[56]

The story of big-league pitcher **Sam Nahem**'s crusade to integrate overseas military baseball during World War II is ripe for a Hollywood movie. Nahem was a right-handed pitcher with left-wing politics. He may have been the only major leaguer during his day who was a member of the Communist Party. He grew up in a Syrian Jewish family in Brooklyn, was a baseball and football star at Brooklyn College, and earned a law degree during the offseasons when he was in the minor leagues. He played for the Dodgers, Cardinals, and Phillies for four seasons between 1938 and 1948. Like many other radicals in the 1930s and 1940s, Nahem believed that baseball should be racially integrated.[57]

During the war, the US military ran a robust baseball program at home and overseas. After Germany surrendered in May 1945, the military expanded its baseball program while American troops remained in Europe. That year, over 200,000 American soldiers—including some major leaguers—were playing baseball on military teams in France, Germany, Belgium, Austria, and Great Britain. All the teams were racially segregated.[58]

While serving in the Army in France, Nahem recruited players for his team, the OISE All-Stars, made up mainly of semipro, college, and former minor-league players. Nahem insisted on putting two Negro Leagues stars who were stationed in France—Leon Day and Willard Brown—on the roster, even though military baseball was officially segregated, thus fielding the overseas military's first team known to be integrated. With Nahem pitching, playing first base, and leading the team in hitting, the OISE All-Stars advanced to the finals of the European GI World Series. In the fifth and final game, on September 8, 1945, in Nuremberg, in the same stadium where Hitler had addressed Nazi Party rallies, Nahem's team beat a team stacked with nine major leaguers, the heavily favored 71st Infantry

Red Circlers, representing General George Patton's Third Army. Allied bombing had destroyed the city but somehow spared the stadium. The Army laid out a baseball diamond and renamed the stadium Soldiers Field.

After his playing days were over, Nahem returned to New York, where he pitched for a top semi-pro team, the Brooklyn Bushwicks, but his political activities caught the attention of the FBI, which put him under surveillance. The Cold War blacklist made it difficult for him to find or keep a job. He moved to the Bay Area, where he worked for 25 years in a Chevron chemical plant and became a union leader, even leading a strike in 1969.[59]

Chick Starr, the Brooklyn-born son of Jewish immigrants who had appeared in 13 games for the 1935 and 1936 Washington Nationals, headed a group that purchased the San Diego Padres in the Pacific Coast League in 1944. Four years later, as team president and general manager, he signed Negro League star John Ritchey, who became the first Black player in the PCL.[60]

Hank Greenberg's experience with anti-Semitism made him sensitive to the vicious racism that Jackie Robinson faced when he broke the color barrier in 1947, Greenberg's final season, which he spent playing for the Pirates. In May, during a game against the Dodgers in Pittsburgh, some Pirates players hurled racial slurs at Robinson from the dugout. In the first inning of the third game on May 17, Pirates pitcher Fritz Ostermueller hit Robinson on the wrist, sending the rookie to the ground, writhing in pain. In the top of the seventh inning, Robinson laid down a perfect bunt, making it difficult for Ostermueller to throw the ball to first baseman Greenberg. As he reached the base, Robinson collided with Greenberg. The next inning Greenberg was intentionally walked. When he arrived at first base, he asked Robinson, who was playing first, if he had been hurt in the earlier collision. Robinson told Greenberg that he was fine. Greenberg said, "Don't pay any attention to these guys who are trying to make it hard for you. Stick in there. You're doing fine. Keep your chin up." After the game, Robinson told reporters, "Class tells. It sticks out all over Mr. Greenberg."[61]

Years later, in his autobiography, Greenberg wrote: "Jackie had it tough, tougher than any ballplayer who ever lived. I happened to be a Jew, one of the few in baseball, but I was white and I didn't have horns like some thought I did….But I identified with Jackie Robinson.[62]

In 1970, Robinson and Greenberg, along with journeyman pitcher-turned-writer Jim Brosnan, were the only former players who testified in court on behalf of Curt Flood's challenge to baseball's "reserve" clause. When Greenberg became the Cleveland Indians general manager, he refused to let the team stay in hotels that denied entry to Black players.

Seymour "Cy" Block was among a handful of players (including Danny Gardella, Tony Lupien, and Al Niemiec) who, long before Curt Flood, challenged baseball's monopoly status and its mistreatment of players. Block and Gardella challenged the reserve clause; Lupien and Niemiec sought to regain their jobs on major-league rosters after World War II based on the Serviceman's Readjustment Act. After serving in the military in World War II, Block returned to the Cubs for the 1945 and 1946 seasons and played in the minors until 1950. In 1951, he testified before Congress during hearings on economic concentration in major American industries, including baseball. He described the miserable pay and working conditions of minor-league players and criticized the renewal clause and baseball's exemption from antitrust laws. After 16 days of hearings, 33 witnesses, and 1,643 pages of transcript, Congress decided to do nothing.[63]

Marvin Miller, the players union's first executive director (1966–82), was baseball's Moses, helping lead the players out of indentured servitude by modifying the renewal clause, which had bound players to teams in perpetuity. Legendary sportscaster Red Barber said that Miller, Jackie Robinson, and Babe Ruth were the most influential people in baseball history. Two years after Miller joined the union, it negotiated the first-ever collective-bargaining agreement in professional sports. Two years later, the union established players' rights to binding arbitration over salaries and grievances. Most importantly, he led the effort to overturn the reserve clause, getting the union to support Flood's lawsuit. After the Supreme Court ruled against Flood in 1972, Miller persuaded pitchers Andy Messersmith and Dave McNally to play the 1975 season without a contract, then file a grievance arbitration. The arbitrator ruled in their favor, paving the way to free agency, which allows players with sufficient seniority to choose which team they want to work for, veto proposed trades, and bargain for the best contract.

Under Miller, the union won improvements in pay, pensions, travel conditions, training and locker room facilities, and medical treatment. The owners hated the union and despised Miller. After rejecting him seven times, the Hall of Fame's Modern Baseball Era Committee finally ended its blacklist and voted Miller in at its 2019 meeting.[64] He was inducted in 2021, but the ceremony was bittersweet, because Miller had died in 2012 at age 95.[65]

As early as the 1930s, Jewish sportswriters were among the strongest supporters of integrating baseball. The most influential was **Lester Rodney**. Starting in 1936, he was the sports editor of the *Daily Worker*, the Communist Party's newspaper. The paper forged an alliance with the Black press, civil rights groups, radical politicians, and left-wing labor unions to dismantle baseball's color line.[66] The protest movement published open letters to baseball owners and Commissioner Kenesaw Mountain Landis, polled white managers and players about their willingness to have Black players on major-league rosters, picketed at baseball stadiums in New York and Chicago, gathered signatures on petitions, kept the issue before the public, and put pressure on team owners. One of Rodney's editorials attacked "every rotten Jim Crow excuse offered by the magnates for this flagrant discrimination." When baseball executives told Rodney that Black players were not good enough to play in the majors, Rodney reported about exhibition games where Negro League players defeated teams composed of top-flight white major leaguers. He was joined in that crusade by two other *Jewish Daily Worker* sportswriters, **Bill Mardo** (birth name Bill Bloom) and **Nat Low**.

Shirley Povich consistently challenged baseball's color line as a *Washington Post* sports columnist. Reporting from spring training in Florida in 1941, he watched several Negro League games and reminded readers that the major leagues were missing out on "a couple of million dollars' worth of talent" by excluding Black players. In 1953, Povich kicked off a 15-part series about baseball integration called "No More Shutouts" with this lead: "Four hundred and fifty-five years after Columbus eagerly discovered America, major league baseball reluctantly discovered the American Negro."[67]

Haskell Cohen, a sportswriter for the *Pittsburgh Courier*, a Black newspaper, and several magazines, pushed major-league teams to give tryouts to Black players to demonstrate that they were of major-league caliber. In 1942, the White Sox reluctantly invited Robinson and pitcher Nate Moreland to attend a tryout camp at Brookside Park in Pasadena, California, where the Sox were holding spring training. Manager Jimmy Dykes raved about Robinson: "He's worth $50,000 of anybody's money. He stole everything but my infielders' gloves." The two ballplayers never heard from the White Sox again. But the *Pittsburgh Courier* and Cohen wrote about the tryout as part of their campaign to keep the issue of baseball segregation in the public eye.[68]

Isadore Muchnick, a progressive Jewish member of the Boston City Council, was determined to push the Red Sox to hire Black players, even though owner Tom Yawkey had staunchly resisted integration. In 1945, Muchnick threatened to deny the team a permit to play on Sundays. Working with *Pittsburgh Courier* sports editor Wendell Smith and *Boston Record* sportswriter Dave Egan, Muchnick persuaded general manager Eddie Collins to give three Negro Leagues players—Robinson, Sam Jethroe, and Marvin Williams—a tryout at Fenway Park on April 16. During the 90-minute tryout, the three players performed well. Robinson, the most impressive of the three, hit line drives to all fields. "Bang, bang, bang; he rattled it," Muchnick said.[69] The Red Sox had no intention to hire a Black player. But after the phony tryout, Smith headed to Brooklyn to tell Dodgers president Branch Rickey—who did want to integrate his team and was looking for the right player to do it—about Robinson's outstanding performance.

Sam Maltin, a sports columnist for the *Montreal Herald* and a stringer for the *Pittsburgh Courier*, was Robinson's biggest booster and closest friend during his 1946 season with the Dodgers' Montreal Royals farm team. When Robinson led the Royals to the Junior World Series championship over the Louisville Colonels of the American Association, fans surrounded him and carried him on their shoulders in celebration. In the *Courier*, Maltin wrote: "It was probably the only day in history that a black man ran from a white mob with love instead of lynching on its mind."[70]

Once Robinson joined the Dodgers, he was still subject to a great deal of racial slurs, not only among fans, but among some sportswriters. A small number of white sportswriters, most of them Jews, embraced Robinson and wrote stories and columns supporting him and the "experiment" of desegregating baseball. They included **Dick Young** and **Hy Turkin** of the *New York Daily News*, **Roger Kahn** of the *New York Herald Tribune*, **Joe Reichler** of the Associated Press, **Milton Gross** of the *New York Post*, and **Walter Winchell**, an influential syndicated columnist for the *New York Daily Mirror*.

Although the major leagues have yet to field an openly gay player, **Brad Ausmus**, then a player and later a manager in the big leagues, was outspoken in support of his friend and former teammate Billy Bean when Bean came out of the closet after he'd retired from baseball.[71]

As manager of the Giants, **Gabe Kapler** was the first manager to publicly support Black Lives Matter in 2020, taking a knee on the sidelines before the start of a game and speaking out against racism.[72] He was also a strong advocate for women inside and outside baseball. In 2020, he hired Alyssa Nakken, the first female uniformed coach in major-league history.[73] Kapler and his wife co-founded the Gabe Kapler Foundation, which focused on educating the public about domestic violence and helping women escape abusive relationships. In 2021, he co-founded Pipeline for Change, a nonprofit dedicated to "creating opportunities and breaking down barriers for women, people of color, members of the LBGTQ community, people with physical disabilities and people from underrepresented backgrounds who seek to begin or advance a career in baseball."[74]

Over 600 women played in the All-American Girls Professional Baseball League, which lasted from 1943 to 1954 and was popularized by the 1992 film *A League of Their Own*. Four of them were known to be Jews.

Thelma "Tiby" Eisen (1922–2014) was born in Los Angeles, one of four children of David Eisen, an Austrian immigrant, and Dorothy (Shechter) Eisen, from New York City. She was already participating in semipro softball by age 14. She graduated from Belmont High School in 1941, then attended Santa Monica College part time. An outstanding all-around athlete, at 18 she played fullback in a short-lived professional football league for women in California. When the Los Angeles City Council banned tackle football for women, her team moved to Guadalajara, Mexico. After attending a tryout in Peru, Indiana, she was assigned to the Milwaukee Chicks (who soon moved to Grand Rapids) and later played outfield for the Fort Wayne Daisies and Peoria Redwings. During her AABPBL career (1944–52), she had 3,705 at-bats, a .224 batting average and 674 stolen bases, second-most in league history. Her 591 runs scored rank third. In 1946, she led the league in triples, stole 128 bases, and was selected for the All-Star team. In the winter of 1949, she toured Central America, Venezuela, and Puerto Rico with the AAGPBL.

After the AAGPBL disbanded, she played semipro softball and field hockey for California teams. She was also an outstanding golfer. She gave baseball clinics for children through a number of nonprofit organizations for many years. In 1993, she helped establish the women's exhibit at the National Baseball Hall of Fame and Museum in Cooperstown, and in 2004 she was inducted into the National Jewish Sports Hall of Fame and Museum.[75]

Blanche Schachter (1923–2010), born in Brooklyn, started playing baseball on her synagogue team. She graduated from Hunter College with a degree in physical education and excelled in three sports: tennis, basketball, and field hockey. While working as a New York teacher, she also pitched, caught, and played third base for the Greenwold Jewells of the American Softball League, one of the best teams in the country at a time when women's softball was a popular sport. In 1945, in a game against a women's Army Corps team, Schachter, who was ambidextrous, played one inning at every position. In the ninth inning, as a right-handed pitcher, she struck out the first two batters on six pitches, then switched to throwing left-handed and got the final batter out.[76] Schachter joined the AAGPBL's Kenosha Comets in 1948 as a catcher but she injured her knee and played only nine games in the league. She returned to New York to work as a gym teacher but also played in semipro women's baseball and basketball leagues. After retiring from the New York school system, she moved to western Massachusetts and worked as a high school tennis coach.[77]

Anita Foss (1921–2015) played in only 28 AAGPBL games over two seasons (1948 and 1949), but she wore the uniforms of four teams—the Springfield Sallies, Muskegon Lassies, Grand Rapids Chicks, and Rockford Peaches—pitching and playing second base. (The league frequently moved players around to guarantee a competitive balance). She was captain of her high school softball team in Providence and a star on the Riverside Townies, the Rhode Island women's champion softball team. She joined the AAGPBL after her husband was killed in World War II. Soon after leaving the league, Foss moved to Santa Monica and worked for Douglas Aircraft. The company asked her to train a man for a supervisory job. She complained that she knew how to do the job and deserved to get it. "The next thing you know, I was in charge," she recalled, becoming the first female supervisor in her department, responsible for over 30 employees. She played in local semipro baseball and softball leagues and was also an avid golfer and bowler. In 2005, she earned the Woman of the Year Award from Santa Monica YMCA for her contributions to the community.[78]

Bea Chester (1921–?) was a star athlete at Brooklyn's Thomas Jefferson High School. She excelled in many sports, including baseball, basketball, volleyball, tennis, bowling, table tennis, hockey, the broad jump, and the 100-yard dash. She appeared in 29 games as a backup third baseman for the 1943 South Bend Blue Sox and the 1944 Rockford Peaches. She batted .190 and .214 in those two seasons. Chester was raised at the Brooklyn Hebrew Orphan Asylum. Articles in the *Brooklyn Daily Eagle* in February 1932 and December 1933 mentioned that a student named Bea Chester played mandolin solos at events sponsored by the asylum. Her mother was Hilda Chester, the well-known Dodgers superfan. Hilda's husband (and Bea's father) died, but Hilda lived until 1978 and it's unclear how Bea ended up in the orphanage. Little else is known about her upbringing or post-baseball life.[79]

Sylvia B. Pressler played a key role in opening Little League Baseball to girls. In 1972, a 12-year-old girl, Maria Pepe, played three games for a team in Hoboken, New Jersey, before national Little League officials threatened to revoke the local league's charter if she continued to play. The National Organization for Women sued on behalf of the girl and all others in New Jersey. The next year, Pressler, a hearing officer with the New Jersey Division on Civil Rights, ruled in favor of the girls. "The institution of Little League is as American as the hot dog and apple pie," Pressler wrote in her ruling. "There is no reason why that part of Americana should be withheld from girls." The New Jersey Appellate Court upheld her ruling. In 1974, Little League Baseball agreed to allow girls to play on its teams. Pressler later rose to be the presiding administrative judge of the state's Appellate Division.[80]

Justine Siegal became the first female coach of a professional men's baseball team, when she worked for the Brockton Rox, in the independent Canadian American Association of Professional Baseball, in 2009. In 2015, the Oakland Athletics hired Siegal for a two-week coaching stint in their instructional league in Arizona, making her the first female coach employed by an MLB team. As founder of Baseball For All, she's been a trailblazer in training girls to play baseball, including a growing number now on rosters of otherwise all-male college teams and on women's college teams.[81]

JEWISH CONTRIBUTIONS TO BASEBALL AS POPULAR CULTURE

Although he had never been to a baseball game, **Albert Von Tilzer**, son of Polish Jewish immigrants, composed the music to "Take Me Out to the Ballgame" in 1908. Born Albert Gumm, he took his mother's maiden name and added the Von title to make himself sound less Jewish. Jack Norworth wrote the words. The song was popularized by Norworth's then-wife, Nora Bayes, a popular vaudeville entertainer, whose original name was Rachel Goldberg and who was Jewish. The song was first played at a ballpark in 1934—at a high school game in Los Angeles. It was played during Game Four of the World Series that year, and after that, it became baseball's unofficial anthem, sung during the seventh-inning stretch at ballparks around the country.[82]

Seymour "Sy" Berger, an employee of the Topps Chewing Gum Company, designed the modern baseball card in 1952. Baseball cards had existed since the 1800s, but it was Berger who added colorful player photos, statistics, short biographies, and facsimiles of their autographs.[83]

Mel Allen (real name Melvin Allen Israel), longtime voice of the Yankees, was one of the most influential broadcasters of all time. Other well-known Jewish baseball announcers include **Marty Glickman**, **Bill Stern**, **Howard Cosell**, **Dick Schaap**, **Al Michaels**, **Chris Berman**, **Len Berman**, **Ken Albert**, **Marv Albert**, **Bonnie Bernstein**, **Ken Levine**, **Mitch Melnick**, **Gary Cohen**, **Elliott Price**, and **Charlie Steiner**.

Several Jewish women have reached the top of their profession as baseball writers and broadcasters. **Jane Leavy** is the author of *Sandy Koufax: A Lefty's Legacy*, considered one of the best baseball books of the past century, as well as biographies of Mickey Mantle and Babe Ruth. **Suzyn Waldman** was hired as the New York Yankees' play-by-play announcer on a local TV station in 1996 and in 2005 became the first woman to do color commentary for the team on local radio. Four years later, she became the first woman to work a World Series game from the broadcast booth.[84] **Linda Cohn** has been ESPN's SportsCenter anchor since 1992.[85] **Amelia Schimmel** is the first female public-address announcer at the Oakland Athletics' Coliseum.[86]

Some of the best known and most lauded novels about baseball were written by Jewish authors. These include *The Natural* by Bernard Malamud, *Bang the Drum Slowly* and *The Southpaw* by Mark Harris, *The Celebrant* by Eric Greenberg, *The Great American Novel* by Philip Roth, and *Man on Spikes* by Eliot Asinof.

JEWISH OWNERS AND EXECUTIVES

Beginning in the mid-nineteenth century, anti-Semitism kept Jews—most of them immigrants—from gaining entry into many industries and occupations. As a result, Jews found niches in business sectors that were new and required little capital, typically expanding small initial investments into larger enterprises. These sectors included clothing manufacturing, retail, real estate, liquor, and entertainment, particularly theater and, eventually, movies. Once they gained a foothold in these businesses, they found their way into the early days of professional baseball. At the time, team owners were often deeply intertwined with local politicians, as political connections were often needed to secure stock in local baseball teams.[87]

Since 1880, at least 37 Jews have been full or part owners of major-league teams, as shown in Table 3 in the Appendix online.

Cincinnati was an early center of Jewish population, so it isn't surprising that Jews owned or partly owned the major-league franchise in that city during its early days. **Nathan Menderson** was an immigrant from Bavaria who owned one of Cincinnati's large clothing stores before becoming the vice president, then the president, of the NL's Cincinnati Stars in 1880. **Aaron Stern** owned a clothing firm and was a theatrical producer before purchasing the Cincinnati Red Stockings in 1882. He transferred the team from the American Association to the NL in 1889 and sold it the following year. **Julius** and **Max Fleischmann** were the sons of Charles Fleischmann, a Hungarian immigrant who created America's first commercially produced yeast, which revolutionized baking by making it possible to mass produce bread. Julius became president of Fleischmann's Yeast as well as the mayor of Cincinnati from 1900 to 1905. From 1902 to 1922, he and Max became major shareholders of the Cincinnati Red Stockings. In 1903, Julius also purchased shares in the Philadelphia Phillies, who competed in the same league.

Barney Dreyfuss arrived in the US from Germany in 1886 almost penniless and knowing very little English, and he found work managing the books for his cousins' bourbon distillery in Paducah, Kentucky. He convinced his cousins to join him and other local distillers in investing in the Louisville Colonels of the American Association. By 1899, Dreyfuss was the president of the club, by then a member of the NL. The next year he purchased the Pittsburgh Pirates, which he owned until 1932. In 1903, he helped end the raiding wars between the NL and AL by persuading the pennant winners in both leagues to play a best of nine series. He is thus credited for having re-established the World Series.[88]

Since the early days of the sport, most major-league teams have been owned by wealthy investors who made their fortunes in other industries before investing in baseball. Jewish baseball owners reflect these trends. Among the 23 Jews who have owned teams since the 1980s, six made their fortunes in real estate (**Robert Lurie, Fred Wilpon, Saul Katz, Ted Lerner, Jerry Reinsdorf**, and **Lewis Wolff**) and six got rich in the financial services industry (**Randy Frankel, Stuart Sternberg, Steven Cohen, Bruce Sherman, David Blitzer**, and **David Rubinstein**). Some grew up in modest circumstances while others inherited their wealth, such as **John Fisher** (whose family owns the Gap clothing empire), **Mark Lerner** (whose father was a major real estate developer), **Walter Haas** (heir to the Levi Strauss clothing firm), and **Charles Bronfman** (heir to the Seagram distillery empire). **Jamie Luskin McCourt** was the wife of real estate developer Frank McCourt, who purchased the Dodgers in 2004; she was a part-

owner and eventually CEO of the team. Like their non-Jewish counterparts, many Jewish baseball team owners also own professional football, basketball, hockey, and other sports teams. For example, Reinsdorf, a successful real estate developer, owns both the White Sox and the Chicago Bulls in the NBA.

At least 21 Jews have filled the top management jobs on major-league teams, typically called CEO, president, or general manager. In baseball's early days, the lines between owners, top executives, and even field managers were often blurry. **Connie Mack** managed the Philadelphia Athletics from 1901 to 1950 and was at least part owner from 1901 to 1954. In 1928, **Emil Fuchs**, the Jewish owner and president of the Boston Braves, hired Rogers Hornsby to manage in 1928. But with the team on the brink of bankruptcy, Fuchs was forced to trade Hornsby to the Cubs after the season. During the next season, he decided to manage the team himself, and the Braves finished last in the NL.

For most of baseball history, top team executives came from the ranks of former ballplayers. When their playing days were over, for example, Hank Greenberg served as general manager for the Indians and White Sox and Al Rosen became president of the Yankees and Astros and general manager of the San Francisco Giants, as shown in Table 4 in the Appendix online.

In the twenty-first century, however, owners shifted toward recruiting executives from the ranks of corporate America, particularly those with business and/or law degrees. For example, after graduating from Harvard, **Mathew Silverman** worked at Goldman Sachs, where he helped **Stuart Sternberg** buy the Tampa Bay Devils Rays (now the Rays). After he bought the team, Sternberg hired Silverman as vice president; he later became president.

Another path is to jump from college to an apprentice-type job with a major-league team and climb the ladder to the top. After **Mike Chernoff** graduated from Princeton (where he played shortstop), he worked as an intern in the Indians front office and was gradually promoted to director of baseball relations, assistant general manager, and then general manager. In 2004, **Chaim Bloom** earned a degree in classics from Yale, but his passion was baseball analytics, which he translated into articles for Baseball Prospectus. He worked as an intern for the Padres, Major League Baseball, and the Rays before the last hired him to work full time as assistant director of minor league operations in 2008. He was promoted several times, eventually to senior vice president of baseball operations in 2018. Two years later, the Red Sox hired the 36-year-old Bloom as chief baseball officer.

Larry Baer took both paths. At the University of California, Berkeley, where he majored in political science, he was the sports director and business manager of the student-run radio station as well as a play-by-play announcer on its sports broadcasts. Upon graduation, he joined the Giants as marketing director. He left to get an MBA from Harvard, after which he worked for Westinghouse Broadcasting and CBS, serving as assistant to the CEO. He rejoined the Giants in 1992 and was named the team's president in 2008 and CEO in 2012.

Among recent Jewish team executives, only **Rubén Amaro Jr.** and **Sam Fuld** (both of whom attended Stanford) wore a major-league uniform, although a few other team executives played baseball in college. **Eve Rosenbaum**, who played on the Harvard women's softball team, was named the Baltimore Orioles' director of baseball development in 2019 and its assistant general manager in 2022.[89]

CONCLUSION

In a variety of ways—as fans, players, coaches, managers, umpires, sportswriters, owners, executives, and activists—American Jews have embraced baseball since the 1800s. Their involvement in baseball has reflected changes in American culture and society, changes within baseball, and transformations within the Jewish community. Each generation of Jews has faced different political, economic, social, and cultural obstacles and opportunities. Baseball was a way for Jews to become part of the larger culture, make a living, and enjoy recreational opportunities. Jews' participation at the pinnacle of baseball has ebbed and flowed, but in recent years, more Jews have populated major-league rosters than at any time since the late 1800s.[90] ∎

Appendix

Table 2: Jews Selected for All-Star Teams
Table 3: Jewish Major League Managers and Coaches
Table 4: Jewish Baseball Owners
Table 5: Jewish Major League Baseball Executives

All appendices and tables can be found online at the complete article (Parts One and Two combined): https://sabr.org/journal/article/jews-and-baseball-history-and-demographics-part-one/.

Notes

1. Leonard Dinnerstein, *Anti-Semitism in America* (New York: Oxford University Press, 1994).
2. Max Wallace, *The American Axis: Henry Ford, Charles Lindbergh, and the Rise of the Third Reich* (New York: St. Martin's Press, 2003).
3. Wallace, *The American Axis*.
4. *The Sporting News*, October 16, 1919, 4.
5. Steven A. Riess, "From Pike to Green with Greenberg in Between: Jewish Americans and the National Pastime," in Lawrence Baldassaro and Richard A. Johnson, eds., *The American Game: Baseball and Ethnicity* (Carbondale, IL.: Southern Illinois University Press, 2002); Peter Ephross with Martin Abramowitz, *Jewish Major Leaguers in Their Own Words* (Jefferson, NC: McFarland, 2012), 24–32.
6. Ralph Berger, "Jimmie Reese," Society for American Baseball Research, https://sabr.org/bioproj/person/jimmie-reese/.
7. Christopher Williams and Robert Bigelow, "Barney Pelty," Society for American Baseball Research, https://sabr.org/bioproj/person/barney-pelty/.
8. "Allentown Brooks Hope to Get into Initial Spring Drill This Afternoon," *Allentown Call*, April 7, 1936, 23.
9. Dinnerstein, Anti-Semitism in America; Helen Fein, ed, *The Persisting Question: Sociological Perspectives and Social Contexts of Modern Antisemitism* (New York: Walter De Gruyter, 1987).
10. Ephross, and Abramowitz, *Jewish Major Leaguers*, 45.
11. Donald Warren, *Radio Priest: Charles Coughlin, the Father of Hate Radio* (New York: The Free Press, 1996).
12. Hank Greenberg with Ira Berkow, *Hank Greenberg: The Story of My Life* (Chicago: Triumph, 2001), 103.
13. Richard Bak, *Cobb Would Have Caught It* (Detroit: Wayne State University Press, 1993), 85.
14. Some baseball observers believe that Greenberg was kept off the 1935 All-Star team because of the prejudice of his own manager, Mickey Cochrane. That year, managers selected the teams. Cochrane picked Lou Gehrig and Jimmy Foxx at first base even though Greenberg was having a better season. Greenberg never publicly accused Cochrane of anti-Semitism, but he was so angry that three years later he refused to play in the All-Star Game, even though he was selected for the AL team.
15. Howard Megdal, "Religion Aided a Home Run Chase, and May Have Led to Its Failure," *The New York Times*, March 20, 2010, https://www.nytimes.com/2010/03/21/sports/baseball/21score.html.
16. Ira Berkow, "The Plot Against Greenberg?" in Franklin Foer and Marc Tracy, eds., *Jewish Jocks: An Unorthodox Hall of Fame* (New York: Hachette, 2012).
17. Berkow, "The Plot Against Greenberg?"
18. Ephross, and Abramowitz, *Jewish Major Leaguers*, 33–40.
19. Peter Levine, *Ellis Island to Ebbets Field: Sport and the American Jewish Experience* (New York: Oxford University Press, 1993), 129.
20. Jane Leavy, *Sandy Koufax: A Lefty's Legacy* (New York: HarperCollins, 2002), 72.
21. Leavy, 71.
22. Andrew Hazucha, "Leo Durocher's Last Stand: Anti-Semitism, Racism, and the Cubs Player Rebellion of 1971," *Nine: A Journal of Baseball History and Culture* 15, no. 1 (Fall 2006), 1–12.
23. "Not a Jew," Jewish Baseball News, http://www.jewishbaseballnews.com/not-a-jew/.
24. G. Edward White, *Creating the National Pastime: Baseball Transforms Itself, 1903–1953* (Princeton, NJ: Princeton University Press, 1996), 250.
25. Greenberg, *Hank Greenberg*, 76.
26. Stephen H. Norwood and Harold Brackman, "Going to Bat for Jackie Robinson: The Jewish Role in Breaking the Color Line," *Journal of Sports History* 26 (Spring 1999), 131.
27. "Myer Tells His Side," *Madison Capital Times*, April 27, 1933.
28. Burton Boxerman and Benita Boxerman, *Jews and Baseball: Volume I: Entering the American Mainstream, 1871–1948* (Jefferson, NC: McFarland, 2007); Peter S. Horvitz and Joachim Horvitz, *The Big Book of Jewish Baseball: An Illustrated Encyclopedia & Anecdotal History* (New York: SPI Books, 2001); Erwin Lynn, *The Jewish Baseball Hall of Fame* (New York: Shapolsky Publishers, 1986).
29. Warren Corbett, "Buddy Myer," Society for American Baseball Research, https://sabr.org/bioproj/person/buddy-myer/.
30. Joshua Yaffa, "Florida Team Strikes Out," *Forward*, June 9, 2006, https://forward.com/israel/729/florida-team-strikes-out; Joe Posnanski, "The Curious Case Of Mike Jacobs, My New Favorite Royal," *Sports Illustrated*, April 20, 2009, https://www.si.com/more-sports/2009/04/20/mike-jacobs.

31. For example: Donald Harrison, "Before Melvin, Padres Had 11 Players, 2 Coaches With At Least One Jewish Parent," San Diego Jewish World, May 15, 2002 https://www.sdjewishworld.com/2022/05/15/before-melvin-padres-had-11-players-2-coaches-with-at-least-one-jewish-parent/.

32. The first All-Star Game was played in 1933.

33. The Most Valuable Player has been awarded in each league since 1931.

34. The Gold Glove award began in 1957.

35. The Rookie of the Year Award began in 1947.

36. The Cy Young Award began in 1956.

37. Gregory H. Wolf, "Art Nehf," Society for American Baseball Research, https://sabr.org/bioproj/person/Art-Nehf/; David Cicotello, "Wilbur Cooper," Society for American Baseball Research, https://sabr.org/bioproj/person/Wilbur-Cooper/.

38. Jack Zerby, "April 30, 1944: New York Giants Sscore 26 Runs; Weintraub Has 11 RBIs," Society for American Baseball Research, https://sabr.org/gamesproj/game/april-30-1944-new-york-giants-score-26-runs-weintraub-has-11-rbis/; Retrosheet, https://www.retrosheet.org/boxesetc/1944/B04301NY11944.htm; "Most RBI By a Single Player in a Game," Statmuse, https://www.statmuse.com/mlb/ask/most-rbi-by-a-single-player-in-a-game.

39. "Craig Breslow," Retrosheet, https://www.retrosheet.org/boxesetc/B/Pbresc001.htm.

40. Rossman made his major-league debut on July 13, 2022, under unusual circumstances. Four Phillies, including two pitchers, were ineligible to play the Blue Jays in Canada—where COVID-19 laws were stiffer than in the US—because they were unvaccinated. Philadelphia filled one of the temporary slots with Rossman, who had been playing in Double-A. Stubbs was his batterymate. After the game, Rossman and his fellow replacement pitcher were sent back down to the minors, as expected.

41. Murray Greenberg, "Baseball's Jewist Moment of All," Forward, May 1, 2015, https://forward.com/culture/307228/the-most-jewish-moment-in-baseball-history/.

42. "2021 World Series Game 6, Braves at Astros, November 2," Baseball Reference, https://www.baseball-reference.com/boxes/HOU/HOU202111020.shtml.

43. "Milwaukee Brewers 2, Toronto Blue Jays 1," Retrosheet, https://www.retrosheet.org/boxesetc/1996/B09180MIL1996.htm; "New: Excerpt from umpire Al Clark's memoir," Jewish Baseball News, May 8, 2014, http://www.jewishbaseballnews.com/new-excerpt-from-umpire-al-clarks-memoir/; Lewis Keene, "Jewish in the big leagues: Power hitter Shawn Green dishes at White House event," Forward, May 19, 2022, https://forward.com/news/sports/502989/shawn-green-jewish-baseball-player-on-yom-kippur-and-antisemitism/; Dann Halem, "Jews on First," Slate, April 13, 2001, https://slate.com/culture/2001/04/jews-on-first.html.

44. Howard Wasserman, "Testing the Koufax Curse: How 18 Jewish Pitchers, 18 Jewish Hitters, and Rod Carew Performed on Yom Kippur," Baseball Research Journal 49, no. 2 (Fall 2020), https://sabr.org/journal/article/testing-the-koufax-curse-how-18-jewish-pitchers-18-jewish-hitters-and-rod-carew-performed-on-yom-kippur/.

45. Charlie Bevis, "Jacob Morse," Society for American Baseball Research, https://sabr.org/bioproj/person/jake-morse/.

46. "Louis Heilbroner - 4'9" Cardinals Manager," History of Cardinals, https://historyofcardinals.com/louis-heilbroner-49-cardinals-manager/; "Louie Heilbroner," Baseball Reference, https://www.baseball-reference.com/register/player.fcgi?id=heilbr001lou.

47. Frederick J. Frommer, "He grew up on a Kibbutz. Now he's coaching the Cincinnati Reds," Forward, May 23, 2023, https://forward.com/news/sports/548106/alon-leichman-jewish-cincinatti-reds-kibbutz-pitching-coach/.

48. Associated Press, "Four longtime MLB umpires set to retire," USA Today, February 21, 2017, https://www.usatoday.com/story/sports/mlb/2017/02/21/4-new-umps-as-hirschbeck-welke-davidson-joyce-retire/98224326/.

49. Ralph Berger, "Dolly Stark," Society for American Baseball Research, https://sabr.org/bioproj/person/dolly-stark/.

50. "Controversial Stan Landes Still Mystified Over Losing Job," Ocala Star-Banner, March 15, 1973; "Landes, Dismissed Umpire, Takes Case to N.L.R.B.," The New York Times, March 30, 1973, 45, https://www.nytimes.com/1973/03/30/archives/landes-dismissed-umpire-takes-case-to-nlrb.html.

51. "Notable Deaths," Boston Globe, December 27, 1994, 49.

52. "Warren Giles Will Not Renew Forman's Pact," Altus Times-Democrat, January 23, 1966.

53. "New Jersey Sports," The New York Times, October 31, 1972, https://www.nytimes.com/1972/10/31/archives/new-jersey-pages-umpire-has-a-calling.html;

54. Al Clark and Dan Schlossberg, Called Out But Safe: A Baseball Umpire's Journey (Lincoln: University of Nebraska Press, 2014); Larry Ruttman, American Jews and America's Game: Voices of a Growing Legacy in Baseball (Lincoln: University of Nebraska Press, 2013), 313–22; Murray Chass, "Umpire Is Forced Out, But Details Are Sketchy," The New York Times, June 23, 2001, https://www.nytimes.com/2001/06/23/sports/baseball-umpire-is-forced-out-but-details-are-sketchy.html.

55. Peter Dreier and Robert Elias, Baseball Rebels: The Players, People, and Social Movements That Shook Up the Game and Changed America (Lincoln: University of Nebraska Press), 2002.

56. "Morrie Arnovich: Breaking Ground for Branch Rickey's Bold Move," Chevrons and Diamonds, May 15, 2020, https://chevronsanddiamonds.wordpress.com/2020/05/15/morrie-arnovich-breaking-ground-for-branch-rickeys-bold-move/.

57. Peter Dreier, "Before Jackie Robinson: Baseball's Civil Rights Movement," in Bill Nowlin and Glen Sparks, eds., Jackie: Perspectives on 42 (Phoenix: Society for American Baseball Research, 2021), 27–37, https://sabr.org/journal/article/before-jackie-robinson-baseballs-civil-rights-movement/.

58. It is possible that a few Black players played on otherwise all-white teams during earlier periods. For example, in 1914 Oscar Charleston left school, joined the Army, and was stationed in the Philippines, where he joined the all-black 24th Infantry baseball team that played in the semipro Manila League, which some sourses say was the US Army league. Other sources claim that he was the only Black player in that league. One source suggests that he played on a regular all-Black team but was recruited to play in the league's all-star game with white teammates. Upon returning to the US, he played on all-Black teams and became a superstar in the Negro Leagues. "Charlestown's First Appearance in the Papers," Oscar Charleston: Life and Legend, December 24, 2016, https://oscarcharleston.com/tag/philippines-baseball/; Jeremy Beer, "Hothead: How the Oscar Charleston Myth Began," Baseball Research Journal 46, no. 1 (Spring 2017) https://sabr.org/journal/article/hothead-how-the-oscar-charleston-myth-began/.

59. Peter Dreier, "Sam Nahem," Society for American Baseball Research, https://sabr.org/bioproj/person/sam-nahem/.

60. Gary Sarnoff, "Chick Starr," Society for American Baseball Research, https://sabr.org/bioproj/person/chick-starr/

61. Harry Keck, "Sports: Hank Gives Robinson a Helping Hand," Pittsburgh Sun-Telegraph, May 17, 1947, 11.

62. Greenberg, Hank Greenberg, 191.

63. Warren Corbett, "Cy Block," Society for American Baseball Research, https://sabr.org/bioproj/person/cy-block/.

64. Peter Dreier, "Union Busting at the Baseball Hall of Fame: The Blacklisting of Union Leader Marvin Miller," Labor: Studies in Working Class History of the Americas, Vol. 21, Number 2, May 2024, 94–120. https://peterdreier.com/wp-content/uploads/2024/07/Union-busting-at-the-baseball-hall-of-fame-94dreier-1.pdf.

65. John Helyar, Lords of the Realm: The Real History of Baseball (New York: Villard, 1994); Charles P. Korr, The End of Baseball as We Knew It: The Players Union, 1960–81 (Urbana: University of Illinois Press, 2002); Robert F. Burk, Marvin Miller: Baseball Revolutionary (Urbana: University of Illinois Press, 2015); Marvin Miller, A Whole New Ballgame: The Sport and Business of Baseball (New York: Birch Lane Press, 1991); Peter Dreier and Robert Elias, Major League Rebels: Baseball Battles Over Workers'

Rights and American Empire (Lanham, MD: Rowman & Littlefield, 2022); Peter Dreier, "Union Busting at the Baseball Hall of Fame: The Blacklisting of Union Leader Marvin Miller," *Labor: Studies in Working Class History* 21, no. 2 (May 2024), 94–120.

66. Chris Lamb, *Conspiracy of Silence: Sportswriters and the Long Campaign to Desegregate Baseball* (Lincoln: University of Nebraska Press, 2012); Irwin Silber, *Press Box Red: The Story of Lester Rodney, the Communist Who Helped Break the Color Line in American Sports* (Philadelphia: Temple University Press, 2003); Kelly Rusinack, "Baseball on the Radical Agenda: The *Daily Worker* and *Sunday Worker* Journalistic Campaign to Desegregate Major League Baseball, 1933–1947," in Joseph Dorinson and Joram Warmund, eds., *Jackie Robinson: Race, Sports, and the American Dream* (Armonk, NY: M.E. Sharpe, 1998); Henry Fetter, "The Party Line and the Color Line: The American Communist Party, the 'Daily Worker,' and Jackie Robinson" *Journal of Sport History* 28, no. 3 (Fall 2001), 375–402; Dreier, "Before Jackie Robinson."

67. Shirley Povich, "Negro Has Found Real Democracy in Baseball," *Washington Post*, May 10, 1953, 1C.

68. "They Were Turned Down," *Pittsburgh Courier*, March 21, 1942; Haskell Cohen, "The Negro and Our National Pastime," *PIC*, September 1942. See also: Haskell Cohen, "Negro Baseball Champs," *Sport*, September 14, 1943, 41–43.

69. Howard Bryant, *Shut Out: A Story of Race and Baseball in Boston* (Boston: Beacon Press, 2003); Rebecca T. Alpert, *Out of Left Field: Jews and Black Baseball* (New York: Oxford University Press, 2011), 162–64; Norwood and Brackman, "Going to Bat for Jackie Robinson."

70. John Kalbfleisch, "Robinson and Montreal were a perfect match," *Montreal Gazette*, October 3, 2004, https://montrealgazette.com/sponsored/mtl-375th/from-the-archives-robinson-and-montreal-were-a-perfect-match.

71. Jim Buzinski, "The Gay Baseball Saga: What We've Learned," Outsports, June 2, 2001, https://www.outsports.com/2013/3/4/4063600/the-gay-baseball-saga-what-weve-learned; Billy Bean, *Going the Other Way: An Intimate Memoir of Life In and Out of Major League Baseball* (New York; Marlowe & Company, 2003).

72. Maria Guardado, "Kapler: Movement Has To 'Continue In Perpetuity,'" MLB.com, June 10, 2020, https://www.mlb.com/news/gabe-kapler-outlines-his-support-of-black-lives-matter; Tom Dart, "Gabe Kapler: MLB's Liberal Jock In America's Most Conservative League," *The Guardian*, May 31, 2022, https://www.theguardian.com/sport/2022/may/31/gabe-kapler-san-francisco-giants-manager-anthem-protest-gun-violence-baseball.

73. Adam Wells, "SF Giants' Alyssa Nakken Becomes 1st Woman to Coach During an MLB Game," Bleacher Report, July 21, 2020, https://bleacherreport.com/articles/2901021-sf-giants-alyssa-nakken-becomes-1st-woman-to-coach-during-an-mlb-game.

74. Andrew Baggarly, "Foundational piece: How Giants' Gabe Kapler and a unique co-director seek change," The Athletic, February 9, 2021, https://theathletic.com/2376802/2021/02/09/foundational-piece-how-giants-gabe-kapler-and-a-unique-co-director-seek-change/.

75. Rebecca Alpert, "Thelma 'Tiby' Eisen: An Oral History," *Nine: A Journal of Baseball History and Culture* 22, no. 2 (Spring 2014), 108–31; "Thelma Eisen," All-American Girls Professional Baseball League, https://web.archive.org/web/20240608030646/https://www.aagpbl.org/profiles/thelma-eisen-tiby/400; Melanie Meyers, "Tiby Eisen: Star Player of the All-American Girls Professional Baseball League," American Jewish Historical Society, September 8, 2023, https://ajhs.org/tiby-eisen-star-player-of-the-all-american-girls-professional-baseball-league/; David Spanier, "Thelma Eisen," Shalvi/Hyman Encyclopedia of Jewish Women, May 22, 2023, https://jwa.org/encyclopedia/article/eisen-thelma-tiby;

Ruttman, *American Jews and America's Game*.

76. Haskell Cohen, "Jews in Sports," May 10, 1946, 11.

77. "Blanche Schacter," All-American Girls Professional Baseball League, https://web.archive.org/web/20240423084843/https://www.aagpbl.org/profiles/blanche-schachter/433; "Jewish Women of the AAGPBL," Jewish Sports Collectibles, October 17, 2012, https://web.archive.org/web/20130122103321/http://www.jewishsportscollectibles.com/2012/10/jewish-women-of-the-aagpbl.html.

78. Ruttman, *American Jews*, 39.

79. Rob Edelman, "The Enigma of Hilda Chester," *Baseball Research Journal* 44, no. 2 (Fall 2015), https://sabr.org/journal/article/the-enigma-of-hilda-chester-4/; "Child Box Fund Brings $2,000 to Hebrew Orphans." *Brooklyn Daily Eagle*, February 23, 1932, 6; "Asylum Given Substantial Aid By Auxiliary." *Brooklyn Daily Eagle*, December 14, 1933, 22; "Bea Chester," All-American Girls Professional Baseball League, https://web.archive.org/web/20240224053403/https://www.aagpbl.org/profiles/bea-chester/213.

80. Bruce Weber, "Judge Sylvia Pressler, Who Opened Little League to Girls, Dies at 75," *The New York Times*, February 17, 2010, https://www.nytimes.com/2010/02/17/nyregion/17pressler.html.

81. Glenn Swain, "Advocate for Women in Baseball Finally Gets to Be One," *The New York Times*, February 21, 2011, https://www.nytimes.com/2011/02/22/sports/baseball/22pitcher.html; Susan Slusser, "A's Hire Woman Coach: Justine Siegal To Be Guest Instructor," SF Gate, September 29, 2015, https://www.sfgate.com/athletics/article/Oakland-A-s-hire-woman-coach-Justine-Siegal-to-6538183.php.

82. Robert Thomson, Tim Wiles, and Andy Strasberg, *Baseball's Greatest Hit: The Story of "Take Me Out to the Ballgame"* (New York: Hal Leonard, 2008).

83. Richard Goldstein, "Sy Berger, Who Turned Baseball Heroes Into Brilliant Rectangles, Dies at 91," *The New York Times*, December 14, 2014; James Sullivan, "How Sy Berger Invented the Baseball Card," *Forward*, December 16, 2014, https://forward.com/culture/211032/how-sy-berger-invented-the-baseball-card/.

84. Laura Albanese, "Pioneering Yankees Broadcaster Suzy Waldman Has Had To Deal With Sexism and Abuse Throughout Her Career," *Newsday*, Mach 30, 2019, https://www.newsday.com/sports/baseball/yankees/yankees-suzyn-waldman-s11171.

85. Richard Deitsch, "Linda Cohn's Impressive Run at ESPN," *The New York Times*, July 23, 2018, https://www.nytimes.com/athletic/441835/2018/07/23/media-circus-linda-cohns-impressive-run-at-espn-larry-nassar-survivors-come-together-at-the-espys/.

86. Naomi Blumberg David, "A Voice in Major League Baseball," *Brandeis Magazine*, Spring 2021, https://www.brandeis.edu/magazine/2021/spring/class-notes/alumni-profiles/schimmel.html.

87. Steven Riess, "The Baseball Magnates and Urban Politics in the Progressive Era: 1895–1920," *Journal of Sport History* 1, no. 1 (Spring 1974), 41–62, https://www.slideshare.net/slideshow/the-baseball-magnates-and-urban-politicsin-the-progressive-edocx/253887206.

88. Sam Bernstein, "Barney Dreyfuss," Society for American Baseball Research, https://sabr.org/bioproj/person/barney-dreyfuss/.

89. Nathan Ruiz, "Orioles Promote Eve Rosenbaum to Assistant General Manager for Baseball Operations, *Baltimore Sun*, June 3, 2022, . https://www.baltimoresun.com/2022/06/03/orioles-promote-eve-rosenbaum-to-assistant-gm-of-baseball-operations/.

90. Peter Dreier, "Jews and Baseball: History and Demographics (Part One)," *Baseball Research Journal* 53, no. 1 (Spring 2024), 115–23. Sourcing details are in endnote 1 of Part One.

Contributors

MARK ARMOUR is a baseball researcher and writer living in Corvallis, Oregon. He founded SABR's Baseball Biography Project and its Baseball Cards Committee.

MASON CLUTTER is a student in the combined Doctor of Optometry and Master of Science program at the Ohio State University.

ED DENTA is a retired professional engineer and lifelong baseball fanatic. He umpired Florida high school baseball for eighteen years. He combines his analytical background and fervor for history/statistics to research and author sports related artifacts. Ed is an active member of the Roush-Lopez Chapter of SABR in the Tampa Bay area.

CONNELLY DOAN, MA, is a data analyst in Las Vegas who has applied his professional skills to the game of baseball, both personally and for RotoBaller.com. He has been a SABR member since 2018 and has contributed to the *Baseball Research Journal*. He can be reached on X.com (@ConnellyDoan) and via email (doanco01@gmail.com).

PETER DREIER is the E.P. Clapp Distinguished Professor of Politics at Occidental College and coauthor of *Baseball Rebels: The Players, People, and Social Movements That Shook Up the Game and Changed America* (University of Nebraska Press, 2022) and *Major League Rebels: Baseball Battles Over Workers' Rights and American Empire* (Rowman & Littlefield, 2022).

DR. WOODY ECKARD is a retired economics professor living in Evergreen, Colorado, with his wife Jacky. Among his academic publications are five papers on the economics of Major League Baseball. More recently, he has published in SABR's *Baseball Research Journal, The National Pastime*, and *Nineteenth Century Notes*. A Rockies fan, he has been a SABR member for over 20 years.

NICK FOGT grew up in western Ohio during the Cincinnati Reds' "Big Red Machine" era. He is a professor at the Ohio State University College of Optometry, combining his baseball interests with his work in eye and head movements.

HERM KRABBENHOFT is a retired chemist (PhD, University of Michigan, 1974) and author of *Leadoff Batters of Major League Baseball* (McFarland, 2001). Among various baseball research topics he has pioneered are: Ultimate Grand Slam Homers, Consecutive Games On Base Safely (CGOBS) Streaks, Quasi-Cycles, Imperfect Perfectos, Downtown Golden Sombreros, Pitcher's Cycles. Krabbenhoft has received three SABR Research Awards (1992, 1996, 2013).

Born and raised on Chicago's north side, **JAMES MUSSO** is a life-long Cubs fan who somehow does not despise the White Sox. He was first drawn to baseball history and numbers in the early 1970s by the now-classic *Sports Illustrated* All-Time All-Star Baseball board game. After graduating from Northwestern University Law School, he spent the 1990s at STATS, Inc.

CHARLIE PAVITT has been a SABR member since 1983. His Statistical Baseball Research Bibliography is now integrated into SABR's Baseball Index; his Sabermetric Research Literature Review (https://charliepavitt.home.blog/) is intended to be a complete survey of the literature and consistently gets updated. Charlie is responsible for defining the sabermetric terms in the fourth edition of the *Dickson Baseball Dictionary*. Online version: (https://www.baseball-almanac.com/dictionary.php).

JOHN RACANELLI is a Chicago lawyer with an insatiable interest in baseball-related litigation. John is membership director for the Chicago SABR Chapter and founder of the SABR Baseball Landmarks Research Committee. A regular contributor to the SABR Baseball Cards Research Committee, his "Death and Taxes and Baseball Card Litigation" series of articles was a 2023 McFarland-SABR Baseball Research Award winner.

RICK REIFF is Editor at Large of the *Orange County* (California) *Business Journal*. He lives in Gavy Cravath's hometown of Laguna Beach, roots for and suffers with the American League franchises in Chicago, Cleveland, and Anaheim, and cherishes his 1959 Topps Keystone Combo (Fox-Aparicio) baseball card. He has written thousands of news stories. This is his first article for SABR.

BARRETT SNYDER holds an MS in Sports Management and a Master of Business Administration (MBA) from Drexel University. He is currently enrolled at West Chester University studying Exercise Science with a concentration in Sports Psychology.

SAM ZYGNER, a SABR member since 1996, is the author of *Baseball Under the Palms: History of Miami Minor League Baseball Volume Two: 1962–1991* (Sunbury Press, 2022), *Baseball Under the Palms: History of Miami Minor League Baseball The Early Years: 1892–1960*, and *The Forgotten Marlins: A Tribute to the 1956–1960 Original Miami Marlins* (Scarecrow Press, 2013). He received his MBA from Saint Leo University.